CLEAN EATING

with

a Dirty Mind

over 150

PALEO-INSPIRED
RECIPES FOR EVERY CRAVING

Written and photographed by **VANESSA BARAJAS**

Foreword **BY** **Juli Bauer**, *New York Times* bestselling author

Victory Belt Publishing Inc.
Las Vegas

Interior design by Yordan Terziev and Boryana Yordanova

Interior lifestyle photography by Patty Brutlag, Petula Pea Photography,
www.petulapea.com

Printed in the U.S.A.
RRD 0115

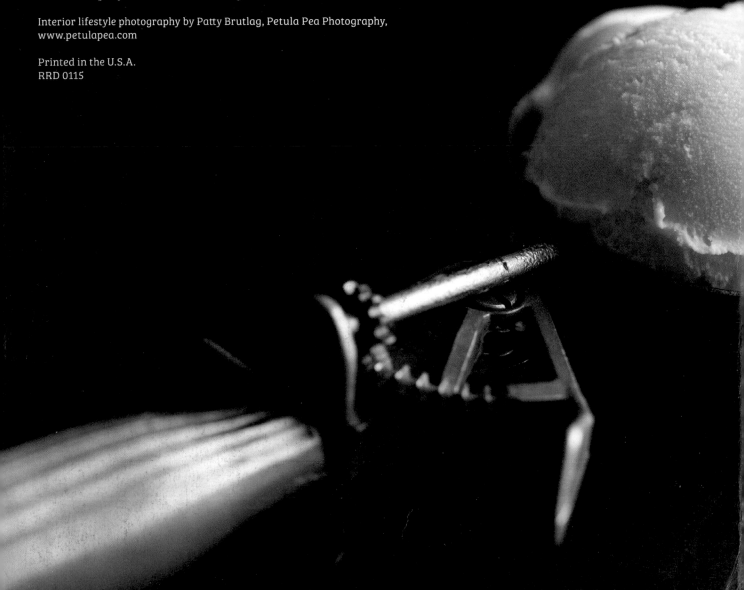

For my grandmother Peggy,
because she would have been prouder
than anyone

CONTENTS

FOREWORD

Forewords are hard. You sit there, staring at your computer, Googling big words that will help evoke the emotion you feel for the person. And then you're left sitting there, wondering how many days . . . weeks . . . maybe even months it may take to make those big words sound natural.

I've given up on the big words. I'm ready to just throw my emotions onto the paper. I need to get 'em all out there. Because I have a lot to say when it comes to Vanessa.

I found out about Vanessa and her jaw-dropping recipes through the creepy World Wide Web in 2013. And with the name *Clean Eating with a Dirty Mind*, I knew we would be best friends in about four minutes. No, scratch that, let's be real, more like thirty seconds. As I skimmed through her recipes online, I was blown away by what her mind could come up with. She was taking treats from my childhood and reinventing them into even more delicious masterpieces. With recipes on her website like Salted Nutella Stuffed Cookies, McGriddle Sandwiches, and Browned Butter Snickerdoodles, pre-Paleo memories were brought to life with healthier, grain-free alternatives. I became pretty much obsessed with Vanessa and would check her website every day in hopes of some new creation to blow my mind.

But it wasn't until 2014 while writing *The Paleo Kitchen* that I actually met Vanessa in person for the first time. She owned the room: walking in holding a bottle of champagne in one hand and orange juice in the other, with her famous Reese's Cheesecake in tow. She oozed excitement and confidence, and basically threw up glitter. She was a ball of energy and I ate it up. I wanted to be around her, I wanted to sip mimosas and talk dessert with her, and I wanted to learn from her. Her personality was so infectious, and her Reese's Cheesecake made life worth living.

I know I sound a bit over the top, but every single word I say about Vanessa is true. Our friendship has grown from sipping champagne during our first encounter to sipping champagne for five hours in Austin, Texas, while we waited in line for brisket at Franklin Barbecue. She is a person you want to be around and cannot wait to see again. She lives life in a constant state of excitement, and that's exactly what you see in her recipes. You see life, you see beauty, and you see a "diet" that sparks your senses.

When you open this book, you may have a hard time figuring out what to make first. With over 150 gorgeous recipes, where the hell do you even start? Don't worry, I'm here for you. Feelin' bitchy? It's cool, make yourself a batch of Better than Box Brownies. Have a little holiday spirit in your step? Try her Eggnog Chiffon Pie. Need a little Sunday brunch without the gut aches later on? Make her Biscuits and Cajun Sausage Gravy. Any recipe you try, you'll love. Believe me, I've tried many, and every time, I've gone back for seconds . . . and thirds. Okay, and fourths.

Vanessa is unlike anyone I know, and her Paleo take on food is unlike anything I've seen. With this cookbook, Vanessa is going to get you excited about cooking and excited about food again. No need to feel deprived or miss the foods you had before you hopped on the Paleo train, because Vanessa has you covered. She's going to keep your family excited about weekly meals with her Chiles Rellenos Casserole. She's going to keep birthday parties tasty with her Hot Fudge Sundae Cupcakes. And she's going to make bake sales possible for the gluten-intolerant souls with her Simple Chocolate Chip Cookies. Vanessa is going to keep your new grain-free lifestyle the best it could ever be. No need to miss any food; *Clean Eating with a Dirty Mind* has your back. Time to get cooking and fall in love with every recipe you try. Be careful, you may just fall in love with Vanessa along the way.

Juli Bauer,
New York Times bestselling author

Preface:
MY STORY

If you were to ask me what I love most about food, I would simply tell you, "Everything." I love the entire experience. I love that every single human sense is involved in the process: sight, sound, touch, smell, and, best of all, taste. I love sitting down to a meal and using all of these senses, one at a time, to experience food. I even love the little details that go along with a meal, the ones that most people just don't seem to notice. Like how the linen napkin feels in my hand as I set it on my lap; is it soft or crisp? The weight of the utensil in my hand and how it clinks ever so lightly against the plate as I take each bite. The gratification of flavor and texture working together like a symphony. Up until a few years ago, however, I absolutely hated one key component of the process, and perhaps the most crucial of them all. I completely and utterly loathed . . . cooking.

My excuses were never-ending. I would claim anything negative about cooking that I could, from it being too time-consuming or expensive to it being too difficult or simply not worth it. If I wanted decent food, I would go to a restaurant and have it cooked for me, or I would throw something in the microwave and be done with it. These were obviously the days before Paleo. Maybe I was averse to cooking because I didn't understand the power of real food and the effect it has on the body. Maybe I was just lazy. Maybe it was a combination of both. Who knows?

I totally remember the days when I hated cooking. It's so funny to me now, because cooking has become such a passion of mine and is something I really look forward to. It's become a part of the whole food experience for me. When I walk into my kitchen, it's like a blank canvas waiting for me to create something. The details have become just as important, and again, like when eating food, I find myself using every sense. How the light reflects off my stainless-steel measuring cups hanging over the sink. The warmth that comes from a preheated oven. The texture of the fabric of my apron as I tie it around my waist. The way the house smells when a batch of cupcakes is just minutes away from being done. The brief scent of spices that escapes my cupboard when I open the door to grab an ingredient. The long dried chocolate that I just can't seem to scrub out of the grout on my kitchen counter. Everything in cooking is an experience. Just like food itself, it's magic.

I've always loved food, but food hasn't always loved me. I've been on some kind of diet since the age of ten. Name it and I've tried it. I vividly remember being made fun of in the fifth grade for being overweight and then going on a diet. I also remember being so insecure about my Latin curves at age twelve, when I was in seventh grade, that I would take diet pills and drink SlimFast. I didn't want hips or a booty; I just wanted to look skinny in my Bongo jeans like all the other girls. These were the pre–Jennifer Lopez days. (That woman alone has done wonders for us curvy ladies. J.Lo, I will forever be grateful for you.)

I remember being on Weight Watchers and Jenny Craig around that same age and having to weigh and measure my food. I would feel ashamed if I ate pizza or Oreos or anything else a normal twelve-year-old kid would want to eat. I went to Weight Watchers meetings with my mom and was the youngest person in the room.

As I reached my early twenties, my weight hit an all-time high. For years I struggled with the same twenty pounds, losing it and gaining it back. In my late twenties I did Weight Watchers again and managed to lose it all and then some by eating lots of really low-calorie, low-fat, processed food. I remember being hungry ALL THE TIME. I remember feeling tired, run down, and starving. Right after I ate, I was hungry again. I never felt full or satisfied, but I thought that's just what it takes to weigh that perfect number on the scale. I remember having a "Cheat Day" every Saturday when I would weigh in and then immediately go scarf down three donuts. All I thought about was food and when I would be able to eat it again. By Tuesday I was already counting the days until Saturday when I could eat and actually feel full again. If I went one "*Point*" over my allotment for the day, I felt awful about myself. Obviously, this was no way to live, and it was certainly not a healthy relationship with food. So I stopped.

Around the same time, a new trend was popping up all over the interwebs: "eating clean." What the heck does that mean? Like eating off of clean dishes? Maybe you scrub the food really well before you eat it so it's super clean? I had no idea. After reading more and more about it, I realized that the eating clean movement is advocating eating real food—nothing more, nothing less. So I started reading food labels to filter out preservatives, additives, and MSG. I researched the names of food additives and taught myself what to look for. I didn't eat anything I couldn't pronounce, and I learned everything I could about my food and where it came from.

I traded my sugar-filled fat-free yogurt for high-protein, grass-fed yogurt and blueberries. Instead of being afraid of fat, like I had been taught to be my entire life, I started to embrace eating fat. Avocados and almonds became staples in my diet. I learned to enjoy a few blocks of dark chocolate for a treat instead of a pint Ben and Jerry's. I still indulged, of course; after all, "Everything in moderation, including moderation." For the first time in my life, though, I wasn't hungry all the time, and I began to understand that I could actually have a healthy relationship with food without feeling deprived or guilty. Did I gain a few pounds? Sure. But I learned a lot in the process. Instead of trying to hit some unreachable number on the scale, I learned to make better choices for my body.

So how did I go from Weight Watcher to clean eater to Paleo? Strangely enough, it all started with a Groupon. Yes, a Groupon.

Bored and tired of my current workout routine, I wanted to try something new. I had heard a lot about a new exercise program called CrossFit, and I was dying to try it. Apparently Groupon was hip to this, so they emailed me an offer I couldn't refuse. Of course I couldn't just go by myself; that would have been crazy. Luckily for me, I was able to recruit one of my friends to go with me—you know, for moral support, or at least to go get a drink with after, when it all turns out to have been a terrible idea. When we showed up to our first class, I remember being so intimidated that I almost didn't get out of the car. People with six-packs were running by me, stopping only to lift really heavy-looking barbells, and then went right back to running. What had I gotten myself into?

It turned out to be love at first lift. I got better and better in my new workouts. I did things I'd never thought possible, like pull-ups and seven-minute miles. I could lift things over 200 pounds and squat more than I weighed. I immediately thought I was pretty much the coolest person on earth. But how could I up my game? I Googled. In all my research I found that progressing in your workouts is completely dependent on how you fuel your body.

The CrossFit folks already knew this. They are huge advocates of the Paleo diet and eating to fuel your workouts.

I remember the first time I Googled "What can you eat on a Paleo diet?" I immediately started laughing. It seemed a little ridiculous. No peanut butter? Lame. No dairy? Super-lame. No bread? Ultra-lame. So I put it on the back burner and stopped thinking about it. Shortly thereafter, as fate would have it, my CrossFit gym announced a Thirty-Day Paleo Challenge. I remember thinking, "Eh, it's only thirty days, that's not that long. I'm going to suck it up and give it a whirl." Here's how it went:

THE FIVE STAGES OF PALEO

1.
PANIC.
"WHAT? I CAN'T HAVE ANY BREAD? WELL. WHAT AM I SUPPOSED TO EAT, THEN?"

2.
DENIAL.
"HOW CAN FAT BE GOOD FOR YOU? I ALREADY HAVE ENOUGH ON MY THIGHS. THANK YOU."

3.
BARGAINING.
"WHAT IF I ONLY HAVE MILKSHAKES ON THE WEEKENDS? OR DAYS THAT END IN -Y?"

4.
GOOGLING.
"WHAT'S A LEGUME?" "IS BEER PALEO?"

5.
ACCEPTANCE.

The first two weeks I was so irritable that it made my PMS look like a good mood. I was tired. I was cranky. I had no energy. I would have cut someone for a Reese's Peanut Butter Cup—not even the whole thing, just a bite. I was . . . detoxing. My body was going through withdrawal from gluten, sugar, artificial sweeteners, and who knows what else. And then let's not forget beer withdrawal! Beer. Sigh, don't get me started.

Then, all of a sudden and completely out of nowhere, the sun came out from behind the clouds, and I arrived at what I call "The Magic Day." It happened around day twelve to fourteen, and it was like a runner's high but better. It was like when Dorothy landed in Oz, opened the door, and walked out into a world in full color.

I wake up and . . . wait, what's this? I feel so rested. I have so much energy I feel like bouncing off the walls. I'm in the middle of a crazy-intense workout and, wait, what? My body wants to go faster! And what about you, you complete and total stranger in the elevator, you held the door for me—I love you! I hope you have the most glorious day ever! Then I get to work and, what? A full inbox? Good thing multitasking is my name and e-mail is my game! Oh, it's rush hour traffic and you just cut me off? No worries—in fact, why don't the other three of you jump on into my lane, too? We'll make it a party up in here!

All of the above is based on actual events, and it was like nothing I'd ever experienced before. At the end of the challenge I knew there was no way I could ever go back to eating the way I had been. I realized that there are actually quite a few foods that my body doesn't tolerate well. Before Paleo I never even knew food intolerance was a thing. Sure, I knew people had allergies to nuts, shellfish, wheat, and stuff, but I had never omitted anything from my diet before, so I had no idea that I was actually sensitive to certain foods this whole time.

One of the main culprits I discovered was gluten. I think the gluten-free lifestyle gets such a bad rap these days. People end up thinking, "Oh great, another person jumping on the gluten-free bandwagon. Unless you are allergic to gluten or have been diagnosed with an autoimmune condition by a doctor, then you should stop acting like you can't eat it." I've heard stories about restaurant servers rolling their eyes at people who request gluten-free options because they think it's just some fad diet. Here's how I see it: I'm the only person who lives in my body. Period. Therefore, I'm the only one who knows how I feel every second of every day. Thus, I should be considered an expert in the field of my body.

The same goes for you and everyone else on the planet. Having someone else tell you that what you feel after eating a certain food isn't valid just because a doctor hasn't diagnosed you with something is absurd. The fact that you have the ability to recognize when something isn't right with your body after eating a certain food should be celebrated, not looked down upon or punished.

Another thing I learned really fast was that if you're going to eat real food that nourishes your body, you actually have to cook it . . . so cook I did. I Googled dumb cooking questions. I read all the Paleo blogs. I tried all the recipes. Most were great, but some . . . not so much. I remember baking muffins for my friends that were hard as rocks, and so dry you might as well have been eating the Sahara Desert. I thought to myself, "Is this the be-all and end-all? It can't be."

Enter baking. I'd always glossed over the magazine stands in supermarket checkout aisles, leafing through while waiting for my turn, admiring the painstakingly detailed cakes and pies. Beautiful, an art form even, though not something attainable for the average person, and certainly not something I would ever be good at. Then, on top of that, add to the equation being unable to use such simple ingredients as flour, sugar, and baking powder. It might as well have been mission impossible. But I wasn't going to let that stop me, or the dry, flavorless, rock-hard muffins. I was determined to make Paleo baked goods that actually—*gasp*—taste good. (Insert mental image of me, whirling my ugly apron around to become a superhero cape, hands on my waist, one foot forward, in the obligatory superhero stance.) I was going to bake the world a better place, one recipe at a time.

So I got in my tiny kitchen and started experimenting. It wasn't very pretty at first. Though in my head I was a master chef—whirling around in my beautiful copper pot–lined French kitchen, baking and sautéing impossible French entrees that were simmering to perfection over my mammoth Viking range, humming and chopping away so elegantly that even Julia Child would be envious—in reality, I was a red-in-the-face cook, frustrated and sweaty, with hair flying in every which direction and smudges of ingredients all over my face and clothes, working on the smallest of counter spaces in the tiniest of inglorious, non-French, late '70s, 2-foot-square kitchens, trying to cook on that left burner, the crooked one that tilts. Do I smell something burning? Oh yeah, that hot spot on the left side of the oven, it burns everything. My sad cooking journey might have ended there. It probably should have, but I'm just too stubborn.

I think it all basically comes down to inspiration. What inspires you? Chocolate is what inspires me. Period. I remember when I was about five years old, coloring with crayons in my grandmother's kitchen, and came across the brown color. Being the child genius that I was, I realized, hey, this is the color of chocolate; I wonder if it tastes like chocolate? It didn't. Has someone ever asked you what your dream job would be if money and experience were no object? Some people answer architect, rock star, fashion designer, astronaut, you get the idea. Me? My dream job would be . . . drumroll, please . . . professional chocolate taster. A fancy one, though. Okay, sure, it would be awesome and delicious to sit in the Hershey factory and eat Reese's Cups all day for quality control purposes, but the weird white clean suit with matching hat and booties that I would probably have to wear is a total turnoff.

When I say "chocolate taster," I mean, like, I live in the south of France. I travel to places like Germany and Switzerland to taste the world's finest chocolates. I pair them with different wines and the finest cuisine. Then I travel to South America and study the subtle differences between Columbian chocolate and European chocolate. I would be a sommelier of chocolate. Give me the tiniest bite and I could tell you which region of the world the cacao beans came from and if it was raining when they were harvested. I could tell you what kind of wine would pair best with it and whether or not the beans were harvested too early, too late, or right on time. I would be able to tell you what kind of chocolate is best for each time of day, in each month of the year. Can you tell that I've actually had long daydreams about this? Okay, back to reality, where I have a full-time day job and sit in rush-hour traffic, and the closest I might ever get to that dream job is this book. But it's mine, it's home, and it's in my tiniest of kitchens that I can bring the Paleo world big things. So I'm here to share with you what I've learned along this journey and show you how to re-create your favorite sweets and treats using better ingredients. I hope you find it useful and delicious.

How to use
THIS BOOK

I'm sure this book would make an excellent beverage coaster on your coffee table. Maybe you just bought it because you know me personally and I threatened you with violence or bribed you with baked goods. I'm not saying any of that is beneath me. However, if on the off chance you bought this book because you want to practically apply my techniques and recipes in your own kitchen, then thank you! This is how I recommend you approach it:

If you are familiar with Paleo, the rules and regulations, the haves and have-nots, and are pretty confident in your baking and cooking abilities . . . I applaud you! You get a gold star on your Paleo baking chart. Go straight to Part 2, find your favorite recipes, and get started!

The recipes are structured to make the process easier and to help you strategize your time in the kitchen. At the top of each recipe you will find the following keys:

An asterisked key indicates that an ingredient must be substituted or omitted to make the recipe dairy-free, egg-free, or nut-free; this info is relayed in the Notes at the end of the recipe. You will also see prep and cook times listed as well as resting or setting time, when applicable. The "Ready In" time is the minimum amount of time it will take to make the recipe from start to finish, including any resting time. This will help eliminate surprises along the way—such as time involved to make the subrecipes, or components, in the ingredient list, which are not always included in the stated prep and cook times—and allow you to set aside the time you need. Some of the subrecipes can be made ahead of time; doing so will make the day-of assembly less time-consuming. All make-ahead components are listed at the end of the recipe, below this logo:

For example, if you are making cupcakes, the cupcakes themselves can be made a day ahead and then frosted on the day you serve them. Approaching more complex recipes this way will make your time in the kitchen much more efficient. (I highly recommend that you make the multilayer, tiered cakes this way.) Do you have to approach each recipe this way? Not at all! Sometimes you just want some cupcakes and you want them now. I get it.

For the rest of you who don't know a boiled egg from a poached one, or how Paleo is even pronounced ("PAY-lee-oh"), this book is set up to guide you through everything. Don't worry, I'll hold your hand; we'll go through everything together in Part 1 and take it one step at a time.

First we will dive into what the Paleo diet is and how you can apply it to fit your lifestyle. We'll put the debate about whether dessert is actually Paleo to rest once and for all. You will notice that some of the recipes in this book are not 100 percent Paleo, but are more Paleo inspired. I wrote this book with everyone in mind. A lot of folks with food intolerances, like those with celiac disease, use Paleo cookbooks because they know that they are 100 percent gluten- and grain-free, even though they really don't care about the Paleo diet itself. Many recipes throughout the book use dairy. In most cases I've offered substitutions so you can keep those recipes dairy-free, and thus more Paleo, if needed. Some recipes are not dairy-free in the slightest and are meant to cater more to a gluten- and grain-free audience. My goal was to have something for everyone, helping people create indulgent recipes at home, using quality ingredients, while still keeping dietary restrictions in mind.

I will also guide you through the tools of the trade. What are the absolute necessities that you need to have in your kitchen for baking and cooking? Which appliances are the quality ones to buy? I've got you covered. I won't let you waste your money on crap you don't need, let alone sucky products. Let my failures and triumphs be your guide.

Next we'll get into ingredients—the Who, What, When, Where, and Why. I'll also take you through some simple baking lessons and tricks of the trade to help you get started, including how to use grain-free flours. Don't you already feel like a pro?

My wish is that this book will become a staple in your kitchen, and that you will find it helpful, quirky, and well loved. The more chocolate smudges on it, the better. If you have any questions about the book, please feel free to reach out to me on my blog at www.cleaneatingwithadirtymind.com. Whisks up, happy cooking, and here's to your health and happiness!

Your friend in chocolate,

Vanessa

PART ONE

the ESSENTIALS

CHAPTER 1

What Exactly Is the PALEO DIET?

The Paleo diet, in a nutshell, is meant to remove modern foods with little nutritional value that are eaten in today's standard diet and simply go back to eating whole foods in order to create better health. The word *Paleo* actually stems from the word *Paleolithic,* and it is used to convey the idea of adopting a diet similar to what our ancestors ate before the agricultural revolution and before genetically modified foods and Pop-Tarts were staples in our everyday diets.

So do you actually have to eat like a caveman? I think Michelle Tam of *Nom Nom Paleo* said it best: "The caveman's just a mascot. For me, Paleo's not about historical reenactment. It's a framework for improving health through real food." I couldn't agree more. In today's world it would be almost impossible to eat a true Paleo diet. You would have to live in the woods, hunt all your own food for every meal, and sleep in a cave. Could it be done? Sure. Would you want to? Probably not. I think the Paleo diet gets a bad rap in some nutrition circles because of this. I'm not sure why people want to be so literal about it.

So what did cavemen eat? From what I've read, they basically ate whatever they could eat, whenever they could get it. Grain didn't exist yet, refined sugar didn't exist yet, and modern agriculture didn't exist yet, so this leads people today to believe our forebears basically ate meat that they hunted; fish that they caught; vegetables, fruit, nuts, and seeds that they picked off bushes or trees; and honey when they were lucky enough to find it, which was also obtained at great sacrifice. Ouch.

Today we can walk into any store, pretty much any time of the day, and get whatever we want to eat, whenever we want it, hungry or not. We have gotten so lazy that we can't be bothered to park our cars and walk into a restaurant to get food; we just drive through. This has led to massive health epidemics, especially here in America, where we have probably the worst diets on the planet. I recently read an article about how to not look American while visiting other countries. One of the things on the list was eating while walking. The United States is the only country in which eating and walking at the same time is considered totally normal. In other countries, people sit down together at meals and take time to enjoy their food. This really stuck out to me and made me realize how oblivious we are about eating.

People argue all the time that cavemen lived to be only about thirty years old. This is accurate, but by the same token, their lifespan was likely so short because in addition to hunting every meal, they were also part of the food chain. They had no access to medical care or solid shelter, and absolutely none of the modern conveniences we enjoy today. When we fall and break a bone, we can go get it fixed. A broken limb meant life or death for our ancestors. In fact, tons of research shows how healthy cavemen actually were despite all that, presumably because they ate a simple diet, slept when the sun went down, rose when it came up, ate when they could, and exercised quite a bit. Today we are pretty much the antithesis of that scenario. We eat like crap, plop in front of the TV or our computers for hours, tinkering with our smartphones, and only exercise in the month of January for our New Year's resolutions. We go to bed way too late, wake up way too early, and have lots of health issues because we live like this. I'm totally guilty of these things too, but we are lucky enough to live in an age when we can change our lifestyle and make healthy choices.

This isn't a Paleo science book, obviously, so if you want more information about the science and ideas behind the Paleo diet, I've included a Resources section at the back of the book where you can find more information (see page 418).

So what exactly are the Paleo diet guidelines?

MEAT FISH EGGS
VEGETABLES FRUIT
NUTS SEEDS
Healthy fats and oils
GRASS-FED
BUTTER or GHEE
SPICES

MEAT

Any meat is fair game. Get it? See what I did there? I punned. Ostrich, alligator, snake, you name it. Not that adventurous? You can stick to the basics: beef, chicken, pork, and lamb. Not all meat is created equal, though. Just like shoes. You know a quality pair of shoes from a pair you picked up on sale for $10. A good general rule to remember is, "You are what you eat, eats." So if you're eating an animal that's been fed GMO grains, well, guess what you're eating, too? Grass-fed, pasture-raised meat is preferred. Cows and livestock naturally eat off the land. This means lots of rich green grass on pastures. Feeding animals grains is a practice that was invented because grains are an inexpensive form of food that makes the animals fatter. I think the key point here is that feeding livestock grains fattens them up. What makes us think that eating a diet made up almost entirely of grains wouldn't do the same to us? The animals are also given hormones to make them grow faster and antibiotics so they can survive the crowded and unsanitary conditions in which they are raised. Just like us, animals store toxins in their fat, so when we eat animals, we are essentially eating the toxins found in their fat as well. When an animal eats what was originally intended, the meat contains less toxins along with some really healthy nutrients, like omega-3s and conjugated linoleic acids (CLAs).

FISH

The same goes for fish. These days fish are farmed and raised in terrible conditions, just like livestock. Opt for wild-caught sources instead. That means the fish were caught in the open sea or in streams and until then lived in the wild eating their natural food sources.

EGGS

Eggs are one of the healthiest foods on the planet. They are full of protein and tons of vitamins and minerals. They can also be a great way to get your omega-3s. Eggs are similar to meat in that they are classified in several different ways according to how the hens are kept and what they're fed, which offers varying amounts of health benefits. Usually in a store you will find conventional, cage-free, free-range, and sometimes pasture-raised eggs. I usually think of eggs in terms of *good, better,* and *best, good* being cage-free, *better* being free-range, and *best* being pasture-raised. Pasture-raised eggs can sometimes be found in stores but more often at a local farmers' market. These eggs come from hens that are raised in their natural environment, are free to come and go as they please, and eat a natural diet. They are similar to grass-fed beef in the fact that they have the most nutritional value. Choose these eggs when you can; their shells come in a rainbow of colors, and they have the most orange yolks you've ever seen.

VEGETABLES

Vegetables are awesome because there are literally hundreds of them, in all different shapes, colors, and sizes. I think you could probably go your whole life and not be able to eat every vegetable out there. Before Paleo the thought of vegetables made me shudder. Now I look forward to the produce aisle because it's so colorful and flavorful! Vegetables are among the most nutrient-dense foods on the planet.

In my opinion, all vegetables are fair game, even white potatoes, which are technically a vegetable, even though they are considered more of a starch. Depending on what your goals are, you may or may not want to include potatoes in your diet. Sweet potatoes have a lower glycemic index and more fiber than white potatoes, so they are more widely accepted in the Paleo community. Potatoes are a great source of carbohydrates if you find that you need to incorporate more carbs into your diet to accommodate heavy exercise loads or aren't getting enough carbs elsewhere in your Paleo diet. I personally think that potatoes are an "in moderation" food. I wouldn't eat them every day, but I wouldn't exclude them from my diet completely.

Also, while we are in the vegetable gray area, peas are technically a legume, not a vegetable. Is the world going to end if you eat peas? No. Try not to get so strict that you make yourself miserable.

TO BUY ORGANIC OR NOT TO BUY ORGANIC? THAT IS THE QUESTION

When you see a food labeled as organic, it means that the food was grown without the use of pesticides, synthetic fertilizers, or genetically modified organisms (GMOs). Buying everything organic all the time can get expensive. When it comes to produce, a good general rule to follow is to buy organic if you are going to eat the skin. So if it's a food like strawberries, grapes, or apples, where you eat the skin along with the fruit, then your best bet would be to buy organic. If you are buying something that has a thick rind, peel, or skin that will be removed prior to eating, like pineapples, bananas, and avocados, then nonorganic would be fine.

"The Dirty Dozen" is a list of the produce that contains the most pesticide residues. "The Clean Fifteen" is a list of the produce that is the least likely to contain pesticide residues. These lists can be really helpful to refer to when shopping and deciding whether to spend the extra money on organic vegetables and fruits.

THE DIRTY DOZEN

APPLES
CELERY
CHERRY TOMATOES
CUCUMBERS
GRAPES
NECTARINES
PEACHES
POTATOES
SNAP PEAS
SPINACH
STRAWBERRIES
SWEET BELL PEPPERS

THE CLEAN FIFTEEN

ASPARAGUS
AVOCADOS
CABBAGE
CANTALOUPE
CAULIFLOWER
EGGPLANT
GRAPEFRUIT
KIWI
MANGOES
ONIONS
PAPAYAS
PINEAPPLES
SWEET CORN
SWEET PEAS (FROZEN)
SWEET POTATOES

Note:

The Environmental Working Group updates these lists yearly. To check out the latest versions, visit www.ewg. org. Also, please note that though these lists are useful generally, they were not created specifically for a Paleo diet. This is why you will find sweet corn on the Clean Fifteen list, which is considered a grain and generally not eaten on a Paleo diet.

FRUIT

Fruit is another nutrient-dense food source of vitamins, fiber, and carbohydrates. Since the Paleo diet is naturally less carbohydrate-dense than a standard diet, and because grains are omitted, some people tend to feel that they can't get enough carbs and therefore don't have a lot of energy to fuel them through workouts and such. Fruit is a great natural carb source to give you energy. Again, though, depending on your goals, you may not want to go fruit crazy. After all, fructose may be a natural sugar, but it's still sugar. If you're trying to lose weight or aren't very active, you may want to approach fruit in moderation. Play around with a template and see what works for you. You can also try eating fruits that are lower in natural sugar, like berries and green apples. Fruits like grapes and mangoes tend to be the highest in sugar.

Also, you may want to stay away from dried fruit. Dried fruit has had all the water extracted, which makes the sugar more concentrated. I personally love dried fruit and can't be trusted around it. It might as well be a bag of chocolate chips. But dried fruit is a great and portable source of fuel for long hikes and endurance activities. I also use it in recipes because it adds a ton of flavor.

NUTS

Nuts are amazing. They are full of protein as well as healthy fats to keep you satiated and give you sustainable energy. Some of the healthiest nuts out there are almonds, macadamia nuts, and pistachios. Nuts can be tricky to portion, though, since you can grab handfuls at a time. I recommend using an espresso cup to portion out your nuts; that way you aren't sitting there counting them out obsessively, but you are eating a reasonable amount.

SEEDS

Flax, chia, sunflower, pumpkin (pepitas)—what's your favorite? Seeds are full of all kinds of healthy goodies, from omega-3 fatty acids to protein and fiber. You can make chia seed pudding or add flax to your smoothies. You can pretend that it's Halloween in the middle of winter and roast pumpkin seeds in your oven. Like nuts, seeds add texture to baked goods for that little extra something.

HEALTHY FATS AND OILS

Fat is my favorite. Of all the foods, just give me the fat. Fat is flavor. Fat is also an essential nutrient. Unfortunately, it was demonized in a well-meaning anti-fat campaign that got underway in the 1970s and had become fully entrenched in the American food psyche by the 1990s. The Fat Scare of the '90s led to low-fat food products in every grocery store aisle and left behind a nation full of unhealthy, sugar-addicted, and sick people. Fat is responsible for providing satiety, telling our bodies that we are full, giving us long-lasting energy, and helping the body absorb vitamins. Be sure to eat fat from high-quality food sources, like avocados, nuts, olive oil, and coconut oil, and use organic pasture-raised animal fats like lard and tallow for cooking. Fat is your friend!

GRASS-FED BUTTER OR GHEE

The benefits of grass-fed butter are astonishing. It packs so much great nutrition in such a small package. Grass-fed butter is full of healthy omega-3 fatty acids, conjugated linoleic acids (CLAs), and vitamins A, D, E, and K, and it also has anti-inflammatory properties. Lactose intolerant? Try ghee, also known as clarified butter. It has gone through a heating process to remove all the milk solids. What you're left with is literally liquid gold. Most people with dairy intolerances have no problem eating ghee since the milk solids have been removed. Ghee also has a super-high smoke point, so it is a great fat for cooking; again, just make sure that it comes from organic grass-fed sources to get the most bang for your nutrition buck.

SPICES

Spices equal flavor. When I was a kid in history class learning about Christopher Columbus and how he was commissioned by the queen to bring back spices from the New World, I remember thinking, "Spices? Who the hell wants spices?!" Now I understand just how valuable spices are. Spices give food life; they can take a dish from simple to spectacular. Tons of spices out there have amazing health benefits, too, like cinnamon, cumin, nutmeg, and turmeric.

WATER
CARBONATED WATER
RAW COCONUT WATER
(NO ADDITIVES)
TEA **COFFEE**
(IN MODERATION)
Kombucha
COCONUT MILK
NUT MILKS
PALEO-FRIENDLY ALCOHOL
(IN MODERATION), SUCH AS WINE, CHAMPAGNE, GIN,
TEQUILA, VODKA, HARD CIDER, & GLUTEN-FREE BEER*

DRINK ME

* Even alcohol made from grains, such as whiskey, is considered gluten-free because the gluten is removed in the distillation process. However, be sure to check that there are no caramel colorings or additives (usually added to lower-grade alcohols); those could add gluten back into the alcohol and cause a reaction. Another option is to stick to nongrain-based alcohols, like wine, gin, or vodka made from grapes or potatoes.

DAIRY (WITH SOME EXCEPTIONS: SEE NOTES BELOW)
GLUTEN GRAINS
SOY and LEGUMES
Refined vegetable oils
REFINED SUGAR
and ARTIFICIAL
SWEETENERS
PROCESSED FOODS

DAIRY

Dairy is another one of those foods that typically is not eaten on a Paleo diet. The reason stems from the fact that a huge portion of the population has some sort of lactose or casein intolerance (casein is a protein found in dairy), and from the belief that it is not natural to consume dairy products. The theory goes like this: We, like most animals, drink milk as babies to help us grow and develop our digestive systems, but once we're grown, we no longer need it.

I think dairy can definitely be incorporated into a healthy Paleo diet, depending on your goals and how well you tolerate dairy. Dairy is a great source of protein and fat, and if it's grass-fed, you are reaping all those amazing benefits as well. I recommend eating only high-fat grass-fed sources because they are the most nutritious. Remember, fat helps deliver vitamins to your body. If you are drinking fat-free milk, you aren't getting the vitamins. People who eat Paleo but include high-quality dairy in their diets are usually referred to as "Primal." I have no idea why; I just work here.

GLUTEN

Gluten is a protein found in grains. It's basically what gives bread and baked goods their texture and binds them together. The gluten in today's diet is completely different from the gluten our grandparents ate. Over the years grains have been modified through GMOs and pesticides, and because of that our bodies are becoming more and more intolerant of them. Many people have been diagnosed with celiac disease, an autoimmune condition that causes the body to attack itself when gluten is eaten. Some people have an actual food allergy when they eat gluten, where they break out in hives or start vomiting after ingesting gluten. Then there is a population of people who have gluten sensitivities or intolerances. Symptoms can range from intestinal bloating, stomach cramping, headaches, and irritability to brain fog and fatigue.

GRAINS

As a general rule, grains are not eaten on a standard Paleo diet. However, some grains, like rice, are making their way back into some iterations of the Paleo diet. Rice is naturally gluten-free and is an excellent source of carbohydrates. If you have a heavy training load, whether for endurance sports or for high-intensity activities like CrossFit, rice can be a valuable addition to your diet. If you aren't under a heavy training load, then you can probably find other acceptable sources of carbs. Some people who are sensitive to gluten find that grains like rice and corn give them a similar reaction. Today, grains like corn are almost all genetically modified. If you do choose to eat grains, be sure to buy ones from trusted GMO-free sources.

SOY AND LEGUMES

Soybeans are part of the legume family, or bean family, as we more commonly know it. Most of today's soy, like corn, is genetically modified and treated with pesticides. Soy also contains large amounts of isoflavones, which can interfere with hormone function. But wait, Asian cultures eat tons of soy and are known to be among the healthiest cultures on the planet, so what gives? They mostly use soy sauce and miso, both of which are fermented, as condiments only. Soy is not the basis of an entire meal, three times a day, like it can be for us. Soy is probably the number-one food additive (along with sugar) in the standard American diet.

Legumes are not eaten in conjunction with a Paleo diet because they contain phytates, which sound fancy, but all you need to know is that they prevent minerals from being absorbed into the body. (It should be noted that soaking legumes in warm water overnight can reduce the phytic acid and help the absorption of minerals.) Legumes are also really hard for the body to digest because they block digestive enzymes and contain lectins. Lectins are basically a built-in predator defense system for the plant that our bodies find difficult to break down. That's what causes you to get gassy after you eat beans. Stay classy, not gassy!

REFINED VEGETABLE OILS

Due to the Fat Scare of the 1990s, "foods" like Crisco are used to replace lard, margarine to replace butter, and refined vegetable oils to replace healthy cooking fats. I want to scream at us in the '90s, while shaking our shoulders vigorously and shouting, "What is wrong with you?!" What essentially happened was that we took away all the fat (basically the nutritional value of the food), added sugar to make it taste good, smacked a label on it that said "fat-free," and sold the world a sugar-and-carbohydrate Molotov cocktail.

So what's wrong with Crisco, margarine, and refined vegetable oils? Well, in the case of Crisco and margarine, the manufacturers took out the real animal fat and replaced it with partially hydrogenated oils. These oils are loaded with trans-fatty acids, which are the worst of all the fats out there. Trans fats not only raise your LDL, or bad, cholesterol levels, but also lower your HDL, or good, cholesterol levels. *No bueno.* Our bodies are designed to break down animal proteins and fats, but definitely not the partially hydrogenated ones created in a lab. As for refined vegetable oils, the most common one is canola oil. What is a canola? There isn't a vegetable called canola, is there? Canola oil comes from a seed called rapeseed, which undergoes an extensive and unnatural process to create the oil. Not only that, but most refined vegetable oils also contain GMOs and a very unhealthy ratio of omega-6 fatty acids. Vegetable oils are also known to cause inflammation and lead to heart disease.

REFINED SUGAR AND ARTIFICIAL SWEETENERS

Oh, sugar, you little devil, you. How we love to hate you. We all know by now—or at least I hope we do—that refined sugar is bad for you. It has no nutritional value; it's full of empty calories. I like to call them fun calories. Just kidding. Not really. "Refined sugar" typically means highly processed sugar in the form of table sugar, cane sugar, cane juice, or brown sugar (which is just white sugar

colored with molasses). The natural or unrefined forms of sugar are honey, because it's made by bees; maple syrup, because it comes from trees; date sugar, which is made from dried and ground dates; maple sugar, which is just a condensed granulated form of maple syrup; and coconut sugar, which is made from the sap of the coconut tree. Though not heavily used in Paleo baking, molasses has a place in this list because it has some nutritional value, unlike refined cane sugar, which is derived from the same plant. (Molasses is made by boiling the juice squeezed from the sugar cane plant that is left over after the sugar crystals, or refined sugar, have been extracted.) Regardless, sugar is sugar. I think the unrefined, natural sugars are just the lesser of two evils. Again, sugar should always be eaten in moderation, even natural, unrefined sugars. All the sweet treats in this book use natural, unrefined sugars whenever possible.

Artificial sweeteners are just that: artificial. Most are made in a lab and can cause severe stomach distress, including bloating, gas, belly rumbling, and diarrhea. Also, new findings are showing that artificial sugar actually increases your cravings for real sugar. When you eat artificial sweeteners, your body gets the signal that something sweet is coming down the hatch, so it sends out the troops to break it down. And when nothing actually comes, it starts to crave something sweet so the troops can have something to do. See how science-y I get? (Yes, *science-y* is too a word.) Examples of artificial sweeteners include Splenda, NutraSweet, Equal, xylitol, and sorbitol. Some folks have turned to stevia as a natural sweetener to use in place of sugar. I dislike the taste of stevia, so I don't include it in any of my recipes, but if you like it, go for it.

PROCESSED FOODS

By today's standards, almost all food is processed; it's just a matter of degree. If someone in Florida picks an orange off a tree and then washes it, puts it in a box, and ships it to California, that fruit, organic or not, has undergone a process. Even if you picked the fruit from the tree yourself and ate it right there, technically it still underwent the process of being picked. Let's not split hairs. What we really mean by "processed food" is food that has undergone a process to strip nutrients and add preservatives **and** artificial anything to increase flavor, nutritional value, or shelf life, and then is packaged in a box or bag and put on a shelf. Basically, if you can't pronounce or define an ingredient on the package, don't eat it. Simple.

Other components of
A PALEO DIET

I recommend that anyone who is interested in a Paleo diet or lifestyle should embark first on a thirty-day elimination plan. Follow the Paleo guidelines strictly for thirty days and then incorporate the omitted foods back into your diet one at a time and see how you feel. That way you will have a better template for which foods you react positively or negatively to, and then you can base your normal everyday eating around that template.

Other factors to take into consideration that are just as important as food are sleep and exercise.

In a perfect world, there would be no alarm clocks. We would fall asleep when we were tired and wake up when we were rested. Since we live hectic lives, this isn't always achievable. There are some tips that you can incorporate to help you, though. Cover your bedroom windows with blackout curtains and remove all electric sources of light in your bedroom, like those from alarm clocks, modems, and cable boxes. Winding down with a real book instead of an electronic device will help you fall asleep. When we watch TV or tinker with our electronic devices right before bed, the blue light that they omit tells our brains to stay awake and active. You can also purchase blue light blocker glasses, which help block the blue light if you can't detach yourself from technology. Guilty as charged.

Whether you run, walk, bike, do yoga, CrossFit, Orange Theory, or Turbo Kickbox, get active! Our bodies were meant to be active and work best when they are active. A body in motion stays in motion—so keep moving! Whatever you do for exercise, be sure to find something that you enjoy. If you do, you will be that much more inclined to stick with it. Exercise is known to help relieve stress and improve mood and sleep.

Invest in a stand-up desk for home and work, or ask your workplace services team to order one for you. Sitting is the new smoking. Make sure to get up from your desk and walk around often.

Clean eating can be life-changing. It can also be challenging. If a thirty-day challenge isn't for you, don't fret. Start slow. Remove one thing from your diet at a time and see how you feel. Commit to trying out one new exercise activity, or download an exercise app. Give yourself an extra thirty minutes before bed to wind down. Meditate, pray, or do aromatherapy—whatever helps you relax and de-stress. Just find what works for you. You may get it right the first month, or it may take you a year of tweaking to get it just right. Above all, remember that no one is perfect. No one. You have to find what works best for you in your life. There are so many resources out there. I hope that this book becomes one of those resources for you in times of dessert crisis. Yes, needing chocolate can be considered a crisis. Trust me.

CHAPTER 2

Are You There, DESSERT? It's me, PALEO

IS DESSERT PALEO?
THIS IS PROBABLY THE MOST WIDELY AND HEAVILY DEBATED TOPIC
ON ANY PALEO WEBSITE OR BLOG IN THE UNIVERSE.
AND THE ANSWER IS . . .
IT DEPENDS.
THAT'S THE SIMPLE TRUTH. AND IN THE WORDS OF
WHO WANTS TO BE A MILLIONAIRE, IT'S MY *"FINAL ANSWER."*
I SAY, "IT DEPENDS," FOR A FEW REASONS.

First, WHAT ARE YOUR GOALS?

If your goal is to lose weight, lean out, or build muscle, eating dessert—Paleo or not—probably isn't going to be the best way to get those results. You know that, I know that. A Paleo cupcake is still a cupcake. Just because a dessert is Paleo doesn't mean that you should eat it with reckless abandon. I know, I love eating dessert with reckless abandon too, but I also like fitting into my jeans. You wouldn't bake a dozen cupcakes and eat all twelve in one sitting, would you? (Well, maybe you would; I won't judge.) So why would Paleo cupcakes be any different? They still contain calories, fat, and sugar; they are just made with better ingredients. Just because it's *natural* sugar doesn't mean that it's not sugar. It doesn't mean that you can never eat dessert, either; it just means that you need to find a balance that works for you.

Paleo people generally fall into two categories: Paleo Police and Everyone Else. You may have met the Paleo Police before. They are the Paleo perfectionists who live, breathe, and eat Paleo, literally. You can usually find them hunting and gathering, openly judging the food choices of others, and carrying around copies of *The Paleo Diet* to reference at all times. They won't eat at restaurants for fear of vegetable oil or legume cross-contamination. And dessert? Don't even get them started. Now, don't get

me wrong, I'm not knocking someone who sticks to the Paleo guidelines 100 percent of the time because that's what makes them feel and function best. I'm knocking the ones who look down on everyone who doesn't follow a strict Paleo diet 100 percent of the time, who leave rude comments on social media outlets, and basically just bring the whole party down. Food is an individual choice.

If you're not a competitive athlete and you aren't looking to drastically change your body composition, then dessert may be in your personal Paleo plan. Your goal may just be to lead and enjoy a healthy lifestyle. And part of a healthy lifestyle is enjoying life. To me, enjoying life involves the occasional splurge or two. This book was written to be a resource for Paleo-ish sweets and treats. I do not endorse eating sweets, Paleo or not, on a daily basis, but rather on occasion. You know your body better than I do, so it's up to you to decide whether eating Paleo treats is a weekly, monthly, or yearly thing. These recipes are meant as a go-to if you are having a dessert crisis or if an event requires you to make something that everyone can eat and enjoy, but doesn't require you to eat ingredients you'd rather not, such as gluten, soy, legumes, and maybe dairy, due to allergies, intolerances, or personal choice.

So why not JUST EAT THE REAL THING?

Well, for starters, a lot of people have genuine food allergies and intolerances. They can't just eat "the real thing." A cupcake or brownie made with wheat flour, whether it's an occasional indulgence or not, could wreak havoc on someone with a gluten intolerance. When they do indulge in a gluten-free or grain-free treat, it may not taste so great, and that just plain sucks. My goal is to make great-tasting treats that don't make people who have dietary restrictions feel deprived. Throughout this book, I've tried to create something to satisfy every craving.

Second, sometimes I want a dessert or treat, but I don't want the consequences that will come from eating it. If I have an alternative that tastes just as good but won't make me feel sick, why wouldn't I eat that instead of the real thing? The chocolate cupcakes in this book taste just as good as their grain-filled counterparts, I swear. I'd much rather make them and get my Paleo dessert on than eat a "real" cupcake and feel like crap. I think a huge percentage of people in the Paleo community feel the exact same way. Sometimes I want a real cinnamon roll out of a pop can, like on Christmas morning, and sometimes I want the Quattro Formaggi pizza from Blind Lady Ale House washed down with a local craft beer. Sometimes feeling like crap is worth it, so I eat what I want. That's just life. It's a give-and-take. It would be unrealistic to expect yourself (or anyone else, for that matter) never to eat dessert again, regardless of the kind of lifestyle you lead. So if you are going to indulge in dessert, why not have the option to make better choices?

It's true, sometimes Paleo desserts and treats don't taste exactly like their regular counterparts, but they're usually close enough to make me feel satisfied and able to move on with my life without feeling deprived. For people in the community to demonize Paleo desserts or baked goods is, to me, just absurd and, honestly, a waste of time. You worry about what's on your plate, and I'll worry about what's on mine. Simple.

But cavemen didn't bake,
SO HOW CAN IT BE PALEO?

Again with the caveman?! There was a really funny cartoon going around the Internet that portrayed two cavemen baking a recipe in a cave with the caption, "This Paleo diet is harder than it looks." When it comes to the whole caveman thing, I think you need to have a sense of humor and not take it so literally. I'm sure that if cavemen could have baked, they would have.

I think most people want to live a life as close to normal as possible, even when suffering from food allergies, intolerances, or autoimmune conditions. Dessert was part of life before Paleo, so why shouldn't it be after Paleo? Again, according to your goals, there is no reason that you shouldn't be able to include desserts and treats in moderation.

On the flip side, though, moderation can be tricky for some people because it's so vague and, by definition, varies from person to person. What I consider moderation may not be what you consider moderation and vice versa. To one person, moderation could mean every day or every week, and to another person it could mean once a month or once a year. Some people can't indulge at all because it takes them too far off-track from where they want to be goal- and health-wise. See what I mean? Is dessert Paleo? **It depends.**

Moderation can be hard for me as well. When I'm standing at my counter with a bag of chocolate chips, it may be the first time I've had chocolate in a few weeks—which is my definition of moderation—but once I start eating them, trying to stop myself after only a handful can be almost impossible. That's why you need to figure out what moderation means for you. I've always been jealous of those people who can eat just one cookie. I could polish off an entire bag of Oreos in one sitting if I wanted to, or an entire pint of ice cream. Sometimes I can eat two squares of dark chocolate and feel perfectly content. Other times I eat everything in sight and move on with my life. Sometimes, I have an all-out bake fest, eat one cupcake, and bring the rest in for my co-workers. It just depends.

If you want dessert to be a part of your life, then I think an easier and perhaps more manageable way to approach moderation is to have desserts and treats on special occasions. Special occasions, by definition, don't happen all the time. That's what's so special about them. Holidays, birthdays, anniversaries, promotions—you get the idea. Saturdays might be considered special occasions because they fall on the weekend, and if that weekly indulgence works for you, great. If not, then that's fine too. Again, you need to find what works best for **you**. No Paleo book, blog, or website can tell you that. It might take some tinkering to figure out the right balance, but pay attention to how your body feels and use it as a guide.

We live in the twenty-first century. We've grown up baking cookies with our families and making cakes to celebrate birthdays and special occasions. We have dinner parties with friends and like to impress them with our latest culinary creations. Food is a huge part of our lives and is tied to many happy memories, experiences, and emotions. In fact, during the writing of this book there were many trips to the grocery store to buy things like chocolate chips, nuts, vanilla, spices, and eggs. I can't tell you how many times the cashier ringing me up got genuinely excited about what I was buying and wanted me to tell them all about what I was going to bake when I got home. In fact, a few even tried to invite themselves over.

There are definitely healthy and responsible ways to incorporate desserts and treats into your Paleo or clean eating lifestyle. I truly hope that this book can be a resource in helping you find that balance. So is dessert Paleo? See what I mean? It really all depends.

Danielle's Note:

If you doubt how good a Paleo dessert can be, start with the Chocolate Cupcakes on pages 226 and 227.

CHAPTER 3

Bitchin'

KITCHEN

SO WHAT ARE THE MUST-HAVES YOU WILL NEED TO COOK
AND BAKE YOUR WAY THROUGH THIS BOOK?
I'M SO HAPPY YOU ASKED!
YOU MAY ALREADY HAVE SOME OF THESE TOOLS.
PERHAPS YOU DON'T AND ARE IN THE MARKET FOR STUFF:
EITHER WAY. LET ME BE YOUR GUIDE.
I GEEK OUT OVER KITCHEN TOOLS. SO PLEASE BEAR WITH ME.

Small APPLIANCES

A good rule to keep in mind when buying pricier kitchen items like stand mixers and food processors is that you get what you pay for. When you purchase these items, you don't want to skimp on price. Buying one high-quality thing will be less expensive than buying less expensive things multiple times.

STAND MIXER

A stand mixer is definitely more of a luxury item, and by no means a must-have for every kitchen. I wrote this entire book without one. I did, however, get a KitchenAid one for Christmas, and let me tell you, it's like going from an old Ford Pinto to a brand-new, fully loaded BMW. Wowza! Not only that, but they are really pretty to look at and come in every color known to man. I would cuddle with mine if it weren't so heavy.

HAND MIXER

A hand mixer is a staple that should be in every kitchen. This light and portable tool can handle small jobs and big jobs alike. A hand mixer is used for everything from beating egg whites and mixing cookie doughs to making frostings and sauces. I recommend one that has at least five speeds. I did, in fact, write this entire book using one. Good models start at around $45. Amazon usually has amazing deals on these.

FOOD PROCESSOR

If you had to choose one kitchen tool to spend the most money on, I would say that a food processor would be the best choice by far. A food processor does EVERYTHING, including mixing and blending doughs and batters. In fact, it may be my desert island tool of choice. Don't skimp on size or quality. For foods that can be harder to process, like nuts, you want a high-powered, high-quality food processor, because the motor will have to run for longer periods. Better quality means not only a more powerful motor, but also better blades. Better blades and a better motor combined mean better processing for the life of your appliance. I bought my Cuisinart 11-cup (2.6-liter) food processor two years ago at Costco for around $140. At the time it seemed like a lot of money to spend on a kitchen item. Let me tell you, though, it's been worth every penny and then some. Knowing what I know now, I would have paid double for it. For the recipes in this book, a 10- to 12-cup (2.3- to 2.8-liter) food processor is the way to go. It can hold large amounts of food, and the majority of the cake recipes in this book are made using a food processor of this size.

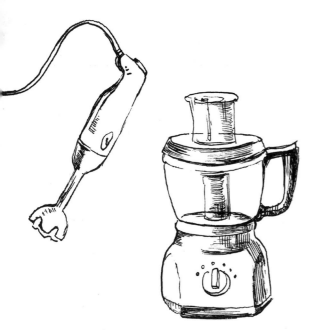

BLENDER

A blender is a great tool to have; that's why you can find one in almost every kitchen. You can use it to make smoothies, soups, quick breads, ice cream, and tart fillings—and an immersion or "stick" blender, like the one shown below, is great for making mayonnaise (page 78). Blenders are another one of those things where quality counts. Honestly, I would love a $300 to $400 blender, but that's unrealistic for me budget-wise, as I'm sure it is for most people. On the other hand, a $40 blender probably isn't going to do much for you and will likely break in the middle of a recipe. I know this from experience. For me, the middle ground is around $100. You can get something that will last and work well enough until you win the lottery and can afford the $400 blender.

SLOW COOKER

A slow cooker is a must-have for any kitchen, regardless of diet and lifestyle. There is a reason why slow cookers are so popular. Who doesn't want to "Set it, and forget it!" Just show me the person. Throw literally anything in there and it will slow-cook to perfection. Set it before you go to work and let your food cook for 8 hours. Or set it before you go to bed. Whatever you do, just set it. Pretty much all good slow cookers fall in the same very reasonable price range, which is anywhere between $30 and $40.

ICE CREAM MAKER

Making your own ice cream is not only easy and delicious, but you can get super creative and make all your favorite flavors. Not only that, but you can control every ingredient that goes in there. This gives you the freedom to use grass-fed milk products or keep it dairy-free! You can buy a quality ice cream maker for $60 to $80, or even get an ice cream attachment for your KitchenAid stand mixer. I love my Cuisinart ice cream maker; I think I paid about $60 for it.

TOOLS

FOOD SCALE

The most accurate way to measure ingredients is to use a food scale. Measuring ingredients by weight is not only more accurate, but it's a simple way to get consistent results when baking. This is common practice in most countries but is still up-and-coming here in the United States. A good food scale should run you about $20, but I've seen them priced as low as $13.

MEASURING CUPS AND SPOONS

A must-have. Or you can use a food scale. Either way, you need to measure things, especially for baking. When it comes to measuring cups, there are two types: one for dry ingredients and one for liquids. Dry measuring cups are the metal or plastic ones that come in a set of four, usually connected on a ring. They are flat across the top so that you can use the side of a knife (or other similar tool) to scrape off the excess and level the contents. Liquid measuring cups are sold singly and usually come in 1-cup (240-ml), 2-cup (1-pint/475-ml), 4-cup (1-quart/1-liter), and 8-cup (2-quart/2-liter) sizes. They are usually made of glass and have a spout for easy pouring.

Dry and liquid measuring cups don't always equal the same amount when it comes to measuring, which is why they can't be used interchangeably. It should be noted, however, that some sets of dry measuring cups will be exactly on par with their equivalent liquid measuring cup. To test yours at home, fill your dry measuring cups with water one at a time and then pour each of them separately into the corresponding glass measuring cup to see where they line up. If they are exact, you won't need to worry about using separate dry and liquid measuring cups for recipes.

I find measuring cups and spoons to be very personal items. I need mine to work for me. I need them not to be fussy and get locked on a key ring because when I need them, I need them. I found a great set of Oxo stainless-steel ones that I like, where the cups and spoons easily snap off their ring. Not that they ever make it back onto the ring, but you get it.

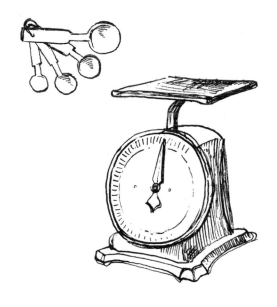

KNIVES

Knives are among the most important—and personal—tools a chef can own. Quality knives can be very expensive. That said, take a look at your budget, assess your needs, research, and then purchase. Treat buying knives like you would buying a new car. Take them for a test drive at your local cooking store. Shop around to get the best prices. Learn how to care for them properly. If you just need something that works well and doesn't break the bank, Costco sells a great set of J.A. Henckels knives for about $140.

When buying knives individually, I find that there are a few must-haves. First on the list is a basic 8- to 10-inch (20- to 25-cm) chef's knife. This is great for cutting, chopping, and dicing and even works well for cutting tougher foods like spaghetti squash. I also like Santoku knives (all-purpose Japanese knives) for chopping and scooping up chopped ingredients to transfer them to a pot or bowl, and a 4-inch (10-cm) paring knife for smaller jobs. Again, these are personal choices. Ask five other chefs and they'd probably all give you different answers. These are the knives that I use the most.

KITCHEN SHEARS

A pair of nice kitchen shears is a very handy thing to have. It's by no means necessary, but shears make quick work of so many tasks, such as cutting bacon into pieces or snipping herbs.

FLOUR SIFTER

It's not just for white flour anymore! The only flour I work with that I sift is almond flour. The rest are so fine that you really don't need to sift them. Even when using finely ground almond flour, I still sift it to get the finest powdery texture possible. I prefer the type of flour sifter that has a handle you turn. The squeeze one makes my hand tired. There is no wrong choice here, though; it's whatever works best for you! I bought mine at the grocery store for $4. Best $4 I ever spent. That thing has stood the test of time!

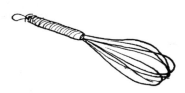

WHISK

If I'm going to be perfectly honest, I have no idea what the differences are between all the whisks. There are hundreds, I swear. They have balloon ones, and flat ones, and piano ones, and ones you only use on Tuesdays. Not really. Well, maybe. I just use a regular 8-inch (20-cm) whisk, most often called a sauce, French, mixing, or kitchen whisk—or just plain "whisk." I actually have two, a metal one and one with the wires coated in silicone. I'm assuming that's so you don't scratch the bottoms of your pans and bowls when whisking, but what do I know? I never said I was a whisk expert.

RUBBER SPATULAS

A rubber spatula would have to come with me to the deserted island. Or would it be the desserted island? I use this tool more than any other tool in the kitchen, hands down. It's great for stirring, scraping batter from the bottom of a bowl, and scooping frosting and marshmallow crème. You name it and I've probably used a rubber spatula to do it. I use this tool so much, in fact, that I own three, because there is a 100 percent chance that the other two are dirty. The sweetest gift I ever got was a set of two rubber spatulas with hooks on them so that they can be placed on the side of a pot or bowl while cooking.

MIXING BOWLS

Mixing bowls are essential items for any cook or baker. You use them to make cookie doughs, batters, and frostings, to cream butter, to beat eggs, and to combine meat loaf ingredients. Everything. A standard set of mixing bowls includes one small, one medium, and one large bowl. I probably own two sets and then some. I find that I need every size of mixing bowl that exists, from micro, mini, small to medium, medium-large, large, and extra-large. I'm not kidding, check my cupboard. You'll be fine with three. Choose either stainless steel or glass; both work great. Stainless-steel sets can be good quality and inexpensive. I recently picked up an amazing set at Costco that I love dearly for $13. Yep. Thirteen bucks. I'm sure you could pay upwards of $100 for a set at a high-end kitchen store. Here is where I think it's okay to skimp on price. Stainless steel and glass are pretty solid materials, so you'll be fine not breaking the bank on this one. Pyrex is a good material because it's heat-safe, so you can use it in the oven or on the stovetop too.

CANDY THERMOMETER

Candy thermometers are very inexpensive. I bought mine at the grocery store for $4. You can pay more for a digital one, but why? A candy thermometer is essential because it can register way higher temperatures than a meat thermometer can. This is necessary for candy making, marshmallows, and even when making maple sugar. Get one; you'll need it.

FINE-MESH SIEVE

A sieve works great for straining things when you want to remove clumps. You can use it with dry or wet ingredients. I often use mine when making curds or sifting my homemade maple sugar. A sieve is super inexpensive and a very handy tool to have.

MICROPLANE

You can get a Microplane for so little money these days. I use mine primarily for grating citrus zest. Zest is more important in baking than you might think. I have a big ol' Microplane because I'm clumsy and always end up scraping my knuckles when I zest, so I want to get it over with as soon as possible, and a big one makes the process way faster. It's so fun to grate lemon zest, knick your finger, and then squeeze the lemon juice. So fun.

COOKIE SCOOP

Cookie scoops come in handy for more than just cookies. These spring-loaded trigger scoops are great for transferring batter to cupcake liners and even just scooping small things to make desserts look fancy, like a small scoop of gelato next to a slice of cake. Yum, I want that. They release the contents in a smooth motion, and if you want a bigger scoop, you can round it at the top. Cookie scoops are cheap and come in a few varieties. Try out a few to see which one works best for you and feels comfy. I once spent thirty minutes in the cookie scoop section. I am now the proud owner of the best cookie scoop out there. Again, this is a personal preference; spend all the time you need to find the right one.

Cookie scoops come in two common sizes: small and large. A small cookie scoop usually has a capacity of about 1 tablespoon, and a large one has a capacity of anywhere from 2 to 4 tablespoons. For the recipes in this book, you will need a small cookie scoop.

ICE CREAM SCOOP

I use a spring-loaded ice cream scoop for many tasks. I love to use mine for cupcake frosting. It's a quick, easy, and fun way to make the cupcakes look irresistible. I also use it to make side dishes look fancy on my plate. Mashed cauliflower looks way fancier when scooped. And sometimes I use it for actual ice cream. Duh. My ice cream scoop has a capacity of ¼ cup (60 ml).

Cookware and
BAKEWARE

You can usually find a good-quality set of pots and pans at Costco or on Amazon for a great price. This is another of those items that I recommend spending more money on to get better quality. Higher-end pans will be made of a more durable material, will heat better and more evenly, and of course will last longer.

MEDIUM SAUCEPAN (2½ QUARTS/2.3 L)

This is a great size saucepan because it's not too small, but it's not gigantic, either. I mainly use this size for making sauces, browning butter, and setting up a water bath to temper chocolate.

LARGE SAUCEPAN (3½ QUARTS/3.3 L)

This is a great saucepan to use for making marshmallows and candy or for anything that will rise in the pan as it heats up.

STOCKPOT OR SOUP POT (8 QUARTS/7.5 L)

It's the perfect size for cooking large batches of soup and steaming artichokes.

10-INCH (25-CM) CAST-IRON SKILLET

Cast iron is an amazing material to work with. Not only does it look old-timey, but it cooks foods amazingly well. Cast iron gets really, really hot. It's great when you want to put something in the oven but you don't have a pan that can withstand the oven temperature. It's also great for searing meat (like steak) on the stove and then transferring it to the oven to cook further. I use mine for baked desserts too. Be sure to treat your cast-iron skillet properly. Most brand-new skillets must be seasoned before use (the manufacturer will provide instructions). After washing with just water (or mild soap if needed), you want to dry it immediately so it doesn't rust. You also want to make sure that it's properly seasoned with oil. Most manufacturers recommend vegetable oil, but I find that olive oil or coconut oil work great. I'm sure you could even use ghee or lard.

6-INCH (15-CM) CAST-IRON SKILLET

This size skillet is perfect for desserts, egg dishes, and anything else you want to divide into individual servings. And it is really cute. I found mine at Cost Plus World Market for about $8. (See the following entry for notes on caring for cast-iron pans.)

12-INCH (30.5-CM) SKILLET (STAINLESS STEEL OR NONSTICK)

One of my biggest pet peeves is not having enough room in the pan while I cook. This size skillet has enough room for a pound of meat, veggies, and some sauce. You can use it for cooking anything from bacon to asparagus. Skillets can get pricey. Just look for something that feels solid in your hands.

BAKING SHEETS (COOKIE SHEETS)

Baking sheets are another must-have item. They are so inexpensive that there really is no reason not to have at least two in your kitchen. Baking sheets are great for cookies and biscuits and for chocolate-covered items like strawberries. The size I use is 11 by 17 inches (28 by 42 cm). This is a common size for most home cooks and can be found anywhere cookie sheets are sold.

RIMMED BAKING SHEETS (SHEET PANS)

A rimmed baking sheet, also called a sheet pan, is basically just a cookie sheet with a 1-inch (2.5-cm) rim around the edges. These pans are great for baking bacon, roasting nuts, and even making certain types of cakes. The most common size is 18 by 13 inches (46 by 33 cm).

12-CUP MUFFIN/CUPCAKE PAN

These pans are used for making cupcakes and muffins. The standard size is 12 cups, but you can also find others, like a 6-cup pan for jumbo muffins and a 24-cup pan for mini ones. Muffin pans are inexpensive, and a quality one will literally last you forever.

8-INCH (20-CM) SPRINGFORM CAKE PAN

The 8-inch (20-cm) cake size is my favorite. It's big, but not too big. You can layer it tall or keep it short. This is the primary pan size used for the larger cakes in this book. Amazon sells a great set of Wilton springform cake pans for about $25. They come in three sizes: 8-inch (20-cm), 9-inch (23-cm), and 10-inch (25-cm). I actually own two sets of these because it speeds up the process of making multilayer cakes.

I prefer springform pans because cakes come out clean and in one piece. Getting cakes to come out of a standard aluminum cake pan intact can be challenging. Why make it harder than it has to be? You can find springform pans in both regular and nonstick finishes. I prefer nonstick because cakes come out a little easier, but any cake pans will work for the recipes in this book. Please note that if using lighter-colored aluminum pans, you may have to add additional baking time. I find that darker pans bake faster.

6-INCH (15-CM) SPRINGFORM CAKE PAN

I'm obsessed with 6-inch (15-cm) cakes. This size pan makes the most gorgeous petite cakes. I use it for a few of the cake recipes in the book, such as the Death by Chocolate Cake on pages 238 to 241. I own two of these pans, and I love to make this size cake with three or four layers. I use a Wilton brand nonstick springform pan that I purchased on Amazon for about $12.

4½-INCH (11.5-CM) SPRINGFORM CAKE PAN

This is more of a specialty-sized pan, and it's not an absolute necessity. I do have an amazing Mississippi Mud Pie recipe (pages 178 and 179) that calls for this size, but an 8-inch cake pan will work just as well. Wilton makes a great set of three mini pans for around $8. I love making cute little cheesecakes with these guys.

9-INCH (23-CM) PIE PAN

This pan is the classic size for making pies.

9-INCH (23-CM) OR 11-INCH (28-CM) TART PAN

Tart pans are great for making fruit tarts as well as quiches and other baked egg dishes. I like the kind with a removable bottom because it makes it easy to remove the tart from the pan without having to cut into it. Push on the bottom and out comes your tart.

4¾-INCH (12-CM) MINI TART PANS

As you can probably tell by now, I like mini pans. They give desserts and baked goods a great appearance. These pans are also great for dinner parties where you may want to make tartlets and serve them to 4 to 6 guests. Again, I love the removable-bottom pans because of the ease of use. I bought a set of Wilton ones for $13, and they work great.

SPECIALTY TART PANS

Tart pans come in all kinds of cool shapes and sizes. A few of the recipes in this book were made and photographed in square or rectangular tart pans. All the tart recipes can be made in round tart pans (just use the equivalent dimension or volume), but these distinctive-shaped pans can be fun to work with and add a pleasing and elegant aesthetic for special occasions. The two specialty tart pans that I own are a 9-inch (23-cm) square pan and a 14 by 5-inch (35.5 by 12.75-cm) rectangular pan.

8 BY 8-INCH (20 BY 20-CM) SQUARE GLASS BAKING DISH

This is my go-to dish for anything that needs to be baked in the oven. I cook chicken, casseroles, dessert bars, and egg dishes in this bad boy. I can't live without it. Pyrex is a great material because it can withstand high temperatures without cracking or breaking. You can find these on the cheap just about anywhere, from Amazon to Bed Bath & Beyond.

9 BY 5-INCH (23 BY 12.75-CM) GLASS LOAF PAN

This is my go-to loaf pan. I find I get the most consistent quick breads and baking times with this. I also use it for meatloaf. When I use aluminum or metal pans my baking times are usually off, so I turn to this loaf pan 100 percent of the time. Another really inexpensive item that is a must-have.

MISCELLANEOUS

PARCHMENT PAPER

And lots of it. I could probably circle the world twice with the amount of parchment paper I've gone through in my lifetime. I use it for EVERYTHING. From lining baking sheets for cookies or candy to lining loaf pans and cake pans, it's the absolute best material for baking. Nothing sticks to it. If you want to go green, some folks are turning to silicone baking sheets. It is a reusable option that runs about $20 to $30. Amazon is always having sales on different-sized Silpats (the most well-known brand of silicone baking sheets). I prefer parchment paper because I don't have to wash it, and in some situations, like when baking cookies, you can flip it over and reuse the other side. This is definitely one of those personal preference situations. Costco has great deals on huge rolls of parchment paper that will last you a long while.

If you use regular cake pans instead of springform pans—I don't recommend it, but I know you might be attached to your old cake pans—you can purchase precut rounds of parchment paper, eliminating the step of hand-cutting parchment paper circles to the size of your cake pans. The precut rounds are available at specialty cookware shops and online. If you will be using springform pans to make the cakes in this book, regular parchment paper is fine (see page 199 for an easy method of lining springform cake pans).

The easiest way to line a glass or metal baking dish or loaf pan with parchment paper is to cut two sheets of parchment sized to fit evenly in the bottom of the pan. Lay one sheet horizontally across the bottom and the other sheet vertically on top of the other, letting the extra paper hang over the sides, as shown in the photo, opposite. Then, when your baked goods are ready, you can use the overhang as handles to lift everything out of the pan and have a clean area for cutting. The parchment also prevents baked goods from sticking to the pan.

COOLING RACKS

Cooling racks help with cooling foods like cakes and cookies (especially those cookies that are meant to be crisp), but often are optional. I find them most useful when I need to glaze something or cool cakes after removing them from the pan. I also use them for making savory items, like baking bacon. In most cases, though, I prefer to cool things on the counter on the parchment paper they were baked with. If you have the counter space, it's so easy to just slide the cookies off the baking sheet and onto the counter while still on the parchment paper. Parchment paper with baked goods on it can also be slid onto a cooling rack to free up counter space or for faster cooling.

DECORATING BAGS (AKA PASTRY BAGS)

These bags come in reusable and disposable varieties. Again, it's personal preference: Do you want to wash or toss? An easy substitute for decorating bags is resealable plastic bags, like the Ziploc brand. You can fill them with your desired frosting and then just snip off one corner. You can also snip a corner first, add the desired decorating tip, and then fill with frosting to pipe on your desserts. Plastic bags are great in a pinch, but I definitely feel like I have more control with a standard decorating bag. I usually use a 16-inch (40.5-cm) bag.

PIPING TIPS

I use only large piping tips. You can find piping tips in smaller sizes at stores like Target and even at grocery stores. I find that the smaller ones are best for detailed decoration, which I don't do. The larger ones are what you want for placing frosting on cakes and cupcakes. My go-to tip set, the Ateco #786 Large Tube Set, is only $23 on Amazon. In addition to that set, I highly recommend getting a Wilton 1M tip because it's probably my number-one favorite. See what I did there? The Wilton 1M tip is a large tip that is used for creating rose piping on cakes and cupcakes. It's super easy to use and yields amazing results. It's maybe $3 at Michaels. I also like using the 1A tip, which is just a plain round tip used to easily apply frosting on cupcakes. Another favorite of mine is the 2C, it creates a really cool looking designs when piped. Decorating tips will last you forever; grab a set today. (*Note:* Sprinkled throughout the recipes, you will find references to the specific piping tip(s) that I used to frost or decorate a particular dessert, in case you want to recreate what's shown in the accompanying photo; however, you may use any tip you like. A more detailed description of the applications of various piping tips is included on pages 203 and 204.)

COOKIE CUTTERS

I grabbed a great set of Wilton metal cookie cutters at Michaels for about $10. I have a set of plain round ones and a set of square ones too. Six come in a set, and they range in size from small to large. They are dual-sided, with a straight edge on one side and a curved edge on the other.

PAPER BAKING CUPS (STANDARD AND MINI)

You can grab paper baking cups at any grocery store. You'll find plain, foil, and fun colored varieties. I mostly use the standard size for cupcakes and muffins. I do, however, use the mini size for the Salted Caramel Cheesecake Bites (pages 256 and 257) in this book. Not only are they delicious, but they are oh so cute and fun-sized!

SILICONE BAKING CUPS (STANDARD SIZE)

I actually can't stand baking cupcakes in silicone baking cups. I just don't like it. The cupcakes never come out. What I do use my silicone baking cups for is making candy, and lots of it! These are the absolute best molds for

Almond Butter Cups (pages 146 and 147), Salted Caramel Cups (pages 148 and 149), and plain ol' homemade chocolate (pages 140 to 143). I use them for quite a few recipes in this book, and I literally can't live without them. As far as price goes, you can pick up a set of 12 for about $6.

CHOCOLATE SILICONE MOLDS

I use chocolate bar–shaped silicone molds for making white and dark chocolate (pages 140 to 143). Silicone works best for popping hardened chocolate out, and cleanup is a breeze. You can find these in all different shapes, sizes, and designs for a few bucks on Amazon.

OFFSET SPATULAS (AKA ICING KNIVES)

These stainless-steel knives are used to spread frosting on the tops and sides of cakes and the tops of cupcakes. They come in all different sizes. I have a two-piece set from Oxo that covers all my needs: a larger knife with a 6-inch (15-cm) blade, which Oxo calls a "bent icing knife," and a smaller one with a 4½-inch (11.5-cm) blade, which Oxo calls a "cupcake icing knife." Again, this is personal preference. I recommend trying out a few sizes in the store to see what feels comfortable in your hand. A set of two can range in price from about $25 for professional ones to $10 for general consumer-oriented ones. Personally, I think they work the same. It also depends on which material you like best. Some are made with wooden handles, and some with plastic or silicone handles. If you don't have an offset spatula, you can use a rubber spatula; offset spatulas are longer and flatter, which makes spreading frosting on a cake quicker and the results a little cleaner.

CANDY-DIPPING FORK

Candy-dipping tools are used for coating things in chocolate. The tool resembles a fork and gives you an easy and mess-free way to dip, swirl, and coat your item while providing a stable base to remove the item from the chocolate without ruining your beautiful coating. You can usually find these for under $5 at Michaels craft stores and online. An easier and less-expensive option is to snap off the two middle prongs of a plastic fork. It provides the same ease of use and stability.

DOUBLE BOILER

A double boiler, or bain-marie if you're fancy, is essentially just a two-piece pot that is used to gradually heat things or to keep things warm over time. There is a larger pot on the bottom in which water is simmered and a smaller pan or insert that rests on top in which the ingredients are gently heated or kept warm. When the water in the bottom pot is heated, it creates steam that slowly and steadily heats the item in the top pan. Double boilers are sold at home goods stores like Bed Bath & Beyond and online at Amazon. The capacity of most double boiler inserts ranges from 1½ to 2½ quarts (1.4 to 2.3 liters), with the smaller size of 1½ quarts (1.4 liters) being most common followed in popularity by the 2-quart (2-liter) size and then the 2½-quart (2.3-liter) size.

If you don't own a double boiler, which I don't, it's simple to create one at home with tools you already have. Take a small or medium-sized saucepan, fill it halfway with water, and place it on the stove. In a separate larger heatproof bowl, place the ingredient you would like to heat. For the recipes in book, those ingredients will be mainly chocolate and eggs. Then place the bowl on top of the saucepan. Make sure that the bowl is big enough to rest snugly on the lip of the pan so that no steam escapes and the bottom of the bowl doesn't touch the water. Then turn the heat on low or medium to maintain a simmer and heat your ingredient. This is the best method for melting chocolate and heating eggs to a temperature that makes them safe to consume without the risk of curdling.

WOODEN SPOONS

The wooden spoon is probably the most historical kitchen tool. It's likely been used since the advent of cooking! Chop wood, carve spoon, stir food. There's caveman for you. The wooden spoon is my favorite tool for making homemade maple sugar and ice cream. It won't scrape the bottom of your pots and pans, and you can honestly use it for anything cooking or baking related. In fact, I'm 80 percent sure that you have one in your kitchen right now.

KITCHEN TORCH

A kitchen torch is such a fun tool! Is it essential or absolutely necessary? Not really. But it's awesome for making crème brûlée and s'mores-type desserts. You can pick one up on Amazon or at Bed Bath & Beyond for about $40. This is one of those kitchen tools that would be great to ask someone for on your next birthday. That way, you get one to play with, but you don't have to pay for it!

CHAPTER 4

POLITE

PROVISIONS

FLOURS

COCONUT FLOUR

Coconut flour is made from the dried pulp of coconuts after making coconut milk. Coconut flours tend to be fairly similar in texture and taste, unlike almond flour. However, I have tried several brands of coconut flour, and I find that I prefer the Nutiva brand. It comes in 3- and 5-pound (1.4- and 2.3-kg) resealable bags and is inexpensive. I like this brand because the bag makes it easy to work with, and I find the quality to be higher than other brands. Sometimes you can find a 3-pound (1.4-kg) bag at Costco for about $5.

www.nutiva.com

TAPIOCA FLOUR (AKA TAPIOCA STARCH)

Tapioca flour is made from the starch of the South American cassava pant. It's very fine in texture, almost powderlike, and is another inexpensive, easy-to-find provision. I use Bob's Red Mill brand, which is available at stores like Whole Foods, Sprouts, and Amazon. It's sold in 20-ounce (467-g) bags.

www.bobsredmill.com

ALMOND FLOUR

Almond flour is definitely my most used flour of them all. Essentially, it's just super finely ground blanched almonds. My absolute favorite brand, hands down, is Honeyville. It's the most fine-textured almond flour available. This makes a huge difference in the texture of your baked goods. You can purchase 3-pound, 5-pound, and 25-pound quantities at Honeyville.com and Amazon.

www.honeyville.com

ARROWROOT FLOUR (AKA ARROWROOT STARCH)

Arrowroot flour comes from the starch of the arrowroot plant. It is used primarily as a thickener in soups and sauces in place of cornstarch, but also works well in baking. It's a very fine, tasteless powder. I use Bob's Red Mill brand, which is widely available at stores like Whole Foods, Sprouts, and Amazon. Most grocery stores carry the 16-ounce (455-g) size.

www.bobsredmill.com

SWEETENERS

RAW HONEY

Buy organic local raw honey if you can, because it has the most health benefits. Your local farmers' market would be a great place to find it. (Locally produced honey has the advantage of helping with pollen allergies.) If you can't find local honey, try the Honey Gardens brand. Of all the store-bought raw honey options, it is my favorite. It has the most amazing flavor. Honey makes a great sweetener for baked goods and helps with texture and leavening properties in some cases. Honey is also an amazing replacement for corn syrup. You can boil honey to make candy and marshmallows.

You will notice that some of the recipes in this book call for "light-colored raw honey" and some for just "raw honey." The reason for this is that in recipes where you want a light color, like white chocolate and vanilla ice cream, you want to use the lightest-colored honey possible. Using a dark-colored honey may cause discoloration. For some folks this may not be an issue, since the taste is the same, but we eat with our eyes first, so it's very important to me that things look like they should! I like to say that I'm just detail oriented.

www.honeygardens.com

100 PERCENT PURE MAPLE SYRUP

No Aunt Jemima stuff here, folks. I'm talking about the stuff tapped straight from trees. Make sure that it says 100 percent pure maple syrup on the bottle. Maple syrup comes in multiple varieties, or grades—from light (currently called "golden," but previously known as "fancy"), which has the least strong maple flavor, to dark (previously called Grade B). I prefer different grades for different uses. When making maple sugar, I use golden maple syrup, but when baking I turn to dark maple syrup because it has a richer flavor and is more mineral rich than its lighter counterparts.

COCONUT SUGAR

Coconut sugar is a popular natural sugar because it's got a very low glycemic index, which means that it won't spike your insulin levels. It has a neutral, mildly sweet flavor. It's a great replacement in any recipe that calls for brown sugar, since they taste somewhat similar. Coconut sugar is made by draining the liquid sap from the flower of the coconut palm and then placing it over heat until most of the water has evaporated, leaving sugar granules. Try to buy your coconut sugar from organic, sustainable sources. My absolute favorite brands are Nutiva Organic, Navitas Naturals, and Madhava Organic. When you open the bag, you can just smell the quality. These brands also tend to be finer in grain and clump less. You can find them at most health food stores as well as on Amazon.

www.nutiva.com
www.navitasnaturals.com
www.madhavasweeteners.com

MAPLE SUGAR

My favorite of all the sugars I use is maple sugar. It can be used in a 1:1 ratio for white sugar in recipes. Making it yourself is a very simple and easy process that will save you a ton of money. You can find a 32-ounce bottle of maple syrup at Costco or Trader Joe's for about $13, which will yield about 3 to 4 cups (195 to 260 grams) of maple sugar, about double the amount for the same price when buying maple sugar at the store. I also find that homemade maple sugar works better in recipes like crème brûlée, where the sugar needs to be torched. Store-bought brands tend to be a little drier and don't work well for this purpose. My preferred store-bought brand of maple sugar is Aunt Patty's, which you can find at Whole Foods. You can also try Etsy, where a lot of maple syrup producers sell high-quality homemade maple sugar for cheap.

www.auntpattys.glorybee.com

DATE SUGAR

Date sugar is another great sugar to bake with because it's completely natural and has such a neat flavor. The flavor resembles graham, and I use it in all my graham cracker recipes. Date sugar is made by grounding dried dates into a fine powder. It is very inexpensive; you can grab a 13-ounce bottle of Aunt Patty's brand at Whole Foods for about $6. Bob's Red Mill brand makes an inexpensive date sugar as well.

MOLASSES

I use two types of molasses in the recipes in this book: light, which is sometimes referred to as "regular," and blackstrap. Blackstrap has a very strong flavor and is called blackstrap because it's almost black in color. Light molasses is more amber in color and tastes sweeter. Molasses is a great way to add flavor to your baked goods and is a must-have for gingerbread recipes. A little goes a long way, particularly with blackstrap! I use Grandma's Original molasses in recipes that call for light molasses and Wholesome Sweeteners in recipes that call for blackstrap, but any brand will do.

CHOCOLATE

Most chocolate is made from a combination of cacao butter or liquor, sugar, an emulsifier, and vanilla. In pure form, chocolate is considered a superfood full of antioxidants. There are two homemade chocolate recipes in this book: one for regular chocolate and one for white chocolate. Making chocolate at home is actually very easy and can be a lot of fun. You can get super creative with different-shaped molds.

The main ingredient in chocolate is cacao butter. You can find a variety of brands of cacao butter online. Just be sure to look for something that is organic and comes from a sustainable source. I find that Amazon has great prices. Cacao butter is similar to coconut oil in that it melts at warmer temperatures, so be sure to store in a cool, dry place.

When you see the percent symbol next to a number on chocolate label, it is referring to the total cacao content of the chocolate. So if you see 85 percent cacao, for example, you know that 85 percent of that chocolate comes from cacao ingredients. The higher the percentage, the less sugar the chocolate contains. Anywhere from 60 to 100 percent is considered dark chocolate, with 60 percent (usually called "bittersweet") being the sweetest and 100 percent containing no sugar at all. Milk chocolate is usually around 30 to 45 percent cacao because milk is added to the ingredients, diluting the cacao content further and making it the sweetest chocolate of all. Semisweet would be, you guessed it, smack dab in the middle.

Never let anyone tell you that all chocolate is created equal. Below is a list of my favorite brands: They make delicious, high-quality chocolate and, better yet, none of them use soy lecithin as an emulsifier in their products. Honestly, I could write an entire book about the chocolate brands I like and why, but I'll spare you.

Feel free to use any form of chocolate you like when making the recipes in this book. I mainly use chocolate chips because they are widely available, easy to measure, and the least expensive form to work with. Also, unless a recipe calls for a specific type of chocolate or chocolate chip, please use whatever you prefer. A recipe may call for a certain type—semisweet or dark, for example—because it yields better results. Better results means less chance for error, and less chance for error means less chance for failure.

» **AlterEco** – AlterEco makes tasty chocolate bars with sustainable practices. I adore their truffles and dark mint bars.

www.alterecofoods.com

» **Askinosie** – Single origin, direct trade, and they make a white chocolate bar from goat's milk that is to die for.

www.askinosie.com

» **Eating Evolved** – Known as the Paleo-friendly chocolate, these guys use only organic maple sugar to sweeten their chocolate and use only the highest-quality fair-trade cacao. Because chocolate is food, not candy!

www.eatingevolved.com

» **Guittard Chocolate Company**– Guittard (pronounced GHEE-TARD) is my absolute favorite chocolate to bake with. It contains only four ingredients, including sunflower lecithin instead of soy lecithin. Guittard was one of the first big chocolate companies to make this switch. You can find at least four bags of their extra-dark chocolate baking chips (63% cacao) and another four bags of their semisweet chocolate baking chips (46% cacao) in my kitchen at all times. Guittard chocolate can be found at Sprouts Farmers Market, Albertsons, Safeway, and Vons stores.

www.guittard.com

WHITE CHOCOLATE

Before making any of the white chocolate recipes in this book, I researched many white chocolate options for you. Hey, I did say that I wanted to be a professional chocolate taster when I grew up, didn't I? I contacted several chocolate companies around the country to find you the best soy-free, non-GMO white chocolate with the highest-quality ingredients and best taste possible. Here are the winners:

In first place we have **Askinosie White Chocolate Bar** (34% cacao), which is made with goat's milk (I'm obsessed with this white chocolate bar). Second place goes to **Stella Bernrain Swiss White Chocolate with Cacao Nibs**; and third place goes to **Olive & Sinclair Buttermilk White Chocolate Bar** (45% cacao). Honorable mention goes to **Alter Eco,** which was developing a white chocolate bar at the time this book went to print, but guaranteed me that it would be soy-free, organic, and delicious. In a pinch, **Ghirardelli White Chocolate Chips** and **Whole Foods 365 Brand White Chocolate Mini Chips** work well, but both do contain soy. On the other hand, they were the only white chocolate chips I could find in grocery stores that didn't contain partially hydrogenated oils, which you want to avoid completely.

CACAO POWDER/UNSWEETENED COCOA POWDER

There isn't much difference between cacao powder and unsweetened cocoa powder. Each is made by grinding cacao nibs into a paste. The fat is then removed, and what remains is ground up again, creating a fine dust, which becomes the cacao or cocoa powder. The two can be used interchangeably in recipes with no difference in taste or richness. According to the FDA, the term "cacao powder" is mostly used to describe the powder in its raw form, made from unroasted cacao beans; whereas the term "cocoa powder" is made from cacao beans that were roasted during processing and may still have a small amount of cocoa butter present.

Dutch-processed cocoa power, on the other hand, has undergone a process to neutralize the acidity of the cacao, and for this reason, Dutch-processed cocoa will not react with baking soda. The process also strips away most of the nutritional value. I never bake with Dutch-processed cocoa. In fact, it's rare that I will buy something if the package says, "cocoa processed with alkali." Translation: Dutch-processed cocoa, and no nutritional value.

GRASS-FED BUTTER

Grass-fed butter might qualify for a place on my list of my favorite things on planet earth. I use butter for everything, especially in baking. Kerrygold makes a delicious grass-fed butter that is available pretty much anywhere. The best prices I have found are at Costco and Trader Joe's. Kerrygold comes in both salted and unsalted varieties; I use both for baking and cooking, depending on what works best in a given recipe. Unsalted butter works amazingly well for buttercream frostings. When a recipe contains butter, either salted or unsalted is specified.

www.kerrygoldusa.com

GHEE

I love ghee. I have been known to sit and sniff a jar of ghee. Ghee is a great alternative to butter for those with dairy allergies and sensitivities. My favorite brands are Tin Star and OMghee. As with butter, you really want to eat only grass-fed varieties of ghee.

www.tinstarfoods.com
www.omghee.com

COCONUT OIL

Coconut oil is taking the world by storm. It has so many health benefits and so many incredible uses! I can't even begin to list them all. Coconut oil becomes solid at about room temperature, or 70°F (21°C). Most of my recipes call for melted coconut oil. The easiest way to melt it is to throw the jar in the microwave for a few seconds, just long enough to liquefy it, and then pour it into a measuring cup. Coconut oil is great for baking; I use it all the time. There are literally hundreds of coconut oil brands out there, and I wouldn't say that I prefer one brand over another. I usually just grab what's on sale. I think anything goes in this department.

PALM SHORTENING

Palm shortening is derived from palm fruit oil. This oil has equal amounts of saturated and unsaturated fat and contains vitamin E and antioxidants. It behaves just like regular shortening in that it makes baked goods tender, springy, and moist and remains solid at room temperature. Palm shortening, however, has none of the bad partially hydrogenated oils (trans-fatty acids) that regular shortening like Crisco does. Palm shortening is my go-to fat when making cakes or cupcakes. It creates a texture that is as close to the real thing as you can get. Palm shortening sometimes gets a bad rap environmentally, mainly due to misinformation and people not doing research to find out which companies use sustainable sources. These are the companies that I found use sustainable sources, operating much like small family farms, and have great information about their practices and environmental impact on their websites.

www.tropicaltraditions.com
www.spectrumorganics.com
www.nutiva.com

PASTURED LEAF LARD

Oh, glorious pastured leaf lard, how I adore you! Lard is one of the best ingredients to bake with. It gives anything a nice flavor and texture. Sometimes I wish I lived in the 1950s, when everything was made with lard. In fact, the first milkshakes that McDonald's served were made with lard. #funfact. Leaf lard is the finest lard available and is the best for making pie crusts nice and flaky. Be sure to use only leaf lard from pasture-raised pigs. Check out more information on lard and animal fats at Fatworks.

www.fatworks.com

COCONUT BUTTER

Coconut butter is great for baking. Or just eating off a spoon. It has a nice subtle sweetness and coconut flavor, but it's not overpowering. I mostly use coconut butter as a glaze, drizzled over baked goods, instead of making one out of powdered sugar. I usually just heat a little up in the microwave, drizzle, and voilà! You can also make coconut butter at home. My favorite brands to drizzle are Nikki's Coconut Butter and Artisana Organics. They are also great for spreading on fruit and baked goods. The You Fresh Naturals brand is great for baking and for eating straight out of the jar.

www.nikkiscoconutbutter.com
www.artisanafoods.com
www.youfreshnaturals.com

DAIRY

CREAM CHEESE

Cream cheese makes one heck of a frosting. Several recipes throughout the book call for it. If you can, try to find an organic source with no preservatives. You can find good organic brands in most stores, especially Whole Foods. Along with cream cheese, I like to use mascarpone in frostings. Mascarpone is like an Italian cream cheese. It's little sweeter and softer and very spreadable, and best of all it only has three ingredients: milk, cream, and lemon juice or citric acid.

HEAVY CREAM

Heavy cream is full-fat dairy at its finest. It is used to make whipped cream, and you can also find it in some of the cake and frosting recipes in this book. I like to use heavy cream because it doesn't come with a lot of added ingredients. You can even find raw versions sourced from grass-fed animals for sale in health food stores.

SOUR CREAM OR GRASS-FED PLAIN YOGURT

If you go with sour cream, be sure to use a brand that isn't full of additives. I actually use Daisy brand because it contains just one ingredient and you can find it anywhere. I don't eat enough sour cream to worry about whether or not it's organic. If you want another option, plain grass-fed yogurt makes a great alternative and tastes very similar to sour cream, with tons of health benefits since it's made from grass-fed milk.

www.daisybrand.com
www.maplehillcreamery.com

Dairy ALTERNATIVES

COCONUT MILK

Full-fat canned coconut milk is the way to go. To be clear, this is very different from the refrigerated coconut milk sold in cartons next to the almond milk. You can usually find the canned coconut milk in the international section of your grocery store with the Asian cooking ingredients. This is my dairy-free milk of choice. Coconut milk is stored and is easiest to use in most recipes at room temperature; it's usually only when making whipped coconut cream that you will find instructions to chill the milk in the refrigerator prior to using. This is because when cold, the coconut cream (fat) content in the milk separates. Even when stored at room temperature the cream will separate sometimes; for this reason, always shake the can to mix the water and cream back together. I have tried every brand out there, so I know what works and what doesn't. If you are looking for something with no added ingredients because you are sensitive to ingredients like guar gum, then go with Golden Star brand. It contains only coconut milk and water, no gums. It's super thick and creamy, all-purpose, and works great in any recipe, even whipped coconut cream. You can find it at Ralphs, Walmart, and Amazon. If you aren't sensitive to guar gum, then try Thai Kitchen Organic brand, which has only three ingredients. I always have great luck with this brand, especially the organic kind. It's rare that I get a can that doesn't thicken in the refrigerator so I can make whipped coconut cream. Another brand that I frequently use and get consistently get great results with is Sprouts Premium Coconut Cream.

www.goldenstartrading.com

www.thaikitchen.com

www.sprouts.com

ALMOND MILK

Almond milk is super easy to make yourself, but I get lazy. If I'm not lazy, I make my own, because it tastes amazing and has no added ingredients. If you do a Google search for "homemade almond milk," you will find hundreds of recipes on the Internet. The process is simple enough: Briefly, you rinse raw almonds and soak them overnight in twice the amount of water (a ratio of 1:2, nuts to water). After the almonds have soaked, you rinse them thoroughly and add the almonds and fresh water (again, a ratio of 1:2, nuts to water) to a blender. You then blend the soaked almonds and water together with a pinch of salt and any extras you prefer, like vanilla extract or a touch of natural sweetener, until the almonds are broken down into a milky pulp. To remove the pulp, you strain the mixture through cheesecloth or a nut milk bag into a storage container. Refrigerate until cold, then pour yourself a glass and enjoy your delicious homemade almond milk.

When I want a store-bought brand of almond milk, I go for Silk Unsweetened Vanilla. Silk does not contain carrageenan, which can cause stomach problems for some people, and is non-GMO verified.

www.silk.com

CASHEW MILK

Same goes for cashew milk; you can easily make your own if you are so inclined. To make it, simply follow the method in the entry for almond milk, above, substituting raw cashews for almonds. (If you are using cashew milk for a savory recipe, like the Cajun Sausage Gravy on pages 74 and 75, do not add vanilla or a sweetener.) If you aren't so inclined, the Silk brand sells a great-tasting unsweetened cashew milk that is free of carrageenan.

Dried FRUIT

My favorite place to get dried fruit for baking and Paleo snacks is Steve's PaleoGoods. Steve's dried fruit contains no added sugars, and it's the best I've ever tasted! Steve has a great company that makes great products and is constantly giving back to the community.

www.stevespaleogoods.com

Nuts/ NUT BUTTERS

Nuts are used quite a bit throughout this book. In most cases I use raw unsalted nut pieces so I can control the amount of salt in the recipe. The nuts are likely going to be ground down in a food processor anyway, so there's no need to buy them whole, which is typically more expensive. I've found the best prices on nuts at Trader Joe's. They have a huge variety and come in perfectly portioned bags.

I also use almond butter quite a bit throughout this book. Nut butters, like with most food, can be such a personal choice. My favorite almond butter of all time is Barney Butter, the smooth one. The texture is exactly the same as smooth peanut butter, and that makes me really happy because I'm not a huge fan of the grainy, chunky stuff. I'm a smooth operator. Barney Butter also makes each version in a chunky texture for all of you who like to live on the edge. There is a Bare version that contains no sugar or salt: it's just raw almonds and palm fruit oil. There is also a regular version, which is made with roasted almonds, is sweetened with cane sugar, and has a hint of salt. With only 3 grams of sugar per serving, I wouldn't sweat it, but those who are watching their intake of sugar in all forms should stick to the Bare variety. I used the Bare variety to make all the recipes in this book that call for almond butter.

www.barneybutter.com

Note:

I've mentioned a lot of name-brand products in Chapters 3 and 4; I haven't been paid or sponsored by any of the companies endorsed above. These are the brands that I use in my own kitchen and the ones that I used to create the recipes in this book. They are tried and true. After all, if they can stand up to all the wear-and-tear I put them through, testing recipe after recipe, then they deserve to be mentioned. These are the brands that have worked best for me, and I don't mind sharing my experience with you.

CHAPTER 5

Baking *for* SUCCESS

Mise en place
AND OTHER WORDS OF WISDOM

Since Paleo recipes are made from scratch and sometimes use nontraditional ingredients, you may have to take some additional steps to get the same outcome as a traditional recipe, and that can feel overwhelming. Having good cooking habits in place goes a long way toward offsetting kitchen angst.

One of the most fundamental is *mise en place*, a French term for "putting in place," which refers to a system of organization in the kitchen. It basically means, check yourself before you wreck yourself, or get organized before you start cooking or baking. Doing so is going to make the process easier and more enjoyable, and there will be much less chance for error.

Mise en place includes the preliminary steps of organizing your ingredients and recipe components as well as prepping and measuring them: Measure out the flours, clean and chop the vegetables, get the spices you'll need out of the cupboard, beat the eggs, par-bake the crust, etc. This makes it easier to go down the steps of a recipe and throw everything together.

Even before organizing your ingredients, it's good to get into the habit of reading recipes through from start to finish, twice. You will get a general idea of how the recipe is going to flow, you can check to make sure that you have all the ingredients on hand, and you will know how much time you are going to need to make the recipe from start to finish.

To help you manage your time, at the top of each recipe, I've listed the minimum prep and cook times required to make the recipe from start to finish; should you want to make everything the day of, these times will let you know what you're getting yourself into. At the end of each recipe you will find a list of the components that can be made ahead, should you want to get a head start on the recipe.

I've set up the recipes this way because I feel that the common practice of listing just the time to prepare the recipe, not including the time needed to prepare any sub-recipes, such as a pie crust or frosting, is a bit deceptive. For example, if I see a bar recipe that I want to make for an upcoming event and the recipe says that it will take thirty minutes, I will assume that it's going to take thirty minutes to make the recipe in its entirety, from start to finish. This can be a problem if I decide to make the bars on the day of the event and find out, once I get into the recipe, that it actually takes two hours because it involves making subrecipes before I can even begin to prepare the bars. Then I'm mad and I have to rush my hair for the party. No one likes to rush their hair—let's get real!

Here's another good reason to read through a recipe multiple times: If you come across a certain term or method that you haven't encountered before—like browning butter, for instance—you will have a chance to look for additional information, if needed. Enter Google and YouTube videos . . . if only I had a dollar for every cooking technique I've looked up. And reading a recipe twice allows you to catch something you may have missed the first time through.

Baking TERMINOLOGY

Baking terminology can be tricky at first. With time, each of the following terms and techniques will become second nature to you. I will go over the ones that come up throughout this book so you can be better prepared when you come across them.

BROWNING BUTTER

The process of making browned butter involves simmering butter until the milk solids separate from the butterfat, sink to the bottom of the pan, and brown. You are left with two totally magical things: browned bits of milk solids at the bottom of the pan and ghee on the top layer. To make ghee, the browned bits, or leftover milk solids, are filtered out, leaving only the butterfat. This makes it virtually dairy-free while still retaining the flavor of butter. The browned bits, on the other hand, give off an amazing aroma of toffee and add the most incredible flavor to any food. I use browned butter in any recipe I can. It might just be my favorite flavor profile to use when baking.

The recipes in this book that call for browned butter use the entire contents of the pan, the browned bits and all. It's easy to scrape up the browned bits left on the bottom of the pan by using a rubber spatula. If you've never browned butter before or tasted its delectable flavor, I highly recommend that you do.

FOLDING INGREDIENTS

Folding is a process of gently mixing two separate ingredients or mixtures together. It is used to combine ingredients when stirring may be too vigorous. Folding is generally done when adding dry ingredients to wet ingredients (or vice versa) or adding a lighter ingredient to a heavier one, such as whipped egg whites to a batter. Some recipes, like brownies, are prone to overmixing. If the batter isn't mixed very gently, or folded, it can yield uneven results, like sinking in the middle.

To fold ingredients, use a rubber spatula or whisk. Hold the bowl with your non-dominant hand, then slowly turn the bowl toward you, while holding the spatula or whisk in your dominant hand. As the bowl turns, scrape the sides of the bowl and fold the mixture up and over itself toward the middle of the bowl and then gently back to the side. Continue this gentle folding motion as you turn the bowl until the mixture is just combined.

Folding takes some practice; it will probably take you a few tries to line up your movements just right. The next thing you know, all the movements will flow together seamlessly, and you won't even have to think about it.

SOFT PEAKS VERSUS STIFF PEAKS

The terms "soft peaks" and "stiff peaks" usually refer to either whipped egg whites or whipped cream. Both go through various stages, depending on how long you whip them.

The first stage for both eggs and cream is foamy: There are no peaks, but you can see the egg whites or cream becoming denser, and ribbons are starting to form and stay as you pass the whisk through.

The next stage is soft peaks: When you take the whisk out of the egg whites or cream and turn it upside down, peaks are just beginning to hold, but are soft enough to fold back into themselves.

The next stage is firm peaks: You'll know you have them when you turn your whisk upside down and the peaks hold.

Stiff peaks are the final stage: When you remove the whisk, the peaks will hold firmly and stand straight up.

You can usually tell the peak stages by the mixture itself. As you continue to beat, the mixture thickens, leaving ribbon outlines that will disappear at first. Then, as the mixture gets thicker and thicker, they become more prominent and stay in the mixture as it passes through each stage. As you become more familiar with the process, these stages will be easy to spot.

Tips for Whipping Egg Whites:

» Start with a very clean, dry bowl. Be careful not to let any yolk slip in. Egg whites are stubborn and will not want to whip as well if any yolk accidentally gets in. If a tiny bit gets in, don't panic; it probably isn't the end of the world. Just move forward and see how it goes.

» Use room-temperature eggs. Not only do egg whites separate from egg yolks more easily at room temperature, but they also whip better.

» Add a pinch of cream of tartar to the egg whites before whipping them. This helps stabilize the proteins so that they can reach full volume.

» Start mixing on low speed and work up to high speed; this will better incorporate air and create more volume.

Tips for Whipping Heavy Cream and Coconut Cream:

» Prechill a large mixing bowl and mixer whisk attachment(s) for 10 minutes in the freezer. Cream (dairy or coconut) whips better at a colder temperature, and the chilled bowl will keep the temperature more consistent during the process.

» Make sure that the cream (dairy or coconut) is very well chilled.

» To extract coconut cream from coconut milk, place a can of full-fat coconut milk in the refrigerator overnight. The coconut cream will firm up and rise to the top of the can, leaving the more watery coconut milk below. This is due to the fat content in the milk; it works similarly to other fats and solidifies when cold. Open the chilled can and scrape the coconut cream layer off the top and straight into the chilled bowl for whipping.

» Start mixing on low speed and work up to high speed; this will better incorporate air and create more volume.

TEMPERING

Tempering refers to both chocolate and eggs. In the case of chocolate, it's a process of heating or melting chocolate slowly to the point where it becomes the perfect consistency for baking, coating, and dipping. Tempered chocolate has a smooth and shiny finish. When it cools and resolidifies, it has a distinct snap to it, like when you bite into a chocolate-covered strawberry and hear a crack.

There are a few ways to temper or "melt" chocolate. My preferred method is to melt chocolate chips or chopped chocolate in a heatproof mixing bowl set on top of a simmering pan of water. This method gives you the most control over your chocolate. This method is sometimes referred to as a water bath or the double boiler method. Not everyone has a double boiler; the bowl and pan setup is an easy makeshift method that anyone can do.

Another way to melt chocolate is in the microwave using a glass bowl or measuring cup. I dislike this method because it usually gives uneven results. It's very easy to burn or overcook the chocolate this way. On the other hand, it's usually quicker and can work well if you are in a time crunch or need to melt only a small amount of chocolate. If using this method, microwave in 10- to 20-second intervals and stir the chocolate in between so that you can gauge how much longer it needs to be heated. Sometimes the chocolate won't look melted all the way, but stirring will spread the heat and continue to melt the chocolate.

Tempering eggs is a process in which a hot liquid is added to the eggs a little bit at a time to slowly bring the eggs up to a temperature at which they are safe to eat without cooking them all the way, and to keep the eggs from curdling (in other words, scrambling/solidifying) when they come into contact with the hot liquid. Tempered eggs are used in things like ice creams, custards, and puddings. Tempering eggs sounds way more complicated than it actually is. In fact, it's probably as easy as scrambling eggs, if that gives you any indication of the simplicity.

PAR-BAKING AND PREBAKING

Par-baking just means that you partially bake a crust before filling it. This helps ensure that you have a solid, not soggy, base to work with. You bake the crust again after adding the filling ingredients in order to cook them, as is the case with fruit-filled pies and quiches. Other times you prebake the crust until it is entirely done because the crust won't be baked again, as is the case with cream pies and fresh fruit tarts, or on occasions where you are adding precooked ingredients.

Alternative FLOURS

In this book I use four main flours for baking: almond flour, coconut flour, tapioca flour, and arrowroot flour. In Chapter 4, "Polite Provisions," I described how these flours are made, which brands I prefer, and why. Here I will teach you how to use these flours so that they work together to create delicious grain-free baked goods in your kitchen. Alternative flours work best when used in combination. Each one brings a different element to the baking table, so to speak, to work in unison when blended with the others.

ALMOND FLOUR

Almond flour is the starting point and main flour typically found in the majority of Paleo baked goods. In a traditional gluten-free flour blend, you would probably find a rice-based flour like white rice flour or brown rice flour. Since Paleo omits grains, almond flour makes a suitable replacement. Due to its high fat content, almond flour is very heavy in comparison to rice flour and standard white flour. Because it's so heavy, it works best when you use a super finely ground version, like the Honeyville brand, and then sift the flour to get it as fine-textured as possible. You don't want to skimp on quality here. The difference between using a fine-textured almond flour and almond meal will be very noticeable. The finer texture creates a lighter crumb, making baked goods as similar to their grain flour–based counterparts as possible. Almond flour is the flour glue that holds a recipe together. I like to use it in combination with other flours, using almond flour for the majority of the blend. Its report card would say, "Works well with others."

COCONUT FLOUR

Coconut flour is a great flour to use in combination with almond flour. Coconut flour absorbs liquid and gives structure to baked goods. It cannot be subbed in a 1:1 ratio with almond flour due to its very high fiber content. The fiber acts like a sponge, absorbing moisture. When working with coconut flour, you typically need to add more liquid to a recipe to account for the sponge effect.

Coconut flour is also a great alternative flour for those with nut allergies. Using it in a blend with other nut-free flours can make some very tasty baked goods. Using coconut flour on its own can be tricky, though, as it tends to make baked goods very dense. This is why it's common for recipes that contain only coconut flour to call for six or more eggs.

TAPIOCA FLOUR

Tapioca flour (also known as tapioca starch) improves the texture of baked goods. It's an extremely smooth flour that gives baked goods a nice elasticity and chew. It also helps bind them, similar to the way gluten would. It's superfine and does not need to be sifted. Tapioca flour works best when combined with other gluten-free flours.

ARROWROOT FLOUR

Arrowroot flour (also known as arrowroot starch) works great in place of cornstarch as a thickener for soups and sauces. It also works well to stop ice crystals from forming in homemade ice creams. Arrowroot flour works well in baking because, as a pure starch, it adds carbohydrates to a protein-based flour like almond flour.

How to MEASURE FLOURS

The correct way to measure flour when using a measuring cup is called the *spoon and level method.* Spoon the flour into the measuring cup until it reaches the top, then using the backside of the spoon or the edge of a knife to scrape and level off the top, removing the excess flour. The *easiest* way to measure flour is the *scoop, level, and lift method.* That's not even a legitimate baking term, but most of us are guilty of using it. It's when you take a measuring cup, dip it into a bag of flour, scoop up the flour and scrape it against the bag to level it, and then lift it out and go. Guilty as charged. The problem with the scoop, level, and lift method is that it tends to condense the flour inside the cup, resulting in a greater amount of flour than actually intended. To get a more accurate measurement, you want to spoon the flour into the measuring cup. That way the flour won't be compressed. I would say that the exception to this rule is when you need only a small amount, like ¼ cup or less; especially in the case of measuring spoons, the scoop, level, and lift method works fine.

In this book I always use the spoon and level method for almond flour. In the case of coconut, tapioca, and arrowroot flours, the amount required is so small—a tablespoon or ¼ cup at most—that the method you use doesn't make a significant difference.

Another important distinction when talking about accurate measuring is sifted flour versus unsifted flour. In a recipe, 1 cup of sifted flour is a completely different yield than 1 cup of flour, sifted; in the former, the flour is sifted *before* being measured, and in the latter, it is sifted *after* being measured. These result in different yields because sifting flour loosens the granules and breaks down the flour into a finer grain, allowing it to pack the cup more densely. That means 1 cup of unsifted flour becomes more like 1¼ cups after being sifted. Sifting after measuring rather than before measuring can throw off an entire recipe; baking can be unforgiving. Be sure to pay attention to this when reading a recipe.

To make things easy for you, just remember that every almond flour recipe in this book calls for sifted almond flour. It's also the only flour I use the spoon and level method for, as I mentioned above. First, sift the almond flour into a bowl, then use the spoon and level method to measure out the flour into the correct sized dry measuring cup.

Another way to measure ingredients is by weight, which is the most common method used outside the United States. You will notice that every dry ingredient in each recipe in this book is accompanied by a weight in grams when the amount used is ¼ cup or more. A kitchen scale is a great tool to invest in, because it's the most accurate measuring tool when it comes to baking. It may seem weird at first to weigh everything out, but once you get used to it, you'll wonder how you ever managed before.

PACKED

When a recipe calls for a packed measuring cup or spoon, it means to really pack the ingredient in there firmly. Doing so provides more of the ingredient in the measurement, which is sometimes what you want in a recipe. Writing "packed" makes the recipe flow better than writing something like "1 cup plus 1 teaspoon." You could probably get that extra teaspoon just by packing more in there, hence "packed." To get a packed cup, you use the scoop, level, and lift method, only you want to make sure that it's really packed in there.

SCANT

Sometimes a recipe calls for a scant cup or teaspoon. This means not to fill the measuring cup or spoon all the way to the top. For example, ⅛ teaspoon of salt may not be quite enough, but ¼ teaspoon would be too much. Since there isn't a measuring spoon between the two, the recipe may say "scant ¼ teaspoon" because it requires more than ⅛ teaspoon but not quite an entire ¼ teaspoon.

LEAVENERS

Another important factor in baking is commonly referred to as leavening. Leavening is another word for rising agent, and it is essentially just a reaction between ingredients that incorporates gas into batters and doughs, expanding their air bubbles and allowing them to rise.

Leaveners also give baked goods their texture and color and sometimes even contribute to how they taste and hold together. In most cases, leavening is created by the reaction between a chemical leavener and an acidic ingredient. In other cases, the rising action is aided by a mechanical process, such as whipping air into egg whites, which adds volume and structure to baked goods. Below I list the Paleo-approved leaveners and include information on how to use them.

BAKING SODA

Baking soda is probably the most common of all the leavening agents. It has to be used in conjunction with an acidic ingredient. The combination of baking soda and the acidic component creates carbon dioxide, allowing the baked good to rise. Acidic ingredients to use with baking soda include lemon juice, vinegar, honey, molasses, natural cocoa powder (not Dutch-processed), chocolate, applesauce, sour cream, milk, and cream of tartar.

CREAM OF TARTAR

In Paleo baking, baking powder is usually avoided due to the fact that most commercial products use cornstarch as a stabilizer. Baking powder already contains its own acidic ingredient, usually cream of tartar, so it doesn't need to be paired with an acidic ingredient. (It is activated when it comes in contact with liquid.) The cornstarch helps absorb moisture and neutralizes the acidic reaction so it doesn't react before it reaches the baked good. Cornstarch is derived from corn, and those who are intolerant of grains aren't able to eat corn. It's very easy to make your own baking powder at home, though.

If a recipe calls for baking powder, use a 2:1 ratio of cream of tartar to baking soda, so two parts cream tartar to one part baking soda. For example, if a recipe calls for 1½ teaspoons of baking powder, you would use 1 teaspoon of cream of tartar and ½ teaspoon of baking soda. If you want to premake baking powder at home for later use, follow this same ratio, but add a starch like arrowroot, tapioca, or potato to prevent the acidic reaction from occurring prematurely. The ratio to use in this case is 2:1:1, or two parts cream of tartar, one part baking soda, and one part starch. To make ½ cup (92 g) of baking powder, for example, combine ¼ cup (44 g) of cream of tartar, 2 tablespoons (30 g) of baking soda, and 2 tablespoons (18 g) of starch.

Hain brand also makes a corn-free baking powder.

EGGS

Eggs, both whole and separated, create structure for baked goods. Whisking egg whites separately before adding them to a batter helps increase volume: Air bubbles that are incorporated into the egg whites via whisking expand when heated, making baked goods rise. And when eggs bake, their steam can create a leavening effect as well.

Room-temperature eggs generally work best in baking. Lots of recipes call for the separation of the yolks and whites because you may need to use only one or the other. When eggs are at room temperature, the whites and yolks separate from each other easier. Since the whites are warm, they tend to slide away from the yolks more readily; when they are cold, they are kind of one congealed, slobbery unit. In some recipes, cold eggs will curdle in batters. It will all work out in the end once everything is combined, but it's just easier to work with eggs at room temperature.

Another thing you may come across in baking recipes is the direction to add eggs to the batter one at a time. This tried-and-true method helps the emulsion process and allows the eggs to mix into the batter evenly.

We eat with our eyes first, so it's important to make food look good. This is why chefs are trained on presentation techniques, or how to plate food to make it visually appealing. Desserts are no different; in my opinion, the presentation is even more crucial. After all, the goal is to make your dessert look just as good as it tastes. That said, it can be hard to decorate desserts when you are limited in the ingredients you can use. Making the transition from using decorations that contain refined sugar, like sprinkles and fondant, can be tricky, especially when you are new to Paleo baking. After all, they are so easy and colorful. Below I highlight some options that you can incorporate into decorating your desserts at home.

My favorite way to decorate cakes and cupcakes is with a fancy piping tip and an inedible prop. (*See* pages 200 to 202 for a frosting tutorial.) When it comes to inedible decorations, my favorites are flowers. I also like to use little props that I find in craft stores like Michaels. Scrapbooking items make great cupcake props! You can get so creative, and they are fun for holidays or when you want to convey a theme.

Another trend in cake decorating is to leave the cake layers completely or partially exposed instead of frosting the entire cake. Cakes decorated this way, such as the Blackberry Elderflower Cake on pages 222 and 223, are called "naked cakes." Not only is this easier, but it's way faster too. Just pipe or spread the frosting or whipped cream across the middle layers and leave everything else exposed. Decorate the top with some flowers, fruits, or props and you have a gorgeous cake on your hands.

FLOWERS

Flowers are my absolute favorite cake decorations; they make cakes living things. Flowers are among the most beautiful and colorful things on earth. We use them as decorations in our homes and workspaces, so why not decorate food with them? When using flowers, just be sure to do a quick Google search to make sure that you aren't putting anything harmful or poisonous on your cake. Remove the flowers after presentation, before eating. There are also edible flowers out there that you can use if desired.

FLAGS AND PROPS

You can find all kinds of great things to decorate with at craft stores, especially around the holidays, from cute cupcake liners to flags and stickers. You can cut up colorful paper straws or use bows and ribbons. The sky is definitely the limit here. Let your imagination go wild!

EDIBLE DECORATIONS

Fruits, just like flowers, are incredibly colorful and vibrant. Fruits can add a lot of life to a cake or tart, and bonus—they're edible. Also, any kind of drizzle or chocolate shaving is going to give a dessert a huge wow factor. Here are some examples of edible decorations:

» Caramel drizzle

» Chocolate chips

» Chocolate shavings

» Chocolate curls (opposite)

» Ganache (pages 369 to 370)

» Fresh and/or dried fruit

» Fruit compote

» Nuts

» Sea salt

» Spices like cinnamon sticks or whole nutmeg, as well as ground spices for dusting

» Tapioca flour or arrowroot flour instead of conventional confectioners' sugar for dusting

» Unsweetened cocoa powder for dusting

How to make
CHOCOLATE CURLS

6 ounces (170 g) chocolate chips

2 tablespoons palm shortening

1. Line a small (8 by 4-inch/20 by 10-cm) loaf pan or a 7 by 2-inch (18 by 5-cm/3-cup) square plastic storage container with foil, leaving some overhang, then line a plate with parchment paper; set both aside.

2. In a medium-sized saucepan, combine the chocolate chips and palm shortening. Mix together over medium heat until melted and combined. Remove from the heat and pour the chocolate mixture into the prepared pan.

3. Refrigerate for 1 to 1½ hours or until the chocolate has hardened. Once the chocolate has set, lift it from the pan, using the foil to help. Set the chocolate on top of a sheet of parchment paper large enough to cover the chocolate (or about the size of a sheet of 8½ by 11-inch/21.5 by 28-cm paper).

4. With the parchment paper wrapped around the side of the block of chocolate, hold the chocolate (the parchment paper barrier will allow it to be held longer without melting). Using a vegetable peeler, peel down one side of the chocolate block to make large curls. Set each finished curl on the parchment paper–lined plate. If a curl gets stuck in the peeler, use a toothpick to remove it and transfer it to the plate. Continue until the desired amount of curls is reached or no chocolate remains. If working in a warmer climate, the chocolate may need to be rechilled during the process. If making in advance of garnishing, keep the chocolate curls in the refrigerator or briefly in the freezer until just before using to keep them from softening. When ready to decorate a dessert, use a toothpick to transfer each chocolate curl to the desired location. Chocolate curls can be made ahead and stored in a covered container in the refrigerator for up to 1 week.

Notes:

If the chocolate is too cold or hard to work with or the curls start to break when peeled, let the chocolate sit at room temperature to soften for 15 to 20 minutes.

The cake pictured above is the Chocolate Dream Cheesecake (page 248) made with one recipe of cooled Ganache (pages 369 to 370) poured on top.

TROUBLESHOOTING

Sometimes, despite your best efforts, a recipe just doesn't come out. You would really need a whole other book to go over all the things that could possibly go wrong and how to fix them, but here are some common things that can go astray and what you can do to get better results next time.

SINKING

The worst is when you take something out of the oven and it looks perfect, then five minutes later you turn around and it's sunk in the middle. This could happen for a few reasons:

» **Overmixing:** If you mix ingredients together too vigorously, less-stable air bubbles get incorporated into the batter. As the batter bakes, the air may rise, but since the bubbles are unstable, they collapse. Try mixing gently and slowly by hand or using a hand mixer on the lowest speed until the ingredients are just incorporated.

» **Wrong Oven Temperature:** Check your oven temperature; it may be off. You can buy an inexpensive oven thermometer, set it in your oven, and confirm that it reaches the temperature you set it to.

» **Too Much Liquid:** Too much moisture can spell disaster. You may have overmeasured your wet ingredients. Even things like zucchini and bananas, when incorporated into breads and muffins, release moisture during baking, so be sure to squeeze out the excess water if you can, and be precise when measuring.

» **Greasing the Pan:** Try greasing or lining only the bottom of the pan. This lets the batter cling to the sides as it rises, creating a stable base and a rounded top.

» **Too Much Leavener:** Too much of a leavening agent (such as baking soda) can cause a baked good to rise too quickly and then fall. Try reducing the leavener in ¼-teaspoon amounts.

BURNED BOTTOMS

Sometimes you bake cookies and cakes exactly as written and still end up with burned bottoms or edges. Here are a few possible culprits:

» **Baking Sheets and Pans:** Try using aluminum baking sheets and pans. They don't get as hot as darker-colored baking pans do.

» **Oven Rack Position:** Is your rack in the wrong place? My oven cooks best when the rack is in the middle position and I place everything on the right side. Burned areas can also happen because your oven isn't at the right temperature or has hot spots.

» **Opening the Oven Door:** I'm impatient too. Sometimes I just want to know if the cookies are done already! But opening the door too many times during baking can cause foods to cook unevenly because it lets in cool air, which imbalances the oven temperature. To avoid this, set your timer for the shortest time recommended and then check your yummies through the oven window.

BROKEN SAUCES

When a sauce breaks, it basically has a layer of fat sitting on top that has separated from the emulsion. This can happen when making things like caramel, hollandaise, and mayonnaise. Here's what may have gone wrong:

» **Temperature:** The sauce may have been too hot when you added the fat, like butter or eggs. We all know that eggs will scramble, and if butter melts too fast, it will sometimes cause a sauce to break. Butter should be melted slowly so that it can incorporate into the other ingredients gradually. Start on low heat until all the ingredients are combined and thickened, and then turn up the heat as needed, but be sure to stir and keep an eye on the party. The same goes for cold temperatures: When your sauce cools down or you put it in the refrigerator, it will separate. Make sauces as close to eating time as possible.

» **Timing:** The fat may have been added to the sauce too quickly. Butter incorporates best when stirred in the same direction. You can also try adding the fat in smaller increments.

AVOIDING MORE OOPS

So many things can go wrong when baking; some of it you can't control, and some of it you can. Most of my mistakes happen when I'm trying to take shortcuts, like "softening" butter in the microwave or sloppily measuring my ingredients. Here are some things to keep in mind to get good results:

» Take Your Time: Reading through a recipe, twice, comes in handy. If you notice that you need to use softened butter, you can take some butter out of the refrigerator right then, and then continue gathering your other ingredients. The same goes with room-temperature eggs.

» Let Things Cool: When foods come out of the oven, all you want to do is eat them as soon as possible. Trust me, I get it. But baked goods have to be cooled before being frosted and sometimes cut. So be patient; it will be worth it. Let muffins, cupcakes, and cakes cool for 5 to 10 minutes. Then remove them from their pans and transfer them to a cooling rack. If left to cool completely in their pans, they will start to sweat, leaving them with soggy bottoms.

» Doubling a Recipe: Sometimes when you double a recipe, it just doesn't come out the same. Baking is a science, which essentially means that you need to account for things like ratios, surface area, and chemistry. Just make separate batches; it will be worth the time you save in the end when you aren't remaking stuff.

» Eyeballing Ingredients: Don't do it. Always measure or weigh ingredients. This goes back to the science and ratios thing. Eyeballing may work fine when you're cooking, but it's a disaster in baking. Also, make sure that you grab the right size measuring cup. It seems simple enough, but if I had a dollar for every time I grabbed the ⅓ cup instead of the ½ cup, I'd be rich. Note that dry measuring cups (the ones that often come as a set on a ring) measure differently than liquid measuring cups (the glass ones with handles and spouts). They should be used for their respective ingredients for accurate measurements.

» Making Substitutions: Ask any cookbook author or food blogger how they feel about substitutions. Then immediately run in the opposite direction! As authors who write for audiences with specific dietary restrictions, we test, test, and test again to get our recipes just right. It's completely understood that you may want to use another ingredient for this reason or that, but a lot of times the substitution will throw off the entire recipe, and it will fail. Substitutions that will work are usually listed with the recipe. I encourage you to try what you want, but again, please be prepared if the recipe fails.

KITCHEN HACKS

» When you need to fill a piping bag, set it inside a tall glass. The glass will hold the bag open for you, so you have both hands free to transfer the frosting neatly into the bag.

» Need to cool something in a hurry? Use a fan. It will cool your baked goods in half the time. Another method is to place the baked goods in the refrigerator or freezer for 10 to 15 minutes.

» Need to get your eggs up to room temperature quickly? Submerge them in hot water while you prepare your other ingredients. By the time you need them, they will be ready to go.

» Coat your measuring cup or spoon in oil or cooking spray before using sticky ingredients like honey, maple syrup, and molasses. The ingredients will slide right out, giving you a more accurate measurement, and you won't have a sticky mess on your hands.

» When in doubt, use parchment paper. For everything. To line cake pans, loaf pans, cookie sheets, everything. No one likes it when baked goods stick; it's just not fun. Parchment paper can be cut and trimmed to whatever size you need and can even be reused for things like cookies (just flip it over and use the other side). To line a loaf pan, lay one strip horizontally and one strip vertically across the pan, then use the sides of the parchment to lift the bread out once it's cooled. Ditto for brownies. Voilà.

» Scoop up bits of broken eggshells that fall into a bowl of batter by using the other half of the eggshell. They work together like magnets, saving you lots of time and frustration.

» Keep your almond flour in the refrigerator; it will keep longer. Presift a large batch of almond flour and store it in a resealable plastic bag to save yourself time when baking.

» Cut brownies with a plastic knife: The crumbs won't stick, so you'll get smoother edges. Another tip for brownies is to put them in the refrigerator before cutting them. Brownies cut best when cold.

» Need to soften butter to room temperature? You can speed up the process by cutting the butter into pieces about the size of a tablespoon. You will still need to let it sit out, but it will soften faster.

» Place a wooden spoon across a pot of boiling liquid. It will prevent the liquid from boiling over.

» A 33.8-ounce (1-L) bottle of Smart Water makes the world's best rolling pin at only $1.27. The size fits perfectly in your hands for rolling, and the water inside the bottle gives it the proper weight. A wine bottle will work too in a pinch.

Make your kitchen WORK FOR YOU

Above all, my number-one tip is to make your kitchen work for you. For years I kept my measuring cups and spoons in a drawer. Every time I had to measure something, I had to open the drawer, dig through it, unhook the correct size from the ring, and then do the same thing in reverse when I was done. What a pain. Then one day I decided to hang them on the same rack I use to hang some of my other cooking tools. That was a game-changer. Not only can I quickly grab one now when I need it, but they are all in front of me so I can easily locate the one I need. This one minuscule change made the biggest difference. Another example is parchment paper. I'm a short gal, and for some reason I kept it on a really high shelf over my sink. It was a chore to get it every time I needed it, so I moved it down to where I could easily access it. Problem solved. What bothers you most about cooking in your kitchen? Get in there and really think about it. Is it something you can fix? How can you make things easier for yourself?

This goes for kitchen tools and appliances as well. Do you hate your hand mixer because it's got dried crusty stuff all over it and makes a weird whizzing sound at high speed that almost makes your ears bleed? Just buy a new one. In the long run it will be well worth the investment in your happiness.

You are going to be more likely to cook and get creative in a workable space. It's why companies spend thousands of dollars on things like nap pods and yoga rooms for their employees. You need to be relaxed and comfortable to create. You can create better if you enjoy your space and it functions well for you. Whether it's labeling your spice jars and putting them in magnetic jars to stick onto the refrigerator because it's right next to the stove (another of my personal hacks) or moving something up or down a shelf, make your kitchen personal; make it your own space.

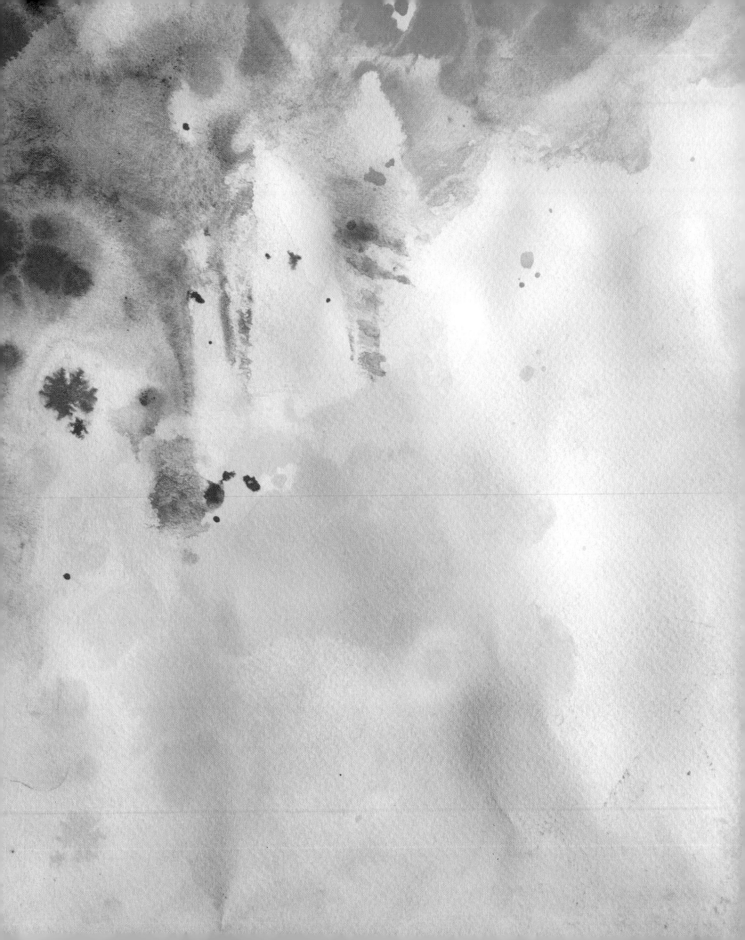

PART TWO

the RECIPES

CHAPTER 6

Meal TICKET

FROSTED "Oatmeal" BREAKFAST SQUARES

PREP TIME: 15 minutes
COOK TIME: 10 to 12 minutes
SETTING TIME: 20 to 30 minutes
READY IN: 45 minutes
YIELD: 1 dozen 2-inch squares

1 cup (130 g) cashew meal (see Notes)

1 cup (50 g) unsweetened coconut flakes

¾ cup (90 g) golden flaxseed meal

1 tablespoon plus 1 teaspoon coconut flour

1½ teaspoons ground cinnamon

½ teaspoon ground nutmeg

½ teaspoon fine-grain sea salt

½ teaspoon baking soda

5 tablespoons (2½ ounces/70 g) cold salted butter

¼ cup (40 g) coconut sugar

¼ cup (30 g) date sugar

3 tablespoons raw honey

1 teaspoon vanilla extract

1 large egg, room temperature

FOR THE FROSTING
¼ cup (60 ml) melted coconut butter

Fun fact: When you combine golden flaxseed meal with date sugar and spices, it tastes just like oatmeal. So I made "oatmeal" breakfast squares. That's what one does when one comes across this kind of information. I love these squares—soft, chewy, and yum.

1 Adjust an oven rack to the middle position and preheat the oven to 350°F (177°C). Line two baking sheets with parchment paper or nonstick baking mats; set aside. (*Note:* If working with only one baking sheet, allow it to cool completely between batches.)

2 In a large mixing bowl, combine the cashew meal, coconut flakes, flaxseed meal, coconut flour, cinnamon, nutmeg, salt, and baking soda. Stir together using a fork until well combined; set aside.

3 Place the butter, sugars, honey, and vanilla in a separate medium-sized mixing bowl. Cream together with a hand mixer set on low speed until combined, about 1 minute. Once combined, add the egg and increase the mixer speed to medium. Continue beating until smooth ripples appear on the surface, about 1 minute. Use a rubber spatula to scrape the creamed butter mixture into the dry mixture and beat on low until combined.

4 Place a Wilton size B square cookie cutter or a 2-inch (5-cm) square cookie cutter on a lined baking sheet and press a portion of the dough into it evenly, about halfway up the sides. (If working without a cookie cutter, see Notes for other options.) Repeat with the remaining dough, leaving about 2 inches (5 cm) between squares or 6 squares per sheet; the dough will rise and spread. Bake each sheet separately for 10 to 12 minutes or until the edges and bottoms of the squares are golden brown. Remove the parchment from the baking sheet and let cool.

5 Once the squares are cool, spread the coconut butter across the top of each square using a butter knife and refrigerate for 20 to 30 minutes to harden and set. Store in the refrigerator for up to 3 days, or freeze in a re-sealable plastic freezer bag. Let thaw for about 15 minutes before serving.

Notes: To make your own cashew meal, place 1 cup (155 g) of raw cashew pieces in the bowl of a high-powered food processor. Process until the cashews turn into meal, 1 to 2 minutes. Scrape down the bowl and continue to process as needed.

If you don't have a square cookie cutter, another method to form the squares is to roll a spoonful of dough into a 2-inch (5-cm) ball, press it down with your palm, and shape it into a square with your fingertips. Or use a greased precut brownie bar pan: Press the dough into the slots and bake for 10 to 12 minutes or until the edges are golden brown.

SOUTHERN BISCUITS

PREP TIME: 10 minutes
COOK TIME: 18 to 20 minutes
READY IN: 30 minutes
YIELD: Five 3-inch (7.5-cm) biscuits

I don't know about you, but I am head over heels in love with biscuits. They're one of the things I miss most from my pre-Paleo life. One of my favorite breakfasts is biscuits and gravy. I also adore any kind of breakfast biscuit sandwich. Well, guess what? We shall want no more! These biscuits are absolutely perfect. It took me five versions to get them just right. In the process I discovered an egg-free variation that I like a lot, so I've included that as well. These biscuits are life-changing. Pair them with anything savory, or even just butter and jam.

2 cups (185 g) sifted fine-ground almond flour

¼ cup (42 g) potato starch

1 tablespoon maple sugar

½ teaspoon baking soda

¼ teaspoon fine-grain sea salt

8 tablespoons (4 ounces/115 g) cold unsalted butter, cubed

1 large egg

1 tablespoon raw honey

½ teaspoon vanilla extract

½ teaspoon apple cider vinegar

¼ cup (35 g) arrowroot flour or tapioca flour, for dusting

1. Preheat the oven to 350°F (177°C). Line a baking sheet with parchment paper; set aside.

2. Combine the almond flour, potato starch, maple sugar, baking soda, and salt in the bowl of a food processor. Pulse 10 times or until combined. Add the cubed butter and process again until smooth, about 15 to 20 seconds. Then add the egg, honey, vanilla, and apple cider vinegar and process once more until combined.

3. Lay a sheet of parchment paper on the counter, then dust the sheet with arrowroot or tapioca flour. Transfer the dough onto the parchment and pat into a mound. The dough will be sticky; sprinkle more flour on top of the dough mound as needed and work the flour into the dough to make it easier to handle. Place another sheet of parchment paper on top of the dough, then roll it out to about 1 inch (2.5 cm) thick.

4. Using a Wilton size A round cookie cutter or a 2½-inch (6.5-cm) round cookie cutter, cut out two biscuits. Remove the extra dough and transfer the biscuits, while still inside the cookie cutter, to the lined baking sheet. Press down lightly to release the dough. Then gather the dough scraps and repeat the process with the remaining dough, using more flour as needed. Bake for 18 to 20 minutes or until lightly browned. Store in a covered container or wrapped tightly at room temperature for up to 1 day, or freeze in a resealable plastic freezer bag. Let thaw to room temperature before eating.

Notes: To make these biscuits dairy-free, use ½ cup (110 g) of ghee or lard in place of the butter.

If you want smaller biscuits or need a higher yield, use a smaller cookie cutter or biscuit cutter (Wilton size B or C) and bake for 15 to 18 minutes.

Subs: An additional tablespoon of honey in place of the maple sugar.

*Variation: **Egg-Free Southern Biscuits.** Omit the egg and replace the potato starch with potato flour. Bake for 15 to 18 minutes or until the bottoms have browned.*

BISCUITS AND CAJUN SAUSAGE GRAVY

PREP TIME: 25 minutes
COOK TIME: 30 minutes
READY IN: 55 minutes
YIELD: 4 servings

I once took a road trip from Alabama to California with my good friend Cassi. Neither of us had been to New Orleans before. We partied all night and had the best hangover breakfast at a little café in the French Quarter. I ordered the Cajun Biscuits and Gravy, and it was extraordinary. I've never seen anything like it on a menu since, and it's stuck with me even after all these years. I made my own version just in case you never come across it on a menu, either, so that you can enjoy a little slice of New Orleans too.

4 Southern Biscuits (page 72)

FOR THE GRAVY

4 tablespoons (2 ounces/56 g) salted butter

8 ounces (225 g) hot pork sausage or andouille sausage

½ cup (80 g) diced yellow onions

1 large red bell pepper, seeded and chopped

1 teaspoon fine-grain sea salt

½ teaspoon chili powder

½ teaspoon garlic powder

¼ teaspoon ground black pepper

¼ teaspoon paprika

¼ teaspoon cayenne pepper

¼ cup (42 g) potato starch

1½ cups (350 ml) unsweetened cashew milk

Chopped fresh parsley, for garnish

MAKE AHEAD
SOUTHERN BISCUITS—1 DAY AHEAD

1. Prepare the biscuits, following the instructions on page 72. While the biscuits are baking, begin the gravy: In a large skillet, melt the butter over medium heat, then crumble the sausage into the pan. Cook for about 5 minutes, until the sausage starts to brown but some pink remains.

2. Add the onions and bell pepper to the pan, stir, and continue to cook on medium heat until the onions just start to become translucent, 3 to 5 minutes. Then add the salt, chili powder, garlic powder, black pepper, paprika, and cayenne pepper to the pan. Use a rubber spatula or wooden spoon to mix the ingredients together until combined. Cook until the sausage is completely brown and no pink remains, another 5 to 10 minutes.

3. Add the potato starch to the pan and mix until combined with the other ingredients. Then add the cashew milk, ¼ cup at a time, stirring well after each addition, and simmer until the mixture has the texture of thick gravy. Remove from the heat.

4. Pour a large spoonful of gravy over the top of each biscuit (or split it in half and fill it with gravy, as pictured) and garnish with parsley.

Notes: To make this dairy-free, make the biscuits with ½ cup (110 g) of ghee or lard and the gravy with ¼ cup (55 g) of ghee or lard instead of butter.

To make this egg-free, use the Egg-Free Southern Biscuits.

Potato starch works just like regular flour for thickening sauces and gravies. Be sure to use potato starch and not potato flour for this recipe. They are two totally different things and work very differently.

I used Silk brand unsweetened cashew milk in this recipe, but feel free to use homemade (see page 50 for the method) or one of the subs listed below. I love cashew milk in place of regular cow's milk for cooking because it has the same consistency and a somewhat similar flavor, more so than almond milk, I think.

Subs: Unsweetened almond milk or boxed coconut milk in place of the cashew milk. Canned coconut milk is too thick; something the consistency of regular cow's milk is needed. If dairy-free gravy isn't required, cow's milk can be used.

Pesto RELOADED

PREP TIME: 5 minutes
READY IN: 5 minutes
YIELD: 1 cup (240 ml)

When I was developing recipes for this book, I originally made a traditional pesto sauce. The whole time I was making it, I was thinking, "You know what would take this pesto up a notch? Truffle oil and arugula." I went ahead and wrote up the traditional pesto recipe, but I couldn't stop thinking about the other pesto I had imagined. As fate would have it, I was rummaging through my veggie drawers to find something one day, and I came across an unopened container of fresh arugula. It was a sign. So I ran to the store, grabbed some white truffle–infused olive oil, and remade the recipe. I love the flavor of this pesto. I'm so glad I followed my foodie instincts.

1½ cups (45 g) packed fresh basil leaves

½ cup (15 g) loosely packed arugula

¼ cup (40 g) pine nuts

¼ cup (32 g) raw walnuts

1 clove garlic

2 tablespoons nutritional yeast

1 tablespoon fresh-squeezed lemon juice

½ teaspoon fine-grain sea salt

¼ teaspoon ground black pepper

⅓ cup (80 ml) extra-virgin olive oil

2 tablespoons white truffle oil

1. Put the basil, arugula, pine nuts, walnuts, and garlic clove in the bowl of a food processor. Process until the ingredients are ground together. Then add the nutritional yeast, lemon juice, salt, and pepper and pulse until combined.

2. With the food processor running, slowly drizzle in the olive oil, then the truffle oil. Continue to process until all the ingredients are combined. Store in an airtight container in the refrigerator for up to 2 weeks.

Notes: Arugula can have a bitter aftertaste, so be sure to not pack the cup too densely; you want just a hint of the flavor to seep through. The majority of the greens should be basil.

I used a combo of walnuts and pine nuts in this recipe; you can use one or the other as well, whichever you prefer.

I use white truffle–infused olive oil; it's relatively inexpensive, and the only other truffle oil I've seen is a vegetable oil. Whomp whomp whomp. Check your local grocery stores or Amazon. Truffle oil is life-changing.

Subs: For a dairy version, substitute ¼ cup (28 g) of shredded Parmesan, pecorino, or Romano cheese for the nutritional yeast.

Easy Immersion
BLENDER MAYONNAISE

PREP TIME: 5 minutes
READY IN: 5 minutes
YIELD: ½ cup (120 ml)

Sometimes I'm lazy. Mayonnaise is no exception. This mayo is so easy, though, that it defies all laziness. I have no problem taking five minutes to whip this up anytime. It also tastes way better than store-bought mayo and is made with way better ingredients. It's really a win-win. I remember the first time I heard of immersion blender mayonnaise, I was like, "Yeah right, that's not going to work." I was wrong. It works, and it works well. Then it was a matter of playing with ingredient ratios to find what I like best. There are two ways to make this recipe: one uses the cup that comes with the immersion blender, and the other uses a glass measuring cup or jar. Pick your weapon; either way, you've got this.

2 large egg yolks

2 teaspoons Dijon mustard

2 teaspoons fresh-squeezed lemon juice

⅛ teaspoon fine-grain sea salt

⅛ teaspoon ground black pepper

½ cup (120 ml) light olive oil or avocado oil

To make with the immersion cup: Combine the egg yolks, mustard, lemon juice, salt, and pepper in the cup of an immersion blender. Add the oil last, on top of the other ingredients. Place the immersion blender stick in the bottom of the cup and begin to blend. The mixture will thicken and lighten as the ingredients start to form an emulsion that looks similar to a cloud. Continue to blend, slowly moving the stick up to the top of the cup. Tilt the cup if needed and continue to blend until the mixture thickens, turns white, and becomes the consistency of mayonnaise.

To make with a glass measuring cup or jar: Combine the egg yolks, mustard, lemon juice, salt, and pepper in a 2-cup (475-ml) glass measuring cup or pint-size mason jar. Place the immersion blender stick in the cup or jar and blend until combined. With the immersion blender on, slowly drizzle in the oil in about 5-second pours, blending well after each addition. Continue to drizzle in the oil in increments and blend until no oil is left or a thick mayonnaise emulsion develops.

Notes: I prefer to make this recipe with light olive oil because the flavor is fairly neutral and the price is right. Avocado oil is also an excellent choice for mayonnaise and is great for cooking at high temperatures, so it's nice to have around. It's usually pricier than olive oil, but Costco sells huge bottles of avocado oil for about $9, and you really can't beat that price. Experiment with both and see what you like; after all, it takes only 5 minutes!

When making the mayo in a glass measuring cup or jar, it's important to add the oil in a nice, slow, steady stream. An option is to buy a dedicated bottle for making mayonnaise and fit it with a bottle pour spout. Measure the oil and then transfer it to the bottle with the spout. This works best for an even, steady drizzle, but a measuring cup will work fine too.

DAIRY FREE*

FRENCH ONION AND BACON TART

PREP TIME: 35 minutes
COOK TIME: 25 minutes
READY IN: 1 hour
YIELD: 4 to 6 servings

French onion soup is amazing. Everything about it. The way the broth is so hearty yet light at the same time. The way the onions are browned to perfection, soft and yet still crisp somehow. The way the cheese melts into the soup and makes its way into my soul with every single bite. French onion soup is romantic. I was so sad to find out that most French onion soup recipes contain flour. I'm sure I could whip up a flourless version, but this tart seemed like way more fun. And it has bacon. This tart has an incredible flavor, and it's one of my favorite recipes to make for an easy but impressive dinner.

1 recipe Old-Fashioned Flaky Pie Crust dough (page 166)

FOR THE FILLING

10 slices bacon

1 large yellow onion, cut into 1-inch pieces, about 4 cups

1 clove garlic, minced

2 teaspoons dried thyme leaves

3 large eggs

½ cup (120 ml) full-fat canned coconut milk

1 tablespoon ghee

¼ teaspoon fine-grain sea salt

⅛ teaspoon ground black pepper

MAKE AHEAD

OLD-FASHIONED FLAKY PIE CRUST—
1 DAY AHEAD

1 Prepare the Old-Fashioned Flaky Pie Crust, following Steps 1 and 2 on page 166. Press the dough across the bottom and up the sides of an 11-inch (28-cm) tart pan. Par-bake the crust following Step 6 on page 166 and set aside. Turn the oven down to 375°F (190°C). Line a rimmed baking sheet with foil; set aside.

2 To make the filling: In a large skillet, cook the bacon over medium heat until crispy, then remove from the pan and set aside. Leave about 2 to 3 tablespoons of bacon drippings in the pan. Add the onion, garlic, and thyme and cook until the onion is soft and browned but not mushy, about 10 minutes.

3 In the meantime, place the eggs, coconut milk, ghee, salt, and pepper in a mixing bowl. Use a fork to beat the ingredients together.

4 When the onion mixture is done cooking, remove from the heat and let cool slightly, about 5 minutes. While the mixture is cooling, cut the bacon crosswise into ¼- to ½-inch (6- to 12-mm) strips; add half of the bacon to the egg mixture and save the other half for sprinkling on top of the tart before baking. Then add the onion mixture to the egg mixture and stir together with a fork until combined.

5 Pour the egg and onion mixture evenly into the par-baked crust and sprinkle the remaining bacon on top. Transfer the tart to the foil-lined baking sheet and bake for 25 minutes or until the egg mixture has firmed up and the top has browned. Store any leftovers covered in the refrigerator for up to 2 days.

Notes: To make this tart dairy-free, use ghee rather than butter in the pie crust.

If you aren't avoiding dairy, Gruyère cheese will take this tart to the next level. After the tart is baked, sprinkle ¼ cup (30 g) of grated Gruyère over the top and bake for an additional 3 to 5 minutes or until the cheese has melted. Or you can melt the cheese under the broiler for 3 to 5 minutes.

DAIRY FREE* NUT FREE

Chiles Rellenos
CASSEROLE

PREP TIME: 20 minutes
COOK TIME: 20 minutes
READY IN: 40 minutes
YIELD: 4 servings

When I was a kid, I hated casseroles. My mom would make this chicken and broccoli casserole that we would eat like four times a week, I swear. I hated it. Sorry, Mom, I hope you aren't reading this. As an adult, though, it turns out that I LOVE casseroles. Go figure. You just throw everything in and bake your way to yum. I'm always looking for new recipes and for ways to turn favorite dishes into casseroles. I love chiles rellenos, so it only seemed right to make a chiles rellenos casserole.

6 cups (1.4 L) water, for boiling

4 poblano (pasilla) chiles or Anaheim chiles (11 ounces/325 g)

1 pound (455 g) ground beef

1 teaspoon fine-grain sea salt

1 teaspoon garlic salt

½ teaspoon chili powder

½ teaspoon ground black pepper

½ teaspoon ground cumin

½ medium white onion, diced

3 large eggs, beaten

4 to 6 slices pepper jack cheese (optional)

½ cup (32 g) crumbled or grated Cotija cheese (optional)

1. Preheat the oven to 350°F (177°C). Bring the water to a boil in a large heavy-bottomed saucepan. While the water is coming to temperature, de-stem and de-seed the chiles. Cut each chile lengthwise into four sections. Place the chiles in the boiling water and parboil for 5 minutes, then drain and set aside.

2. While the chiles are boiling, combine the beef, salt, and spices in a large skillet set over medium-high heat. Cook, stirring intermittently, until the meat has almost browned, then add the diced onion and continue to cook until the meat is completely browned. Drain any excess liquid and set aside.

3. Place a layer of the chiles across the bottom of an 8-inch (20-cm) square glass pan or casserole dish. Top with a layer of beef. Repeat this process, placing the chiles in the opposite direction this time. Next, slowly and evenly pour the beaten eggs across the top of the layers, covering as much area as possible. The eggs will bake into the ingredients and in between the layers, helping them hold together. If using, top with the pepper jack cheese slices and sprinkle the Cotija across the top. Bake for 20 minutes, until the cheese has melted and the chiles have softened and darkened in color. If a crispier top cheese layer is preferred, place under the broiler for 2 to 3 minutes. Let cool slightly before cutting and serving.

Notes: *To make this casserole dairy-free, omit the Cotija cheese and substitute almond milk cheese for the pepper jack, which can be found at most health food stores, or omit the cheese entirely. Don't feel as if you'll be missing out; the beef and chiles offer plenty of flavor.*

When working with chiles, be sure not to touch your face until you are able to wash your hands. The oils can sting your eyes or mouth. Also, if you have asthma, the chiles can aggravate it, similar to the way onions make you cry. Be sure to work in an open area that is well ventilated.

You could also try chopping up the chile peppers and mixing them into the casserole if you don't want a layered look.

Bacon Cheeseburger
STUFFED POTATOES

This recipe started out as a casserole, and then I was like, "You know what? I think it needs a friend." It turns out that potatoes make the perfect companion. It's almost as if you took a bacon cheeseburger and French fries and mashed them together. Makes sense to me.

PREP TIME: 20 minutes
COOK TIME: 1 hour 20 minutes
READY IN: 1 hour 40 minutes
YIELD: 4 servings

4 russet potatoes (3¼ pounds/1.45 kg)

2 tablespoons olive oil, for rubbing

1 pound (455 g) grass-fed ground beef

1 teaspoon fine-grain sea salt, plus more for sprinkling

½ teaspoon ground black pepper, plus more for sprinkling

1 teaspoon garlic salt

½ medium white onion, diced

12 slices bacon

½ cup (120 ml) no-sugar-added pizza sauce

¼ cup (60 ml) mayonnaise, store-bought or homemade (page 78)

1 cup (113 g) shredded mild cheddar cheese (optional)

2 tablespoons chopped fresh chives, for garnish

1 Preheat the oven to 425°F (218°C). Line a rimmed baking sheet with foil or parchment paper. Pierce the potatoes a few times on each side with the tines of a fork; this will allow steam to escape as the potatoes bake. Rub the olive oil over the potatoes, then sprinkle them with salt and pepper. Bake for 50 to 60 minutes, flipping them over about halfway through. Pierce the potatoes with a fork to test for doneness; the skins should feel dry and the insides soft.

2 About 10 minutes before the potatoes are done, combine the beef, 1 teaspoon of salt, ½ teaspoon of black pepper, and the garlic salt in a large skillet set over medium-high heat. Cook, stirring intermittently, until the meat is almost browned, then add the diced onion and continue to cook until the meat is completely browned. Drain any excess liquid and transfer the meat mixture to a medium-sized mixing bowl to cool.

3 Remove the potatoes from the oven and let cool slightly on the baking sheet. Leave the oven on. While waiting for the potatoes to cool, cook the bacon in a large skillet set over medium-high heat. Remove from the heat, pat dry, and then chop the bacon using a knife or kitchen shears; set aside.

4 Slice the potatoes lengthwise down the center, three-quarters of the way through, and pull the two sides apart to create a gap for the toppings. When the beef has cooled some but is still warm, add the pizza sauce and mayonnaise to the bowl and stir until completely combined. (If the beef is too hot, it may cause the pizza sauce and mayonnaise to become watery.)

5 Place a large spoonful of the beef mixture in each potato. Sprinkle a large handful of bacon pieces across the top, then sprinkle shredded cheese, if using, over the bacon. Bake for 5 to 10 minutes or until the cheese has melted. Garnish with chives.

Notes: *To make this dairy-free, omit the cheddar cheese or substitute almond milk cheese, which can be found at most health food stores.*

Subs: *Sweet potatoes or yams for the russet potatoes. In case you weren't sure, yams are the orange-fleshed ones that we commonly call sweet potatoes. Sweet potatoes come in a variety of colors, but their flesh is most commonly white. Both should work fine in this recipe, but personally, I think the flavor of white-fleshed sweet potatoes is most similar to that of white potatoes.*

Chipotle COLESLAW

PREP TIME: 15 minutes
READY IN: 15 minutes
YIELD: 4 servings

This recipe was inspired by my good friend and former neighbor Samantha. She brings this slaw to every BBQ and group event, mainly because I insist on it, and I may or may not throw huge a tantrum if she doesn't bring it. It's my absolute favorite. I've never been a big coleslaw person, but the first time I tried her spicy chipotle version, I couldn't believe how amazing it was. This will be a hit at all your summer barbecues. Serve it alongside some ribs and enter happiness.

1 (14-ounce/400-g) bag ready-to-eat coleslaw mix

1 red bell pepper, diced

1 cup (240 ml) full-fat grass-fed yogurt or sour cream

½ cup (4 ounces/115 g) canned chipotle peppers in adobo sauce

½ cup (15 g) chopped fresh cilantro

1 tablespoon raw honey

1 tablespoon fresh-squeezed lime juice

1 teaspoon grated lime zest

1 teaspoon garlic salt

½ teaspoon fine-grain sea salt

½ teaspoon ground black pepper

1. Place all the ingredients in a large mixing bowl and mix together until combined. Taste and add more seasoning or yogurt or sour cream, if desired. Serve immediately. Store any leftovers in an airtight container in the refrigerator for up to 3 days.

Notes: If you can't find ready-to-eat coleslaw mix in a bag, make your own by very thinly slicing or shredding one head of green cabbage, two large carrots, and half a head of red cabbage and mixing them together.

Be sure to use a clean version of canned chipotle peppers in adobo sauce. Some brands contain gluten and unhealthy vegetable oils. The best one I've found is La Morena, which you can find at Walmart, Amazon, and other large retailers. The ingredients listed are chipotle peppers, tomato puree, paprika, sugar, iodized salt, onions, sesame oil, distilled vinegar, garlic, bay leaves, and oregano. Another option is to make your own! It's a fairly easy process, and there are tons of recipes available online if you're feeling ambitious. In a pinch, San Marcos or La Costena brand will do; they do contain vegetable oil, but since the recipe calls for only ½ cup (115 g), I wouldn't panic over it. Stay far, far away from Embasa brand; it contains wheat flour.

BBQ Pulled PORK NACHOS

PREP TIME: 15 minutes
COOK TIME: 10 hours
READY IN: 10 hours 15 minutes
YIELD: 4 servings

I love making nachos out of plantain chips. They are always delicious, and I never feel disappointed or like I'm missing out in the nacho department. I'm always looking for exciting ways to spice up my nacho creations. These BBQ pulled pork nachos are absolutely perfect. They have a subtle tangy sweetness that goes oh so well with plantain chips. Add your favorite nacho toppings to make the recipe your own.

2 teaspoons cooking oil of choice (optional; see Notes)

4 to 5 pounds (1.81 kg to 2.26 kg) bone-in pork shoulder

1 large yellow onion, chopped

4 cloves garlic, minced

1 cup (240 ml) chicken stock or broth

½ cup (120 ml) apple cider vinegar

¼ cup (40 g) coconut sugar

2 tablespoons light molasses (not blackstrap)

1 tablespoon chili powder

1 teaspoon fine-grain sea salt

1 teaspoon ground cumin

1 teaspoon garlic salt

1 teaspoon onion powder

1 teaspoon cayenne pepper

½ teaspoon ground black pepper

½ teaspoon dry mustard

1 cup (240 ml) Paleo-friendly BBQ sauce

2 (6-ounce/170-g) bags plantain chips

FOR GARNISH

Avocado slices

Fresh chopped cilantro

Sliced jalapeños

Diced red onions

SPECIAL EQUIPMENT

7-quart (6.6-liter) slow cooker

1. If searing the meat—an optional step that gives the meat more flavor—heat the cooking oil in a large skillet over medium-high heat. Add the pork and sear it on each side until browned.

2. Put the rest of ingredients, except for the BBQ sauce and plantain chips, in a slow cooker. Add the pork, then cover and cook on low for 10 hours.

3. When the pork is ready, use a slotted spoon to transfer the meat to a storage container, leaving the liquid in the pot. (Discard the liquid.) Use two forks to pull the pork apart until shredded. Add the BBQ sauce to the meat and stir together using a fork until combined.

4. To assemble: Pour the plantain chips across a large platter or baking sheet. Add large spoonfuls of the BBQ pulled pork across the top of the plantain chips. Garnish with the desired nacho toppings.

Notes: Searing the meat on the stovetop before adding it to the slow cooker adds flavor; for this step, feel free to use your preferred cooking oil (mine is avocado oil). If you're pressed for time, you can always add the meat straight to the slow cooker.

My favorite Paleo-friendly BBQ sauces are Steve's Paleo Goods BBQ Sauce and Stubbs Sweet Heat BBQ Sauce. Stubbs Sweet Heat is the cleanest of all their branded BBQ sauces. It's pretty good for a store-bought brand: Though it does contain sugar and cornstarch, it does not contain corn syrup or modified food starch, which are commonly found in store-bought barbecue sauce. For plantain chips, I love Whole Foods and Sprouts brands.

You will have tons of pulled pork left over either to make more nachos or to use any way you want! It tastes great mixed with eggs in a hash or wrapped in lettuce for BBQ pulled pork tacos.

Subs: A 3- to 4-pound (1.4- to 1.8-kg) boneless pork shoulder instead of bone-in. Raw honey in place of the molasses.

Duck Fat
FRIES

PREP TIME: 10 minutes
SETTING TIME: 30 minutes
COOK TIME: 15 minutes
READY IN: 55 minutes
YIELD: 2 to 4 servings

2 large russet potatoes (1½ pounds/ 680 g)

1¾ cups (14 ounces/400 g) pastured duck fat

1 tablespoon truffle salt or fine-grain sea salt

Chopped fresh parsley, for garnish (optional)

Dipping sauces of choice (optional)

SPECIAL EQUIPMENT

Deep-fry thermometer or candy thermometer

Whenever I'm at a restaurant that is serving duck fat fries, I HAVE to order them. Those and truffle fries. I like to keep my fry game at the top of its game. Now you can make your own duck fat fries at home! These are so easy to throw together and are amazingly delicious. They would be a great companion to lettuce-wrapped burgers straight from the grill for a relaxing Sunday dinner.

1. Scrub the potatoes, then slice them into sticks about ¼ to ½ inch (6 to 12 mm) wide and 3 to 4 inches (7.5 to 10 cm) long. Soak the potato sticks in cold water for 30 minutes. This helps remove the excess starch, preventing the potatoes from sticking together and helping them fry better.

2. After 30 minutes, drain the potatoes and pat dry. Put the duck fat in a large saucepan set over medium-high heat. Using a deep-fry or candy thermometer to gauge the temperature, heat the oil to 325°F (162°C). Add the potatoes a handful at a time and cook until a knife slides through the center with no resistance, about 5 to 7 minutes. Lay the cooked fries on a plate lined with paper towels to drain. Repeat this process until all the potatoes are fried.

3. Turn the heat up to high and bring the oil up to 350°F (176°C). Twice-fry the potatoes a handful at a time. Drain on a plate lined with fresh paper towels. Repeat this process until all the potatoes have been double-fried. Sprinkle the salt on the fries while still hot and glistening with oil to help the salt stick. Garnish with parsley, if desired, and serve with your favorite dipping sauces.

Notes: *The two keys to great fries are the presoak and the double-fry method. The first fry cooks the potatoes, and the second fry gets them nice and crispy.*

I used Fatworks pastured duck fat and an amazing truffle salt from Trader Joe's. Don't toss your duck fat; you can reuse it! Just strain it through a fine-mesh sieve to remove any potato crumbs.

Subs: *Sweet potatoes or yams for the russet potatoes.*

LOADED
MASHED CAULIFLOWER

PREP TIME: 15 minutes
COOK TIME: 10 minutes
READY IN: 25 minutes
YIELD: 2 servings

Call me crazy, but I've eaten so much mashed cauliflower in my time that I've actually started to prefer it to the real thing. I'm not even lying. I have even tricked my loved ones into loving it too. This is my version of loaded mashed potatoes, made with cauliflower instead. I actually find myself craving mashed cauliflower. I'm weird, right? Don't answer that.

1 large head cauliflower

4 tablespoons (2 ounces/56 g) butter or ¼ cup (55 g) ghee

⅛ teaspoon fine-grain sea salt

⅛ teaspoon black ground pepper

⅛ teaspoon garlic salt

5 slices bacon

1 large egg

¼ cup (40 g) coconut flour

4 large yellow onion slices, about ¼ inch (6 mm) thick

2 tablespoons chopped fresh chives or green onions, for garnish

1. Cut the cauliflower florets off the head and place them in a microwave-safe bowl. Microwave for 5 to 10 minutes or until tender and translucent. Another method is to steam them by bringing ⅓ cup (80 ml) of water to a boil in a large skillet. Add the cauliflower florets, cover, and steam until tender and translucent.

2. Place the steamed cauliflower florets and butter in the bowl of a food processor. Puree until a smooth mashed potato–like consistency is reached, scraping down the sides as needed. Add the sea salt, pepper, and garlic salt, then puree again. Taste for seasoning and add more sea salt, pepper, or garlic salt if desired.

3. Cook the bacon in a large skillet set over medium-high heat. When done, remove from the pan and set aside to cool. Leave the bacon drippings in the pan and turn the heat down to low.

4. In a small mixing bowl, whisk the egg using a fork; set aside. Put the coconut flour in a separate small bowl. Dip each onion slice first into the egg and then into the flour until coated. Place them in the pan with the remaining bacon drippings. Turn the heat up to medium-high and fry for about 2 minutes per side or until golden brown.

5. To assemble: Divide the cauliflower mash between two serving bowls. Cut the cooled bacon with kitchen shears and crumble it over the top of each serving. Then sprinkle on the chopped chives and garnish with the onion rings.

Notes: To make this recipe dairy-free, use ghee rather than butter.

When it comes to seasoning, always start with less and add more. You can always add seasonings, but you can never subtract! Once something is too salty, it's going to stay that way.

Pesto
CAPRESE

PREP TIME: 5 minutes
READY IN: 10 minutes
YIELD: 10 pieces

While I was writing this book, the last thing I wanted to do was cook dinner. One of my favorite takeout places has a version of this caprese on their menu, and it's my favorite thing to order. After countless deliveries, I thought to myself, "I could probably make this at home for a lot cheaper." So I did. It literally takes ten minutes to throw together, so I didn't mind making it, even on weeknights when I was exhausted. Needless to say, I ate my fair share of this caprese over the course of this book; it only seemed right to include the recipe.

10 large fresh basil leaves

10 slices fresh mozzarella cheese

10 (¼-inch/6 mm-thick) slices Roma tomatoes

1 recipe Pesto Reloaded (page 76)

½ teaspoon fine-grain sea salt

¼ teaspoon ground black pepper

2 tablespoons extra-virgin olive oil

¼ cup (22 g) sliced almonds

Handful of arugula leaves, for garnish (optional)

1. Lay down a leaf of basil, then top it with a slice of mozzarella and a slice of tomato. Spoon a dollop of pesto on top of the tomato. Sprinkle with salt and pepper and a drizzle of olive oil, then top with sliced almonds.

2. Repeat with the remaining ingredients to make 10 stacks. Sprinkle some arugula leaves around the serving plate as a garnish, if desired.

Notes: *I buy my mozzarella presliced in packs from Costco. Saves you even more time! For a dairy-free version, omit the mozzarella.*

Bacon JALAPEÑO
DEVILED EGGS

PREP TIME: 15 minutes
COOK TIME: 15 minutes
READY IN: 30 minutes
YIELD: 1 dozen deviled eggs

Another thing that I love to order at restaurants is deviled eggs. Deviled eggs are easy to make at home, so I feel a little bit ridiculous ordering them when I'm out. But not so ridiculous that I don't, obviously, because they are delightful. Not only that, but they come in so many varieties; I feel like it's my responsibility to try them all. I love bacon-wrapped jalapeños, so I thought, "What if I made bacon jalapeño deviled eggs?" Yep, it's as amazing as it sounds. These would be awesome for a summer BBQ or as an appetizer for a dinner party. You can even double or triple the recipe depending on how many people you have to feed. I just like to feed myself, so this is the perfect amount. If you're feeling nice, there is enough to share.

4 slices bacon

6 large eggs, hard-boiled

½ cup (120 ml) mayonnaise, store-bought or homemade (page 78)

1 teaspoon Dijon mustard

⅛ teaspoon fine-grain sea salt

⅛ teaspoon ground black pepper

1 jalapeño pepper, seeded and diced

Paprika, for dusting (optional)

1. Cook the bacon in a large skillet set over medium-high heat until crispy. Place the cooked bacon on a plate lined with paper towels to cool and drain.

2. While the bacon is cooling, remove the shells from the hard-boiled eggs and slice the eggs in half lengthwise. The yolks should pop right out; if not, use a spoon to gently scoop them out into a small mixing bowl. Place the egg white halves cut side up on a separate plate.

3. Add the mayonnaise, mustard, salt, and pepper to the bowl with the egg yolks. Use a fork to mix and mash the ingredients together until smooth. Alternatively, for an ultra-smooth mixture, use a hand mixer set on medium speed and beat until smooth and combined.

4. After the bacon has cooled, chop it into small pieces. Transfer the egg mixture to a piping bag or to a resealable plastic bag with a corner cut off and pipe it into each egg white half. Sprinkle with bacon pieces and diced jalapeños. Dust with paprika, if desired.

Notes: *To get perfectly boiled eggs every time, grab an egg timer from a large retailer like Bed Bath & Beyond or Cost Plus World Market.*

Browned Butter Sage AND GOAT CHEESE Spaghetti Squash

PREP TIME: 15 minutes
COOK TIME: 45 to 50 minutes
READY IN: 1 hour
YIELD: 2 servings

As you may or may not know, I'm literally obsessed with browned butter. It's a flavor powerhouse that takes anything to the next level. One of my favorite ways to eat pasta before going Paleo was to use browned butter and Parmesan together as a sauce instead of marinara. So of course I had to include a recipe for you made with everyone's favorite nonpasta friend, spaghetti squash! This recipe is a huge hit in my house, and I hope it will be in yours too.

1 medium spaghetti squash (2 to 3 pounds)

2 tablespoons olive oil

4 tablespoons (2 ounces/56 g) salted butter

10 fresh sage leaves

2 teaspoons fresh-squeezed lemon juice

¼ teaspoon onion powder

¼ teaspoon garlic salt

⅛ teaspoon fine-grain sea salt

⅛ teaspoon ground black pepper

¼ cup (55 g) grated Parmesan cheese

2 ounces (55 g) goat cheese, crumbled

1. Preheat the oven to 350°F (177°C). Line a rimmed baking sheet with foil. Cut the spaghetti squash in half lengthwise and use a spoon to scrape out the seeds. Coat the cut surface and inside of each half with the olive oil. Place facedown on the foil-lined baking sheet and cook for 45 to 50 minutes or until the squash has browned and the strands are translucent.

2. Set the cooked squash aside and let cool until no longer hot but still warm. While it's cooling, prepare the browned butter sage sauce by melting the butter in a large skillet, stirring occasionally, until the butter turns amber in color and browned bits start to appear on the bottom of the pan. Remove the pan from the heat and add the sage leaves and lemon juice. Stir until the sage leaves are covered in butter and the lemon juice is well incorporated; set aside.

3. Using a fork, scrape the squash lengthwise over a bowl to remove all the strands. Add the onion powder, garlic salt, sea salt, and pepper. Use the fork to mix the spices into the squash. Transfer the seasoned squash to the pan with the browned butter sage sauce. Add the Parmesan cheese and toss until the squash is evenly coated.

4. Transfer the squash to a plate and sprinkle the goat cheese crumbles on top, or use the scraped-out squash halves as serving vessels, as pictured. Enjoy immediately.

Notes: To make this recipe dairy-free, substitute ¼ cup (55 g) of ghee for the butter. It won't brown, but it will taste similar. Cook until melted and hot, then add the sage. Omit the cheeses and, if desired, add nutritional yeast to give the dish a cheeselike flavor element: Sprinkle each serving with 1 tablespoon of nutritional yeast just before serving.

Pizza
SOUP

I don't know about you, but I love pizza. Like, love pizza. It's one of those foods that always sounds good to me no matter what. This soup is an easy and delicious way to get your pizza fix. I made a batch and ate the whole thing over three days. The WHOLE thing. This soup would also be great for people who throw their pizza crust away, also known as crazy people. This soup is like squeezing all the toppings from your pizza into a big bowl and eating them with a spoon. Hmm, that sounds kind of gross. I assure you, though, Pizza Soup is anything but gross.

PREP TIME: 15 minutes
COOK TIME: 30 minutes
READY IN: 45 minutes
YIELD: 4 to 6 servings

1 pound (455 g) bulk mild Italian sausage

2 tablespoons olive oil

½ large white onion, diced (1 cup/ 185 g)

2 cloves garlic, minced

2 (14-ounce/415-ml) jars no-sugar-added pizza sauce

3 cups (710 ml) chicken broth

2 tomatoes, chopped (1 cup/215 g)

4 cremini mushrooms, sliced

3 ounces (85 g) sliced pepperoni, chopped

1 green bell pepper, seeded and sliced

1 teaspoon garlic salt

½ teaspoon fine-grain sea salt

½ teaspoon Italian seasoning

½ teaspoon onion powder

¼ teaspoon ground black pepper

1 cup (130 g) shredded mozzarella cheese or Italian cheese blend (optional)

1   In a large skillet, crumble and cook the sausage until no pink remains; set aside.

2   Place the olive oil, diced onion, and garlic in a large heavy-bottomed stockpot set over medium heat. Cook until the onion and garlic are tender, fragrant, and translucent, about 5 minutes. Then add the cooked sausage and the remaining ingredients, except the cheese, and stir until combined. Bring to a boil, then reduce the heat. Cover and simmer for 30 minutes, stirring occasionally. The soup is ready when the mushrooms and bell pepper are tender.

3   Transfer the soup to oven-safe serving bowls. If topping with cheese, turn the oven broiler on and line a rimmed baking sheet with foil. Sprinkle cheese over the top of each soup bowl, place the bowls on the foil-lined baking sheet, two at a time, and broil for 2 to 3 minutes until the cheese is melted and lightly browned.

Notes: *To make this soup dairy-free, omit the cheese.*

Add your personal favorite pizza toppings to make your own custom soup!

Subs: *Marinara sauce (no sugar added) in place of the pizza sauce. The soup will be thinner in texture if marinara is used.*

Chipotle
CHICKEN SALAD

PREP TIME: 10 minutes
READY IN: 10 minutes
YIELD: 2½ cups (350 g)

In addition to running a food blog and writing a cookbook, I work full-time in an office environment. I have brought this recipe to work for lunch several times, and every single time our Top Flight Security guy, Victor, tries to talk me into giving it to him instead. I always tell him that I'll save him a bite, but then I end up eating the whole thing because it's just that good. I should probably be nice and make him his own next time, but again, that just means less for me. Besides lunch, this recipe is also a super easy dinner to whip up on a weeknight in the summer when it's way too hot outside to cook. I know this from personal experience.

2 cups (8 ounces/225 g) shredded cooked chicken

1 cup (125 g) chopped celery

¼ cup (35 g) diced red onions

½ cup (120 ml) mayo, store-bought or homemade (page 78)

2 tablespoons chipotle peppers in adobo sauce

¼ teaspoon fine-grain sea salt

⅛ teaspoon ground black pepper

1 Combine all the ingredients in a large mixing bowl. Stir together using a fork until completely combined.

Notes: *Be sure to use a clean version of canned chipotle peppers in adobo sauce. Some brands contain gluten and unhealthy vegetable oils. The best one I've found is La Morena, which you can buy at Walmart, Amazon, and other large retailers. The ingredients listed are chipotle peppers, tomato puree, paprika, sugar, iodized salt, onions, sesame oil, distilled vinegar, garlic, bay leaves, and oregano. Another option is to make your own! It's a fairly easy process, and there are tons of recipes available online if you are feeling ambitious. In a pinch, San Marcos or La Costena brand will do; they contain vegetable oil, but since the recipe calls for only 2 tablespoons, I wouldn't panic over it. Stay far, far away from Embasa brand; it contains wheat flour.*

One of my favorite ways to eat this chicken salad is wrapped in big fat butter lettuce leaves!

Subs: *Sir Kensington's Chipotle Mayonnaise in place of regular mayo.*

DAIRY FREE*

Shepherd's
POT PIE

PREP TIME: 20 minutes
COOK TIME: 25 minutes
READY IN: 45 minutes
YIELD: 4 to 6 servings

Most shepherd's pie recipes don't call for a crust. Well, that's not fair. Chicken pot pie gets a crust, so why shouldn't shepherd's pie get one? In fact, I think all pie gets a crust, right? I'm not a pie expert, but I do know that I like pie, and I sure as heck like the crust. Well, things are about to get crazy, because I added a crust to my shepherd's pie recipe. It's kind of like if you took a chicken pot pie and a shepherd's pie and combined them. There, now all is right in the world.

---

1 recipe Old-Fashioned Flaky Pie Crust (page 166)

FOR THE FILLING

½ cup (75 g) frozen peas

½ cup (70 g) frozen sliced carrots

2 tablespoons water

1 pound (455 g) grass-fed ground beef

1 small white onion, diced

1¼ teaspoons fine-grain sea salt, divided

1¼ teaspoons garlic salt, divided

½ teaspoon ground black pepper, divided

½ teaspoon onion powder

½ teaspoon garlic powder

1 large head cauliflower

4 tablespoons (2 ounces/56 g) butter or ¼ cup (55 g) ghee

1. Prepare the Old-Fashioned Flaky Pie Crust, following Steps 1 and 2 on page 166. Press two-thirds of the dough into a 9-inch (23-cm) pie pan. Reserve the remaining dough for another use, or, if desired, roll it into a long, thin rope, place the rope evenly around the edge of the pan, and pinch the sides into shape. Bake for 10 to 14 minutes, until the crust is browned and dry to the touch; set aside.

2. Place the peas and carrots in a microwave-safe bowl, pour the water over them, and microwave for 2 to 3 minutes or until thawed. Put the beef in a large skillet set over medium-high heat. Cook until only a small amount of pink remains, then stir in the peas, carrots, and diced onion. Season with 1 teaspoon of the salt, 1 teaspoon of the garlic salt, ¼ teaspoon of the pepper, onion powder, and garlic powder. Continue to cook, stirring intermittently, until the beef is mostly browned. While the beef is browning, prepare the cauliflower mash.

3. Cut the cauliflower florets off the head and place them in a microwave-safe bowl. Microwave for 7 to 10 minutes or until tender and translucent. Another method is to steam them by bringing ⅓ cup (80 ml) of water to a boil in a large skillet. Add the cauliflower florets, cover, and steam until tender.

4. Place the steamed cauliflower florets and butter in the bowl of a large food processor. Puree for 3 to 5 minutes or until a smooth mashed potato–like consistency is reached, scraping down the sides as needed. Then add the remaining ¼ teaspoon of salt, ¼ teaspoon of garlic salt, and ¼ teaspoon of ground pepper and puree again until combined.

5. To assemble: Place an oven rack in the top position and turn the broiler on. Drain the beef mixture, then transfer it to the pie crust. Top with the cauliflower mash, evening it out with a rubber spatula. Broil for 4 to 5 minutes or until the cauliflower and crust have browned.

Notes: To make this dairy-free, use ghee to make the crust and filling.

Need a quick version for a busy weeknight? Skip the pie crust! This filling tastes amazing all by itself. Transfer the beef mixture directly to a dinner plate and top it with a large dollop of the cauliflower mash. The whole thing will take only about 30 minutes!

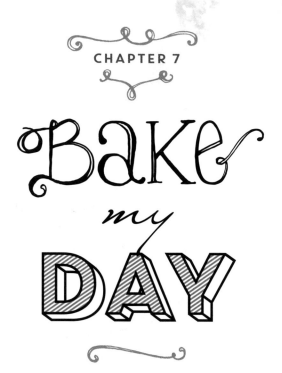

Bake my DAY

EGG FREE*

S'mores
BARS

PREP TIME: 30 minutes
COOK TIME: 25 minutes
SETTING TIME: 4 hours
READY IN: 5 hours
YIELD: 9 bars

1 recipe Graham Cracker Crust dough (page 170)

1 recipe Ganache (pages 369 to 370), any type

1 recipe Marshmallow Crème, regular (page 366) or egg-free (page 368)

SPECIAL EQUIPMENT

Kitchen torch

MAKE AHEAD

GRAHAM CRACKER CRUST—1 DAY AHEAD

I have an obsession with s'mores. I'm not sure you could tell by the 7,139,116,779 s'mores recipes I have in this book. This is one of my absolute favorites. These bars would be great to bring to a potluck or even make for a birthday!

1 Preheat the oven to 350°F (177°C). Line an 8-inch (20-cm) square glass pan with parchment paper.

2 Prepare the Graham Cracker Crust, following Steps 2 and 3 on page 170. Press the dough evenly into the prepared pan and bake for 25 minutes or until the edges turn golden. Let cool.

3 Prepare the ganache, then pour the ganache evenly over the cooled Graham Cracker Crust and place in the refrigerator to chill while you prepare the Marshmallow Crème.

4 When the Marshmallow Crème is ready, use a rubber spatula to spread it evenly on top of the ganache layer. If using the Egg-Free Marshmallow Crème, swirl some into the ganache layer first, then evenly spread the rest on top. Use a kitchen torch to roast the Marshmallow Crème layer until golden brown. Refrigerate for at least 4 hours, until set (overnight is best), before cutting. For a cleaner cut, run the knife under hot water first, then wipe dry with a clean towel. Store any leftovers in the refrigerator for up to 3 days.

Notes: *To make these bars egg-free, use the Egg-Free Marshmallow Crème. If using Egg-Free Marshmallow Crème, the step of using a rubber spatula to swirl some crème into the ganache layer before adding the rest is important. This will ensure that the crème binds to the chocolate; otherwise, it tends to become firm and separate from the chocolate layer.*

The bars pictured were made with Dairy-Free Ganache (page 370) and regular Marshmallow Crème (made with egg whites; page 366).

Better than
BOX BROWNIES

PREP TIME: 15 minutes
COOK TIME: 30 to 35 minutes
READY IN: 45 minutes
YIELD: 1 dozen brownies

Brownies. Need I say more? These bad boys look just like the good ol' out-of-the-box brownies you know and love, but they taste way better. They even have that beautiful sheen and a cracked crust on top. They pair best with red wine, stretchy pants, and a chick flick.

1 cup (7 ounces/200 g) semisweet chocolate chips

6 tablespoons (3 ounces/85 g) salted butter

½ cup (45 g) sifted fine-ground blanched almond flour

¼ cup (20 g) packed cacao powder or unsweetened cocoa powder

¼ teaspoon fine-grain sea salt

1 cup (150 g) coconut sugar

1 teaspoon vanilla extract

2 large eggs, room temperature

Chocolate curls, for garnish (optional; see page 61)

MAKE AHEAD
CHOCOLATE CURLS—1 WEEK AHEAD

1 Adjust an oven rack to the middle position and preheat the oven to 350°F (177°C). Line an 8-inch (20-cm) square glass pan with parchment paper; set aside.

2 Melt the chocolate chips and butter in double boiler over low heat or in a heatproof bowl set over a pan of gently simmering water. Stir frequently, using a rubber spatula, until completely melted and combined. Remove from the heat and let sit until the bowl is relatively cool to the touch. While the chocolate mixture is cooling, prepare the other ingredients.

3 In a medium-sized mixing bowl, combine the almond flour, cacao powder, and salt. Stir together using a fork until well combined.

4 In a separate mixing bowl, combine the coconut sugar and vanilla. With a hand mixer set on low speed, beat in the eggs one at a time for about 5 seconds each, making sure not to overmix.

5 Transfer the egg mixture into the chocolate mixture, scraping down the bowl if needed, and gently mix together using a rubber spatula until just combined. Gently fold the almond flour mixture into the chocolate and egg mixture, being careful not to overmix.

6 Pour the batter into the prepared pan and bake for 30 to 35 minutes, until a toothpick comes out with a few crumbs but isn't wet, and the edges have pulled away from the pan. Let cool in the pan and then, if time allows, place the pan in the fridge to chill before serving (brownies cut best when cold).

7 Garnish with chocolate curls, if desired. Store at room temperature in an airtight container or wrapped well in plastic for up to 2 days.

Notes: To make these dairy-free, use ¼ cup plus 2 tablespoons (85 g) of ghee or ¼ cup (60 ml) of melted coconut oil in place of the butter.

To get that nice crackled brownie top look, as pictured, you have to use semisweet (not dark) chocolate chips.

Brownies are very prone to overmixing. If too much air gets into the batter, it causes the brownies to rise higher during baking, which results in a sunken middle once they are removed from the oven. You want to mix your ingredients so that they are just barely combined.

If you like to eat your brownies warm, straight from the pan, and want that ooey gooey brownie center, decrease the cooking time to 25 to 28 minutes, grab a fork, and go to town.

DAIRY FREE*

Sour Cherry
CRUMBLE BARS

PREP TIME: 30 minutes
COOK TIME: 15 to 40 minutes
SETTING TIME: 1 hour
READY IN: 1 hour 45 minutes
YIELD: 9 bars

I love tart cherries, aka "sour" cherries. I think they make the tastiest fillings for cherry pies and tarts. A little bit of sweet and a little bit of sour, just the way I like it. This recipe was a huge surprise hit with my co-workers when I tested it. In fact, they still talk about it to this day. These bars would be great at any time of year, but I think eating them on the porch on a nice summer day with a slight breeze would be exceptional.

1 recipe Sour Cherry Compote
(page 386)

1 recipe Shortbread Cookie dough
(page 286) or Old-Fashioned Flaky
Pie Crust dough (page 166)

2 tablespoons coconut butter,
melted, for drizzling

MAKE AHEAD

SOUR CHERRY COMPOTE—5 DAYS AHEAD

SHORTBREAD COOKIE LAYER—1 DAY AHEAD

Notes: To make these bars dairy-free, use the Old-Fashioned Flaky Pie Crust made with ghee rather than butter.

This could easily be made into a Sour Cherry Crumble Pie if that's your jam. Just use a 9-inch (23-cm) pie pan instead of a square glass pan. Easy peasy, cherry squeezey.

Subs: The dough for Frosted "Oatmeal" Breakfast Squares (page 70) would make an amazing oatmeal-type crust. Use the dough as instructed above, baking it at 350°F (177°C) for 25 minutes or until a toothpick comes out clean and the edges are golden brown.

1. Make the Sour Cherry Compote. While it cooks and reduces, prepare the rest of the recipe.

2. If using the Old-Fashioned Flaky Pie Crust, jump ahead to Step 3. If using the Shortbread Cookie dough, preheat the oven to 350°F (177°C) and line an 8-inch (20-cm) square glass pan with parchment paper. Prepare the cookie dough, completing Steps 1 through 3 on page 286, without chilling the dough. Set aside about ⅓ cup (85 g) of dough to use for the crumble layer. Use a rubber spatula to transfer and press the remaining dough evenly into the prepared pan and bake for 25 to 30 minutes, until the top is golden. Remove from the oven and let cool on a wire rack. Leave the oven on. Meanwhile, roll out the rest of the dough to ½ inch (1.25 cm) thick on a piece of parchment paper. Slide the parchment paper with the dough onto a baking sheet and bake at the same temperature for 7 to 9 minutes, until the edges are golden. Let cool.

3. To use the Old-Fashioned Flaky Pie Crust dough, preheat the oven to 425°F (218°C) and line an 8-inch (20-cm) square glass pan with parchment paper. Prepare the dough, completing Steps 1 and 2 on page 166. Set aside one-third of the dough to use for the crumble layer, then press the remaining dough evenly into the prepared pan. Use the tines of a fork to pierce the dough along the bottom and sides to allow steam to escape during baking, then place in the freezer for 10 minutes to firm up the crust. Bake for 7 to 10 minutes or until golden. Let cool. Leave the oven on. Meanwhile, roll out the rest of the dough to ½ inch (1.25 cm) thick on a piece of parchment paper. Slide the parchment paper with the dough onto a baking sheet and bake at the same temperature for 5 to 10 minutes, until the edges are golden. Let cool.

4. Pour the compote over the cooled crust layer and use a rubber spatula to spread it evenly across the top and to the sides. Using your hands, crumble the smaller piece of baked dough evenly over the compote layer.

5. Transfer the coconut butter to a piping bag or to a resealable plastic bag with a corner cut off. Drizzle the coconut butter across the top of the crumble layer, then refrigerate to set for at least 1 hour before cutting and serving. Store any leftovers covered in the refrigerator for up to 3 days.

SAMOA BARS

PREP TIME: 30 minutes
COOK TIME: 25 to 30 minutes
SETTING TIME: 45 minutes
READY IN: 1 hour 40 minutes
YIELD: 9 bars

Find me the person who doesn't love Girl Scout cookies—it's a fool's errand, I tell you! When I was mini-me, pushing cookies door to door, Samoas were always one of my favorites. I don't know what it is about shortbread, caramel, chocolate, and toasted coconut that makes Samoas so amazing, but oh my. I think I should earn a baking patch for making these bars. Just saying.

1 recipe Shortbread Cookie dough (page 286)

1 recipe Salted Caramel Sauce (page 374)

1½ cups (120 g) unsweetened shredded coconut

1 (12-ounce/340-g) bag semisweet chocolate chips

MAKE AHEAD

SHORTBREAD COOKIE BASE—1 DAY AHEAD

SALTED CARAMEL SAUCE—2 DAYS AHEAD: WHEN READY TO USE, BRING TO ROOM TEMPERATURE AND THEN STIR IN THE COCONUT

1. Preheat the oven to 350°F (177°C) and line an 8-inch (20-cm) square glass pan with parchment paper. Prepare the Shortbread Cookie dough, completing Steps 1 through 3 on page 286, without chilling the dough. Press the dough evenly into the prepared pan and bake for 25 to 30 minutes or until the top is golden. Remove from the oven and let cool in the pan.

2. While the shortbread base is baking, prepare the Salted Caramel Sauce; set aside.

3. Toast the shredded coconut in a large skillet set over medium heat. Stir frequently using a spatula until the flakes are golden brown and even in color, 5 to 10 minutes. Add the coconut to the caramel sauce and stir until completely combined. Use a rubber spatula to spread the caramel and coconut mixture evenly across the top of the cooled shortbread base. Refrigerate for 30 minutes to firm up and set.

4. Meanwhile, prepare the chocolate topping: Melt the chocolate chips in a double boiler over low heat or in a heatproof bowl set over a pan of gently simmering water. Stir frequently, using a rubber spatula, until the chocolate is completely melted and smooth.

5. Line a baking sheet with parchment paper. Remove the shortbread and caramel base from the pan and cut into 9 squares. Holding it from the top, dip a square into the bowl of chocolate, deep enough to coat the bottom and sides, up to the caramel layer. Use a candy-dipping fork or a plastic fork with the two middle prongs broken off to remove the square from the chocolate, letting any excess chocolate drain back into the bowl. It works best to use the fork to lift the bar from underneath, using the flat cookie bottom for stability. After the excess chocolate has drained, place the dipped square on the parchment paper, chocolate side down. Repeat with the remaining squares.

6. Once all the bars have been dipped, transfer the remaining chocolate to a piping bag or to a resealable plastic bag with a corner cut off. Drizzle chocolate across the top of each bar. Place the tray of finished bars in the refrigerator to set for at least 15 minutes. Store any leftovers in the refrigerator for up to 3 days.

Billionaire BARS

PREP TIME: 25 minutes
COOK TIME: 30 to 35 minutes
SETTING TIME: 1 hour
READY IN: 2 hours
YIELD: 1 dozen bars

These are my take on the millionaire bar. A traditional millionaire bar has a shortbread cookie base, a caramel center, and a chocolate top layer. I upped the richness by replacing the shortbread base with a chocolate chip cookie one and adding two kinds of chocolate for the top layer! Guilty as charged. This recipe is a favorite of my friends and family. It's incredibly rich and indulgent, just like a billionaire should be.

1 recipe Chocolate Chip Cookie Bottom (page 136)

1 recipe Salted Caramel Sauce (page 374)

1 recipe Ganache (pages 369 to 370), any type

1 recipe White Chocolate (page 140)

MAKE AHEAD

CHOCOLATE CHIP COOKIE BOTTOM—
1 DAY AHEAD

SALTED CARAMEL SAUCE—2 DAYS AHEAD

1. Prepare the Chocolate Chip Cookie Bottom.

2. While the cookie bottom is baking, prepare the Salted Caramel Sauce. Place the sauce in the freezer for 15 to 20 minutes to chill and thicken.

3. Once the cookie bottom has cooled and the caramel sauce has cooled and thickened, pour the caramel over the cookie bottom and use a rubber spatula to spread it evenly across the top and to the sides. Place in the refrigerator while you prepare the ganache. Then, while the ganache is cooling, prepare the white chocolate by completing Step 1 on page 140.

4. Once the ganache is fully cool, use a rubber spatula or butter knife to spread it evenly over the caramel layer. (If the ganache is too warm, it will melt the caramel.)

5. Transfer the white chocolate to a piping bag or to a resealable plastic bag with a corner cut off. Drizzle white chocolate across the top of each bar. Place the tray of finished bars in the refrigerator to set for at least 1 hour before cutting and serving. Store any leftovers in the refrigerator for up to 3 days.

Notes: If you don't want to make the white chocolate from scratch, use one of the store-bought brands that I recommend on page 47. If you don't want melted white chocolate on top, another option is to sprinkle white chocolate chunks or shavings on top. You can even use milk chocolate if you want. Make it your own!

S'mores
DONUTS

PREP TIME: 20 minutes
COOK TIME: 15 minutes/40 minutes
READY IN: 35 minutes/1 hour
YIELD: 18 mini donuts, or 1 dozen regular size

1 recipe Chocolate Cupcake batter (page 226)

1 recipe Marshmallow Crème, regular (page 366) or egg-free (page 368)

FOR GARNISH

2 tablespoons melted chocolate, for drizzling

2 tablespoons gluten-free graham cracker crumbs or crumbled Graham Cracker Crust (page 170)

SPECIAL EQUIPMENT

Kitchen torch (optional)

Bring on the s'mores. I can always go for s'more s'mores. These donuts are the perfect treat to treat any s'mores craving. With a rich donut bottom and a creamy and fluffy marshmallow glaze, what's not to love? Nothing. You will love it all.

1 Preheat a mini donut maker or, if using a donut pan, adjust an oven rack to the middle position and preheat the oven to 350°F (177°C). Lightly grease the donut pan.

2 Prepare the Chocolate Cupcake batter, completing Steps 2 through 5 on page 226. Using a rubber spatula, transfer the batter into a large resealable plastic bag and snip off a corner. Squeeze the batter evenly into the donut maker or pan. If using a donut maker that makes six mini donuts, cook the batter in three batches. If using a donut pan that makes six donuts, cook the batter in two batches, filling the pan two-thirds full each time.

3 If using a donut maker, cook for 3 minutes on one side and then flip the donuts, using a knife or fork to help remove them, and bake for another minute. Times may vary depending on the manufacturer. Remove the donuts and place on a wire rack to cool before glazing. Repeat with the remaining batter.

4 If using a donut pan, tap the pan on the counter to remove any air bubbles, then bake for 20 minutes or until a toothpick comes out clean. Let cool slightly, then flip the pan upside down onto a wire rack to cool completely. Repeat with the remaining batter.

5 While the donuts are cooling, prepare the Marshmallow Crème to use for the glaze.

6 Dip the top of a donut into the marshmallow glaze, then place back on the cooling rack. Repeat this process until all the donuts are glazed. Toast the glaze with a kitchen torch, if desired. Transfer the melted chocolate to a resealable plastic bag, snip off a corner, and squeeze to drizzle chocolate across the top of each donut. Sprinkle the graham cracker crumbs across the donut tops, over the chocolate drizzle and marshmallow glaze. Store covered at room temperature for up to 2 days.

Notes: Depending on how "clean" you want to go with this recipe, I've given you two graham cracker crumb options for the garnish. Store-bought crumbs are easier, but most brands contain soy and rice flour. My favorite store-bought option is Gluten-Free Graham Cracker Style Crumbs from Kinnikinnick Foods. You can find them online or at Whole Foods. The second option is to make the Graham Cracker Crust on page 170 and crumble the finished crust into crumbs.

DAIRY FREE*

SKILLET BROWNIE SUNDAE
WITH BROWN SUGAR
Bacon Crumbles

PREP TIME: 35 minutes
COOK TIME: 25 to 30 minutes
READY IN: 1 hour 45 minutes
YIELD: One 10-inch (25-cm) sundae or two 6-inch (15-cm) sundaes; 4 servings

So yeah, candied bacon, brownies, and ice cream is pretty much where it's at. Especially because the brownies are baked in a skillet. How fun are skillets? I want to bake everything in them. You can use either one regular-sized skillet or two mini skillets, depending on the level of cuteness you would like to achieve. The mini skillets are adorable, so you'd be extra-cute, obviously, while the regular size is all business. I'll let you decide where you want to go with it.

1 recipe French Vanilla Ice Cream (page 330)

1 recipe Brown Sugar Bacon (page 158)

Butter or coconut oil, for the skillet

1 recipe Better than Box Brownie batter (page 110)

1 recipe Chocolate Shell Coating (page 376)

MAKE AHEAD
FRENCH VANILLA ICE CREAM—
2 WEEKS AHEAD

1 Prepare the French Vanilla Ice Cream. While the ice cream is setting in the freezer, prepare the Brown Sugar Bacon. Once the bacon is cool enough to handle, cut it into pieces using kitchen shears; set aside.

2 Turn the oven down to 350°F (177°C) and grease a 10-inch (25-cm) cast-iron skillet or two 6-inch (15-cm) cast-iron skillets. Prepare the brownie batter, completing Steps 2 through 5 on page 110. Pour the batter into the skillet(s) and bake for 25 to 30 minutes or until a toothpick comes out with some crumbs but is not wet. (If using two mini skillets, the baking time may need to be reduced.)

3 While the brownies are baking, prepare the Chocolate Shell Coating.

4 To assemble the sundae, scoop some ice cream onto the center of the brownie and drizzle Chocolate Shell Coating on top of the ice cream. Crumble the bacon pieces on top. Leftover naked brownie (not topped with ice cream, chocolate shell, or bacon) can be stored at room temperature in an airtight container or wrapped in plastic for up to 3 days.

Notes: To make this sundae dairy-free, use ghee or coconut oil rather than butter in the brownies.

If you want that ooey gooey brownie center, decrease the baking time to 20 to 23 minutes.

Not a plain-vanilla ice cream fan? Me neither. Jazz it up with any of the ice cream recipes in this book or grab your favorite store-bought brand. Go wild!

DAIRY FREE*

Peaches and Cream
BARS

PREP TIME: 30 minutes
COOK TIME: 15 to 40 minutes
SETTING TIME: 2 hours
READY IN: 3 hours
YIELD: 9 bars

I am obsessed with anything peaches and cream. Remember the peaches and cream–flavored instant oatmeal? That was my favorite. It went especially well with Saturday morning cartoons and pajamas. These bars were inspired by all those things, and also by peach cobbler. Some things in life were just meant to go together. Peaches and cream is definitely one of those combinations.

1 recipe Shortbread Cookie dough (page 286) or Old-Fashioned Flaky Crust dough (page 166)

1 recipe Peaches and Cream (page 384)

FOR GARNISH

2 tablespoons coconut butter, melted

MAKE AHEAD

SHORTBREAD COOKIE LAYER—1 DAY AHEAD
PEACHES AND CREAM—3 DAYS AHEAD

Subs: To make these bars dairy-free, use the Old-Fashioned Flaky Pie Crust dough made with ghee rather than butter.

The dough for Frosted "Oatmeal" Breakfast Squares (page 70) would make an amazing oatmeal-type crust. Prepare the dough, following Steps 2 and 3, then press it into a parchment paper–lined 8-inch (20-cm) square glass pan and bake at 350°F (177°C) for 25 minutes or until a toothpick comes out clean and the edges are golden brown. Note that there is not a dairy-free option for this dough.

1 If using the Old-Fashioned Flaky Pie Crust, jump ahead to Step 2. If using the Shortbread Cookie dough, preheat the oven to 350°F (177°C) and line an 8-inch (20-cm) square glass pan with parchment paper. Prepare the cookie dough, completing Steps 1 through 3 on page 286, without chilling the dough. Set aside about ⅓ cup (85 g) of the dough to use for the crumble layer. Use a rubber spatula to transfer and press the remaining dough evenly into the prepared pan. Bake for 25 to 30 minutes or until the top is golden. Let cool. Meanwhile, roll out the rest of the dough to ½ inch (1.25 cm) thick on a piece of parchment paper. Slide the parchment paper and dough onto a baking sheet. Bake at the same temperature for 7 to 9 minutes, until the edges are golden. Let cool.

2 To use the Old-Fashioned Flaky Pie Crust, preheat the oven to 425°F (218°C) and line an 8-inch (20-cm) square glass pan with parchment paper. Prepare the dough, completing Steps 1 through 3 on page 166. Set aside one-third of the dough (not ⅓ cup) to use for the crumble layer. Press the remaining dough evenly into the prepared pan. Use the tines of a fork to pierce the dough along the bottom and sides to allow steam to escape during baking, then place the crust in the freezer for 10 minutes to firm up. Bake for 7 to 10 minutes or until golden. Let cool. Meanwhile, roll out the rest of the dough to ½ inch (1.25 cm) thick on a piece of parchment paper. Slide the parchment paper with the dough onto a baking sheet. Bake at the same temperature for 5 to 10 minutes, until the edges are golden. Let cool.

3 Prepare the Peaches and Cream and pour it evenly over the cooled crust layer; use a rubber spatula to spread the peaches evenly across the top and to the sides. Crumble the smaller piece of baked dough evenly over the peach layer.

4 Transfer the coconut butter to a piping bag or to a resealable plastic bag with a corner cut off. Drizzle coconut butter across the top of the crumble layer, then refrigerate for at least 2 hours before cutting and serving; the longer they set, the easier they will be to cut. Store any leftovers covered in the refrigerator for up to 3 days.

Barely Legal BARS

PREP TIME: 1 hour
COOK TIME: 30 minutes
SETTING TIME: 30 minutes
READY IN: 2 hours
YIELD: 9 bars

You know how, when something is incredibly delicious, you say, "These are so good they should be illegal"? Well, that was the inspiration behind these bars. The combination of chocolate chip cookies and chocolate dessert cups is so decadent. This recipe is one of my absolute favorites; I love making it for people I really want to impress with Paleo desserts.

1 recipe Almond Butter Cups (page 146) or Salted Caramel Cups (page 148)

1 recipe Chocolate Chip Cookie Bottom dough (page 136)

½ cup (3½ ounces/100 g) chocolate chips

MAKE AHEAD
ALMOND BUTTER CUPS—5 DAYS AHEAD
CHOCOLATE CHIP COOKIE BOTTOM—
1 DAY AHEAD

1 Prepare the Almond Butter Cups or Salted Caramel Cups.

2 While the cups are setting, make the Chocolate Chip Cookie Bottom dough: Place an oven rack in the middle position and preheat the oven to 350°F (177°C). Line an 8-inch (20-cm) square glass pan with parchment paper; set aside. Follow the recipe for the cookie bottom, completing Steps 2 through 4 on page 136. Use a rubber spatula to transfer the dough and press it evenly into the prepared pan.

3 Place 9 Almond Butter Cups or Salted Caramel Cups evenly across the cookie dough, in three rows of three. Bake for 30 minutes or until the edges are golden. Let cool.

4 While the base layer is cooling, melt the chocolate chips in a double boiler over low heat or in a heatproof bowl set over a pan of gently simmering water. Stir frequently, using a rubber spatula, until the chocolate is completely melted and smooth. Remove from the heat.

5 Transfer the melted chocolate to a piping bag or to a resealable plastic bag with a corner cut off. Drizzle chocolate evenly across the top of the base layer. Refrigerate or freeze for 30 minutes or until the chocolate is set and the base is cool. It will be easier to cut after being refrigerated. Cut into 9 squares and serve. Store any leftovers covered in the refrigerator for up to 3 days.

Subs: Use store-bought nut butter cups or sunflower seed butter cups instead of making your own. Justin's, Theo, and Sun Cups brands all make great options.

DAIRY FREE

Brownie
CRUMB DONUTS

PREP TIME: 20 minutes
COOK TIME: 15 minutes/40 minutes
READY IN: 35 minutes/1 hour
YIELD: 18 mini donuts, or 1 dozen regular size

Chocolate donuts? Sign me up. Brownies? Sign me up twice. I love these donuts because they are so easy and fun to make. And they are delicious, so even more reason. You can make them in a donut pan for regular-size donuts or in a donut maker for mini ones. You can find mini donut makers for cheap on Amazon and sometimes for even cheaper at thrift stores. It's a fun specialty kitchen appliance to have when the donut craving strikes. Try making these with the kids on a Saturday morning.

1 cup (92 g) sifted fine-ground blanched almond flour

1 tablespoon coconut sugar

½ teaspoon baking soda

½ teaspoon fine-grain sea salt

⅛ teaspoon ground cinnamon

1 cup (7 ounces/200 g) chocolate chips

½ cup (120 ml) canned full-fat coconut milk, room temperature

¼ cup (55 g) palm shortening

½ teaspoon vanilla extract

2 large eggs

1 recipe Chocolate Shell Coating (page 376), for the glaze

Notes: If you need a coconut-free glaze, use one of the coconut-free ganache recipes on page 369. It will be thicker, but will still taste delicious.

1. Preheat a mini donut maker or, if using a donut pan, place an oven rack in the middle position and preheat the oven to 350°F (177°C). Lightly grease the donut pan.

2. In a medium-sized bowl, combine the almond flour, coconut sugar, baking soda, salt, and cinnamon. Stir together using a fork until combined; set aside.

3. Melt the chocolate chips and coconut milk in a double boiler over low heat or in a heatproof bowl set over a pan of gently simmering water. Stir frequently, using a rubber spatula, until completely melted and combined. Then add the palm shortening and stir it into the chocolate mixture as it melts, until completely combined. Remove from the heat and let cool slightly, then stir in the vanilla and eggs.

4. Gently fold the dry ingredients into the melted chocolate mixture and stir, using a rubber spatula or whisk, until just combined. Using a rubber spatula, transfer the batter into a large resealable plastic bag and snip off a corner. Squeeze the batter evenly into the donut maker or pan. If using a donut maker that makes six mini donuts, cook the batter in three batches. If using a donut pan that makes six donuts, cook the batter in two batches, filling the pan two-thirds full each time.

5. If using a donut maker, cook for 3 minutes on one side and then flip the donuts, using a knife or fork to help remove them, and bake for another minute. Times may vary depending on the manufacturer. Remove the donuts and place on a wire rack to cool before glazing. Repeat with the remaining batter.

6. If using a donut pan, tap the filled pan on the counter to remove any air bubbles, then bake for 20 minutes or until a toothpick comes out clean. Let cool slightly, then flip the pan upside down on a wire rack to cool completely. Repeat with the remaining batter.

7. While the donuts are cooling, prepare the Chocolate Shell Coating to use for the glaze.

8. Dip the top of a donut into the chocolate glaze and place back on the cooling rack. Repeat the process until all but two mini donuts or one regular-size donut are left. Crumble the donut(s) and sprinkle the crumbs across the donut tops, on the wet glaze. Enjoy immediately or place in the refrigerator to let the glaze harden. Store any leftovers covered in the refrigerator for up to 3 days.

ROCKY ROAD
BROWNIES

PREP TIME: 30 minutes
COOK TIME: 30 to 35 minutes
SETTING TIME: 1 hour
READY IN: 2 hours
YIELD: 1 dozen brownies

Sometimes you just need extreme brownies. That's life, people; I don't write the rules, just the recipes. This recipe takes regular brownies and kicks them up a notch by topping them with a layer of marshmallow crème and roasted almonds to create an exquisite indulgence of flavors and textures. If you don't do anything else today, at least make these brownies.

1 recipe Better than Box Brownies (page 110)

1 recipe Ganache (pages 369 to 370), any type

1 recipe Marshmallow Crème, regular (page 366) or egg-free (page 368)

½ cup (3½ ounces/100 g) semisweet chocolate chips

½ cup (50 g) unsalted dry-roasted almond pieces

MAKE AHEAD

BETTER THAN BOX BROWNIES—
1 DAY AHEAD

1 Prepare the brownies. Let cool slightly, then transfer the pan to the refrigerator to cool completely, about 1 hour.

2 After about 40 minutes, prepare the ganache, then remove from the heat and set aside until the bowl is cool to the touch. Once cool, transfer the ganache to a piping bag or to a resealable plastic bag with a corner cut off.

3 Prepare the Marshmallow Crème, then transfer it to a piping bag or to a resealable plastic bag with a corner cut off. Once the brownies have cooled, cut them into 12 squares and garnish individually. Drizzle both the ganache and the Marshmallow Crème evenly across each brownie, then sprinkle some chocolate chips and roasted almond pieces over the top.

4 Place the brownies in the refrigerator if not eating immediately. Store any leftovers covered in the refrigerator for up to 3 days.

Notes: To make these brownies dairy-free, use melted ghee or coconut oil rather than butter in the brownies, and use the Dairy-Free Ganache.

Cold brownies cut best. If you can wait, I always recommend chilling brownies in the refrigerator or freezer for at least 30 minutes. Then you don't get crumbs everywhere, and you get nice clean squares. If you want the brownies warmed, you can heat them back up in the oven or microwave before garnishing.

Another option is to toast the marshmallows with a kitchen torch. Do so before adding the chocolate chips and toasted almond garnish.

Pumpkin BREAD

PREP TIME: 10 minutes
COOK TIME: 1 hour 15 minutes
READY IN: 1 hour 25 minutes
YIELD: One 9 by 5-inch (23 by 12.75-cm) loaf

I love pumpkin-flavored everything. I would eat pumpkin-flavored pumpkin. One of my favorite seasonal pumpkin items is pumpkin bread. I would eat the whole loaf if I could; it's so hard to stop at just one slice. This bread is great because it's super easy to whip up, and it makes your house smell like one of those yummy fall-scented candles. Double score. This pumpkin bread would make a great Thanksgiving breakfast or gift for your neighbors or co-workers. You can also get creative and use the bread in other recipes: baked pumpkin French toast, anyone?

1 cup (92 g) fine-ground blanched almond flour

¼ cup (40 g) coconut flour

1 teaspoon ground cinnamon

½ teaspoon baking soda

½ teaspoon fine-grain sea salt

½ teaspoon pumpkin pie spice

¼ teaspoon ground cloves

1 cup (150 g) coconut sugar

½ cup (120 ml) canned pumpkin puree

⅓ cup (80 ml) melted coconut oil

3 tablespoons canned full-fat coconut milk

1 vanilla bean, split lengthwise and seeds scraped, or 1 teaspoon vanilla extract

4 large eggs

1 Adjust an oven rack to the middle position and preheat the oven to 325°F (162°C). Line the bottom of a 9 by 5-inch (23 by 12.75-cm) glass loaf pan with parchment paper; set aside.

2 Combine the flours, cinnamon, baking soda, salt, pumpkin pie spice, cloves, and coconut sugar in the bowl of a large food processor. Pulse 10 times or until mixed. Then add the pumpkin puree, coconut oil, coconut milk, vanilla bean seeds or extract, and eggs and process for 30 seconds or until combined. Scrape down the sides and process again if needed.

3 Use a rubber spatula to transfer the mixture to the parchment-lined loaf pan. Bake for 70 to 75 minutes or until a toothpick inserted into the center comes out clean. Let cool in the pan for 15 minutes, then use a knife to loosen the bread from the sides of the pan. Remove the loaf from the pan by lifting the parchment paper. Let cool completely before slicing and serving.

Notes: Glass and metal pans bake at different temperatures. If you have only a metal loaf pan to work with, try reducing the baking time to 45 to 50 minutes.

Donut Shop
DONUTS

PREP TIME: 20 minutes
COOK TIME: 15 minutes/40 minutes
READY IN: 35 minutes/1 hour
YIELD: 18 mini donuts, or 1 dozen regular size

Donuts are my weakness. Literally like Kryptonite. I usually just walk around pretending that they don't exist. Sometimes I have fantasies about sitting in a donut shop and eating every single one in the display case. Sometimes I want to take road trips to those crazy donut shops with all the weird toppings and flavors and eat all their donuts too. These are normal things to think about, right?

FOR THE DONUTS

2 cups (185 g) sifted fine-ground blanched almond flour

¼ cup (35 g) tapioca flour

2 tablespoons coconut flour

¼ cup (40 g) coconut sugar

2 tablespoons maple sugar

½ teaspoon baking soda

½ teaspoon fine-grain sea salt

½ cup (115 g) palm shortening

½ cup (120 ml) canned full-fat coconut milk

¼ cup (60 ml) light-colored raw honey

1 teaspoon vanilla extract

⅛ teaspoon almond extract

½ teaspoon cream of tartar

4 large egg whites, room temperature

MAKE AHEAD
DONUTS—1 DAY AHEAD

FOR THE STRAWBERRY GLAZE

¼ cup (60 ml) canned full-fat coconut milk

¼ cup (60 ml) no-sugar-added strawberry fruit spread or Strawberry Sauce (page 378)

2 tablespoons melted coconut butter

1 tablespoon melted coconut oil

FOR THE CHOCOLATE NUT GLAZE

1 recipe Ganache (pages 369 to 370), any type

¼ cup (32 g) unsalted dry-roasted almond pieces

FOR THE SHREDDED COCONUT GLAZE

¼ cup (60 ml) canned full-fat coconut milk

2 tablespoons melted coconut butter

1 tablespoon raw honey

1 teaspoon melted coconut oil

⅛ teaspoon fine-grain sea salt

2 tablespoons unsweetened shredded coconut

1 Preheat a mini donut maker or, if using a donut pan, adjust an oven rack to the middle position and preheat the oven to 350°F (177°C). Lightly grease the donut pan.

2 In the bowl of a large food processor, combine the flours, sugars, baking soda, and salt. Pulse 30 times or until combined. Add the palm shortening, coconut milk, honey, vanilla, and almond extract.

3 In a medium-sized mixing bowl, combine the cream of tartar and egg whites. Beat with a hand mixer set on high speed until soft peaks form. Add the beaten egg whites to the food processor and process until combined. Scrape down the sides as needed and process for another 30 seconds, until a smooth and creamy cake batter has formed.

4 Using a rubber spatula, transfer the batter into a large resealable plastic bag and snip off a corner. Squeeze the batter evenly into the donut maker or pan. If using a donut maker that makes six mini donuts, cook the batter in three batches. If using a donut pan that makes six donuts, cook the batter in two batches, filling the pan two-thirds full each time.

5 If using a donut maker, cook for 2 to 3 minutes, then flip each donut, using a measuring spoon or fork to help turn it, and bake for another minute. Times may vary depending on the manufacturer. Remove the donuts and place on a wire rack to cool. Repeat with the remaining batter. While the donuts are cooling, prepare the desired glazes.

6 If using a donut pan, tap the pan on the counter to remove any air bubbles, then bake for 20 minutes or until a toothpick comes out clean. Let cool slightly, then flip the pan upside down on a wire rack to cool completely. Repeat with the remaining batter. While the donuts are cooling, prepare the desired glazes.

7 **To make the strawberry-glazed donuts:** Combine all the ingredients for the strawberry glaze in a small bowl and stir together until combined. Once the donuts have cooled, dip the tops into the glaze and place on a plate. Put the plate with the frosted donuts in the freezer for a few minutes so the glaze can set. Repeat this process, dipping the donuts in the glaze and freezing, until the desired glaze thickness has been reached.

8 **To make the chocolate nut–glazed donuts:** Prepare the ganache. Once the donuts have cooled, dip the tops into the ganache and garnish with a sprinkle of almond pieces. Place back on the cooling rack or in the refrigerator if a thicker glaze is desired.

9 **To make the shredded coconut–glazed donuts:** Combine all the ingredients for the shredded coconut glaze, except the shredded coconut, in a small bowl and stir together until combined. Once the donuts have cooled, dip the tops into the glaze and place on a plate. Sprinkle the shredded coconut over the wet glaze. Put the plate of finished donuts in the freezer for a few minutes to set the glaze.

10 Store any leftover donuts at room temperature for up to 3 days. If the glaze gets too soft, place the donuts back in the refrigerator to harden.

Notes: *To make these donuts dairy-free, use the Dairy-Free Ganache in the chocolate nut glaze.*

Traditional glazes usually call for white sugar and milk. I find that coconut butter and coconut oil are great to use for glazes because they liquefy when heated and then solidify when cooled. This makes dipping easy and then, by chilling them for a bit, they become just like traditional glaze.

For an extra pop of fun, add chocolate or multicolored sprinkles, like I did for the photos.

Chocolate Chip COOKIE BOTTOM

PREP TIME: 25 minutes

COOK TIME: 30 minutes

READY IN: 55 minutes

YIELD: One 8-inch (20-cm) square cookie bottom

Sometimes you need just the bottom of something to be a chocolate chip cookie. Trust me, I get it. This is a great base for all your favorite dessert recipes, from layered bars to cheesecake. Heck, put meatloaf on top of it if you want to; I won't judge.

6 tablespoons (3 ounces/85 g) salted butter

2 cups (310 g) raw cashew pieces

3 tablespoons coconut flour

2 tablespoons maple sugar

1 tablespoon cacao powder or unsweetened cocoa powder

½ teaspoon fine-grain sea salt

⅛ teaspoon ground cinnamon

¼ cup (60 ml) raw honey

½ teaspoon vanilla extract

1 large egg white

½ cup (3½ ounces/100 g) chocolate chips

1. Adjust an oven rack to the middle position and preheat the oven to 350°F (177°C). Line an 8-inch (20-cm) square glass pan with parchment paper; set aside.

2. Brown the butter following the method described on page 360; let cool completely. Meanwhile, prepare the other ingredients.

3. Put the cashews in the bowl of a high-powered food processor and process until they turn to meal. Scrape down the bowl and process for another 5 minutes or so, stopping to scrape down as needed, until the nut oils start to release and the cashew meal turns into a thick dough ball. Add the coconut flour, maple sugar, cacao powder, salt, and cinnamon to the bowl and process again until combined.

4. In a large mixing bowl, combine the honey and vanilla. Use a rubber spatula to transfer the cooled browned butter into the bowl, scraping in the browned bits as well. Mix together with a hand mixer set on low speed, then beat in the egg white and continue to mix until combined. Transfer the cashew dough to the butter mixture and beat on medium-low until smooth ripples start to form and it no longer appears chunky. (Overmixing may cause the butter to separate.) Fold in the chocolate chips with a rubber spatula or wooden spoon.

5. Use a rubber spatula to transfer the dough and press it evenly into the prepared pan. Bake for 30 minutes or until the edges are golden. Let cool completely before using.

Confections OF a DIRTY MIND

White CHOCOLATE

PREP TIME: 10 minutes
SETTING TIME: 20 minutes
READY IN: 30 minutes
YIELD: 4 ounces (115 g)

You know my feelings on chocolate. I don't discriminate; I love chocolate in all its glorious varieties, colors, and percentages. White, milk, dark, 32 percent, 63 percent, 85 percent—bring it on. I've noticed, though, that it's hard to find white chocolate that isn't full of not-so-great ingredients, from partially hydrogenated oils to soy lecithin. I decided that I would take matters into my own hands and make my own. When it comes to dairy intolerance, white chocolate may be a no-go for some; however, I've heard that a lot of people who are lactose intolerant are able to tolerate goat's milk just fine, so I've included it as an option. It lends such a sweet and subtle flavor; I really think you'll love it.

4 ounces (115 g) food-grade cacao butter

2 tablespoons light-colored raw honey

3 tablespoons whole powdered goat's milk or dry milk powder

½ teaspoon vanilla extract

SPECIAL EQUIPMENT
Silicone mold(s)

1 Melt the cacao butter in a double boiler over low heat or in a heatproof bowl set over a pan of gently simmering water. When the cacao butter is almost melted, add the honey and stir together until completely melted and combined. Remove from the heat and stir in the powdered milk and vanilla until well combined.

2 Pour into a chocolate bar–shaped silicone mold or other silicone mold(s) or cups of choice and refrigerate or freeze for 20 minutes or until hardened. Store in the refrigerator for up to 2 weeks.

Notes: *Goat's milk tends to be less problematic to digest than other types of dairy. If you do not have dairy issues, feel free to use dry milk powder instead of powdered goat's milk if you prefer. Whole milk powder is best, but nonfat will work if it is all that's available. Whole Foods and Amazon have great selections of dry milk products.*

This white chocolate is best used for cold applications, such as for making truffles, garnishing, or eating plain; it will revert to a liquid state at baking temperatures.

CHOCOLATE

PREP TIME: 15 minutes
SETTING TIME: 15 to 20 minutes
READY IN: 30 minutes
YIELD: 5 ounces (150 g)

Making chocolate is fun and actually really easy to do. And if you use the right ingredients, it's 100 percent Paleo. This recipe has many health benefits thanks to the cacao butter and cacao powder. You can get really creative with this chocolate: Use it for anything from homemade nut butter cups to flavored chocolate bark, or even something so simple as chocolate chunks in your ice cream. This recipe yields chocolate that is similar to bittersweet chocolate, so it's great to eat as a chocolate bar too.

5 ounces (150 g) food-grade cacao butter

¼ cup (60 ml) raw honey

¾ cup (55 g) cacao powder or unsweetened cocoa powder

½ teaspoon vanilla extract

⅛ teaspoon fine-grain sea salt

SPECIAL EQUIPMENT
Silicone mold(s)

1 Melt the cacao butter in a double boiler over low heat or in a heatproof bowl set over a pan of gently simmering water. When the cacao butter is almost melted, add the honey and stir together until completely melted and combined. Remove from the heat and stir in the cacao powder, vanilla, and salt until well combined.

2 Pour into a chocolate bar–shaped silicone mold or other silicone mold(s) or cups of choice and refrigerate or freeze for 15 to 20 minutes or until hardened. Store in the refrigerator for up to 2 weeks.

Notes: *Just like the white chocolate on page 140, this chocolate should be used for nonheat applications and in recipes in which you want the chocolate to hold its shape, like Almond Butter Cups (page 146). It will return to a liquid state when heated, so it won't work well for things like chocolate chip cookies.*

Chocolate-Dipped
POTATO CHIPS

PREP TIME: 10 minutes
SETTING TIME: 10 to 15 minutes
READY IN: 20 minutes
YIELD: 30 chips

This recipe is for anyone who loves the salty-sweet combination. The best potato chips for this recipe are Jackson's Honest Potato Chips made with coconut oil, Boulder Canyon's Canyon Cut chips made with avocado or olive oil, or Boulder Canyon's Olive Oil Kettle Cooked chips. These can be found in most grocery and health food stores, as well as online. You can do single dip into molten chocolate, or, for extra indulgence, do a double dip of caramel sauce followed by chocolate (see Variation below).

FOR THE CHOCOLATE DIP

1 cup (7 ounces/200 g) dark chocolate chips (63% to 72% cacao)

30 potato chips made with coconut, avocado, or olive oil

FOR GARNISH (OPTIONAL)

½ cup (3½ ounces/100 g) milk chocolate chips, ½ cup (3¼ ounces/ 90 g) white chocolate chips, or 1 recipe Salted Caramel Sauce (page 374)

1 tablespoon sea salt flakes

1 tablespoon unsweetened shredded coconut

1 Line a baking sheet with parchment paper or a silicone baking mat; set aside.

2 Make the chocolate dip: Melt the chocolate chips in a double boiler over low heat or in a heatproof bowl set over a pan of gently simmering water. Stir frequently using a rubber spatula until completely melted.

3 Dip each potato chip halfway into the chocolate, letting the excess chocolate drip back into the bowl, and place on the lined baking sheet.

4 Garnish the dipped chips with the desired toppings. For a milk or white chocolate drizzle, melt either chocolate following the method used to melt the dark chocolate in Step 2, then transfer to a piping bag or to a resealable plastic bag with a corner cut off. Drizzle across the chocolate-covered portion of each chip. For a caramel drizzle, prepare the caramel sauce, let cool, and transfer to a piping bag or to a resealable plastic bag with a corner cut off; drizzle across the chocolate-covered portion of the chip.

5 Immediately sprinkle on the sea salt or shredded coconut or both, if using, while the chocolate dip or drizzle is still wet.

6 Refrigerate the baking sheet with the finished chips for 10 to 15 minutes to set the chocolate. Store any leftovers in the refrigerator or in a cool, dry place for up to 2 days; if stored any longer, the chips may get soggy.

Notes: To make this recipe dairy-free, drizzle the chips with Salted Caramel Sauce made with ghee rather than butter.

For a smoother consistency for the chocolate dip, add 1 tablespoon of coconut oil to the melted chocolate and stir until combined.

Variation: **Caramel and Chocolate-Dipped Potato Chips.** *Before making the chocolate dip, make 1 recipe of Salted Caramel Sauce (page 374) and let cool to room temperature. Dip each chip three-quarters into the caramel sauce, let the excess caramel drip back into the pan, and place the chips on the lined baking sheet. Then dip each chip halfway into the chocolate dip, leaving a line of caramel at the top, and let the excess chocolate drip back into the bowl. Place the chips on the lined baking sheet.*

Almond Butter
CUPS

PREP TIME: 25 minutes
SETTING TIME: 35 minutes
READY IN: 1 hour
YIELD: 1 dozen cups

Almond butter cups are great to make when you're craving peanut butter cups. This was one of the first recipes I made as a treat after going Paleo. These cups are fun to eat alone or to mix into other baked goods. Either way, they are always delicious.

1 (12-ounce/340-g) bag chocolate chips

1 recipe Almond Butter Center (page 362)

⅛ teaspoon fine-grain sea salt

SPECIAL EQUIPMENT
12 standard-size silicone baking cups or foil liners

1. Melt the chocolate chips in a double boiler over low heat or in a heatproof bowl set over a pan of gently simmering water. Stir frequently using a rubber spatula until the chocolate is completely melted and smooth. Remove from the heat.

2. Line a 12-cup muffin pan with silicone baking cups or foil liners. Spoon about a tablespoon of melted chocolate into each cup, about halfway up the sides. Pick up the liner, twirl it slowly, and use the spoon to evenly coat the bottom and sides with the melted chocolate. If the chocolate cools and is not spreading as well before all the cups are lined, gently reheat using the method described above. Refrigerate or freeze the completed pan for 15 minutes or until the chocolate is set.

3. While waiting for the chocolate to set, prepare the Almond Butter Center.

4. Once the chocolate is set, use your fingertips to press the Almond Butter Center evenly into each chocolate cup, filling each cup to about ⅛ inch (3 mm) below the chocolate line. Then use a spoon to spread the remaining melted chocolate over the almond butter. If the chocolate has started to cool, reheat it until it's warm and spoonable again, but not hot. Cover the top of the pan with foil, then refrigerate or freeze for 20 minutes or until the chocolate is set. Store any leftover cups in the refrigerator for up to 1 week.

Notes: You can make these cups in any size you prefer, from 24 mini-sized ones to 6 giant ones. The recipe is totally customizable. To make giant Almond Butter Cups, bring the chocolate all the way to the top of each silicone baking cup, then fill and cover according to the instructions in Step 4. I find that the smaller you go, the fussier the cups can be to work with. Because you don't have a ton of room, it can be difficult to get the Almond Butter Center in. But with some patience, it can be done!

For a nut-free option, use sunflower seed butter in place of the almond butter.

Salted Caramel CUPS

PREP TIME: 25 minutes
SETTING TIME: 35 minutes
READY IN: 1 hour
YIELD: 1 dozen cups

1 recipe Salted Caramel Sauce (page 374)

1 (12-ounce/340-g) bag chocolate chips

Coarse or flake sea salt, for garnish (optional)

SPECIAL EQUIPMENT
12 standard-size silicone baking cups or foil liners

MAKE AHEAD

SALTED CARAMEL SAUCE—2 DAYS AHEAD

I love salted caramel and I love chocolate. So it felt only natural to combine the two. It's like a match made in heaven. Or batch made in heaven. Whatever it is, I want it in my mouth.

1. Make the Salted Caramel Sauce. Transfer to a medium-sized mixing bowl and place in the freezer to thicken while you prepare the chocolate.

2. Melt the chocolate chips in a double boiler over low heat or in a heat-proof bowl set over a pan of gently simmering water. Stir frequently using a rubber spatula until the chocolate is completely melted and smooth. Remove from the heat.

3. Line a 12-cup muffin pan with silicone baking cups or foil liners. Spoon about a tablespoon of melted chocolate into each cup, filling it about halfway up the sides. Pick up the liner, twirl it slowly, and use the spoon to evenly coat the bottom and sides with the melted chocolate. If the chocolate cools and is not spreading as well before all the cups are lined, gently reheat using the method described above. Refrigerate or freeze the completed pan for 15 minutes or until the chocolate is set. While waiting for the chocolate to set, check on the caramel mixture; it should be fairly thick by now. If not, continue to chill until completely thickened.

4. Once the caramel has thickened, spoon about a tablespoon of caramel into each chocolate cup. Then use a spoon to spread the remaining melted chocolate over the caramel and cover the top. If the chocolate has started to cool, reheat it until it's warm and spoonable again, but not hot. Garnish each cup with a pinch of sea salt, if desired. Refrigerate or freeze for 20 minutes or until the chocolate is set. Store any leftover cups in the refrigerator for up to 1 week.

Notes: To make these cups dairy-free, use ghee rather than butter in the Salted Caramel Sauce.

Make sure that your chocolate isn't hot when you add it on top of the caramel, or it will melt and re-liquefy the caramel, leading to streaks in your chocolate once it sets.

The freezer works great for these because it gets the caramel more chewy; placing them in the refrigerator to set will make them more runny.

EGG FREE

White Chocolate Caramel
CASHEW CLUSTERS

PREP TIME: 20 minutes
SETTING TIME: 35 to 40 minutes
READY IN: 55 minutes
YIELD: 1 dozen clusters

One of the things I miss most from my former eating life is yogurt-covered pretzels. I think it's mostly because I'm obsessed with the sweet-and-salty combination. This recipe is simple to throw together and will keep your sweet-and-salty tooth super satisfied.

1 recipe Salted Caramel Sauce (page 374)

1 recipe White Chocolate (page 140) or 2 cups (12 ounces/360 g) white chocolate chips or chopped white chocolate

2 tablespoons melted coconut oil (if using store-bought white chocolate)

2 cups (275 g) unsalted dry-roasted cashew pieces

SPECIAL EQUIPMENT

12 standard-size silicone baking cups or foil liners

MAKE AHEAD
SALTED CARAMEL SAUCE—2 DAYS AHEAD
WHITE CHOCOLATE-LINED CUPS—
2 DAYS AHEAD

1 Prepare the Salted Caramel Sauce. Transfer to a medium-sized mixing bowl and place in the freezer or refrigerator to thicken, about 15 to 20 minutes.

2 If using homemade white chocolate, complete just Step 1 on page 140 (skip the step of molding and chilling it). If using store-bought white chocolate, melt the white chocolate chips and coconut oil in a double boiler over low heat or in a heatproof bowl set over a pan of gently simmering water. Stir frequently using a rubber spatula until the chocolate and oil are completely melted and combined. Remove from the heat and set aside.

3 Once the caramel sauce has thickened, stir the cashew pieces into the caramel, evenly coating them.

4 To assemble: Line a 12-cup muffin pan with silicone baking cups or foil liners. Spoon the caramel-cashew mixture evenly into each cup, about halfway up the sides. Then spoon the melted white chocolate on top. Refrigerate or freeze for 20 minutes or until the white chocolate is set. Store any leftover cups in the refrigerator for up to 1 week.

cookie dough
FUDGE

PREP TIME: 15 minutes
SETTING TIME: 40 minutes
READY IN: 55 minutes
YIELD: 15 pieces

We all know how delicious raw cookie dough is. It can be dangerous to eat, though, because it contains raw eggs. But who are we kidding . . . like that's ever stopped us. This recipe is a game-changer. It tastes just like the real thing, and it's egg-free. Now we don't have to play raw egg roulette. The only dangerous thing about it is that you may not be able to stop eating it.

8 tablespoons (4 ounces/115 g) salted butter

3 cups (465 g) raw cashew pieces

1 tablespoon melted coconut oil

¼ cup (40 g) coconut flour

¼ cup (60 ml) melted raw honey

½ teaspoon fine-grain sea salt

½ teaspoon vanilla extract

⅛ teaspoon ground cinnamon or ground nutmeg

1 cup (7 ounces/200 g) chocolate chips

1. Line a 9 by 5-inch (12.75 by 23-cm) loaf pan with parchment paper; set aside.

2. Brown the butter following the method described on page 360; set aside.

3. Put the cashews in the bowl of a high-powered food processor and process until they turn to meal. Scrape down the sides of the bowl and process for another 5 minutes or so, stopping to scrape down as needed, until the nut oils start to release. With the processor on, slowly drizzle the melted coconut oil into the cashew meal and continue to process until it turns into a thick dough ball or attains a doughlike consistency (it will be much thicker and drier looking than peanut butter).

4. In a medium-sized bowl, combine the cashew butter, browned butter, and coconut flour using a hand mixer or whisk. Add the honey, salt, vanilla, and cinnamon and stir until combined and smooth. Press plastic wrap across the surface of the dough and freeze for 20 minutes.

5. Remove the chilled dough from the freezer and fold in the chocolate chips. (If the chocolate chips are added before freezing, they will melt and sink to the bottom.) Transfer the dough to the parchment-lined pan and press it down evenly. Place back in the freezer for 20 minutes to firm up and set. Cut into 15 pieces before serving. Store any remaining fudge in the freezer; remove from the freezer a few minutes before serving to thaw slightly.

Cookie Dough CUPS

PREP TIME: 40 minutes
SETTING TIME: 30 minutes
READY IN: 1 hour 10 minutes
YIELD: 1 dozen cups

Cookie dough rules. Chocolate rules. Cover cookie dough in chocolate and what do you have? Major ruleage. These things are incredible. They are fun to make, but not really that fun to share. Trust me, you will want them all to yourself. Unless you're nice. Like, really nice.

1 recipe Cookie Dough Fudge (page 152)

1 (12-ounce/340-g) bag chocolate chips

SPECIAL EQUIPMENT

12 standard-size silicone baking cups or foil liners

MAKE AHEAD

COOKIE DOUGH FUDGE—5 DAYS AHEAD

1 Prepare the Cookie Dough Fudge, following Steps 2 through 4 on page 152; set aside.

2 Melt the chocolate chips in a double boiler over low heat or in a heat-proof bowl set over a pan of gently simmering water. Stir frequently using a rubber spatula until the chocolate is completely melted and smooth. Remove from the heat.

3 Line a 12-cup muffin pan with silicone baking cups or foil liners. Spoon about a tablespoon of melted chocolate into each cup, filling it about halfway up the sides. Pick up the cup, twirl it slowly, and use the spoon to evenly coat the bottom and sides with the melted chocolate. If the chocolate cools and is not spreading as well before all the cups are lined, gently re-heat using the method described above. Refrigerate or freeze the completed pan for 15 minutes or until the chocolate is set.

4 Once the chocolate is set, use your fingertips to press the cookie dough mixture evenly into the chocolate cups, filling each cup to about ⅛ to ¼ inch (3 to 6 mm) below the chocolate line. Then use a spoon to spread the remaining melted chocolate over the cookie dough and cover the top. If the chocolate has started to cool, reheat it until it's warm and spoonable again, but not hot. Refrigerate or freeze for 15 minutes or until the chocolate is set. Store any leftover cups in the refrigerator for up to 5 days, or freeze for longer storage.

Chocolate-Covered TOFFEE

PREP TIME: 5 minutes
COOK TIME: 30 minutes
SETTING TIME: 1 hour
READY IN: 1 hour 35 minutes
YIELD: 1 dozen 2-inch (5-cm) pieces

This recipe took a few tries to get right, but was so worth the effort. It tastes just like real toffee. You can eat it plain or get creative, like I did, and dip it in all kinds of fun things, like nuts and chocolate. It would be great to make around the holidays and put in little gift bags for your friends and neighbors. Look how nice you are!

There are two options for coating the toffee: dipping individual pieces in melted chocolate so that they are completed coated or using the heat of the toffee to melt the chocolate on the surface, right in the pan. Though more time-consuming, I prefer to hand-dip individual pieces because the result reminds me of Skor and Heath bars (drool). The latter method makes more of a toffee bark. Try it both ways and see which you prefer!

FOR THE TOFFEE

1 cup (150 g) coconut sugar

2 tablespoons water

½ teaspoon vanilla extract

¼ teaspoon fine-grain sea salt

8 tablespoons (4 ounces/113 g) salted butter, cubed

FOR THE COATING

1 (12-ounce/340-g) bag chocolate chips

½ cup (65 g) unsalted dry-roasted almond pieces (optional)

SPECIAL EQUIPMENT

Candy thermometer

MAKE AHEAD

TOFFEE—3 DAYS AHEAD (FOR INDIVIDUALLY DIPPED PIECES. *NOT* TOFFEE BARK)

Notes: To make this nut-free, omit the almonds from the coating.

Keep an eye on the thermometer as the toffee mixture boils. It will reach 300°F (148°C) a lot faster than you think! Heating the toffee beyond 300°F (148°C) will give it a burned taste.

1. Line a 2-quart (2-L) oblong glass baking dish with parchment paper; set aside.

2. In a large heavy-bottomed saucepan, combine the coconut sugar, water, vanilla, salt, and butter, in that order. Turn on the heat to medium-high and stir the ingredients together in one direction, so the butter doesn't separate, until the butter has completely melted and the ingredients are fully combined. Stop stirring and let the mixture come to 300°F (148°C), or the hard crack stage on a candy thermometer. Once it reaches temperature, remove from the heat and pour into the parchment-lined baking dish. If you're making toffee bark, jump ahead to Step 5.

3. Place the toffee in the refrigerator for 1 hour to harden. After about 45 minutes, melt the chocolate chips in double boiler over low heat or in a heatproof bowl set over a pan of gently simmering water. Stir frequently using a rubber spatula until the chocolate is completely melted.

4. Line a baking sheet with parchment paper. Once the toffee has hardened, break it into pieces using your hands or a knife. Use a candy-dipping fork or a plastic fork with the two middle prongs broken off to dip a piece of toffee into the melted chocolate, turning it over until completely coated on all sides. Let the excess chocolate drip back into the bowl and place the chocolate-covered toffee piece on the parchment-lined baking sheet. Sprinkle with the almond pieces. Repeat this process until all the toffee pieces are coated. Refrigerate for at least 20 minutes to set the chocolate.

5. To make chocolate-covered toffee bark: Sprinkle the chocolate chips over the hot toffee right after transferring it to the baking dish. Let the chocolate sit for a few minutes until the heat from the toffee melts it. Use a rubber spatula to spread the chocolate evenly, then sprinkle the almond pieces over the chocolate. Refrigerate for 1 hour or until hardened. Once hardened, break into pieces using your hands or a knife.

6. Store any remaining toffee covered in the refrigerator for up to 1 week.

BROWN SUGAR
BACON

PREP TIME: 5 minutes
COOK TIME: 20 minutes
READY IN: 25 minutes
YIELD: 8 slices

The first time I had brown sugar bacon, I couldn't believe my taste buds. It was absolutely incredible. I just had to figure out a way to make it without actually using brown sugar. So I got in the kitchen and got to work. Nailed it.

This bacon is great to eat alone or to use in desserts. It also goes great with eggs, making it the perfect side for Sunday brunch.

2 tablespoons coconut sugar
1 tablespoon maple sugar
⅛ teaspoon chili powder
8 slices bacon

1 Adjust an oven rack to the middle position and preheat the oven to 400°F (204°C). Line a rimmed baking sheet with foil and place a wire rack on top of the foil; set aside.

2 Combine the sugars and chili powder on a large plate and mix together by hand. Drag each slice of bacon through the sugar mixture, coating both sides lightly and evenly. Place each slice on the wire rack, spaced evenly. Bake for 20 minutes or until the edges are crispy and the sugar has caramelized.

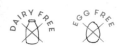

"Reese's" Dessert
SHOOTERS

PREP TIME: 10 minutes
READY IN: 15 minutes
YIELD: 8 shooters

I think dessert shots are so fun. (Who are we kidding? I think regular shots are fun too.) Getting dessert wasted is way more family-friendly, though, and you probably won't be hungover the next day. You can get really creative with how you garnish and serve these shooters. They would be great for a dinner party with little spoons in them!

2 (13½-ounce/400-ml) cans full-fat coconut milk, refrigerated overnight

½ cup (115 g) smooth almond butter

2 tablespoons pure maple syrup, any type

⅛ teaspoon fine-grain sea salt

FOR GARNISH

2 ounces (42 g) dark chocolate (63% to 72% cacao)

3 tablespoons cold water

8 chocolate chips

SPECIAL GLASSWARE

8 shot glasses

1 Place the cans of coconut milk in the refrigerator overnight or for a minimum of 8 hours. The coconut cream should separate from the water and form a firm layer on top. Scrape the cream into the bowl of a stand mixer or into a medium-sized mixing bowl. Discard the water or save it for another use.

2 Add the almond butter, maple syrup, and salt to the bowl and beat on high using the whisk attachment, or using a hand mixer, until creamy and combined.

3 Using a Microplane or cheese grater, grate the chocolate onto a plate. Pour the water onto a separate plate. Dip the rim of a shot glass into the water, shaking off any excess. Then dip the wet rim into the grated chocolate. Repeat with the remaining shot glasses.

4 Transfer the almond butter mixture to a piping bag or large resealable plastic bag with a corner cut off, fitted with the desired tip, and pipe into the shot glasses. Garnish each shot with a chocolate chip.

Caramel
CRÈME BRÛLÉE

PREP TIME: 20 minutes
SETTING TIME: 1 hour 15 minutes
READY IN: 1 hour 35 minutes
YIELD: 2 servings

Crème brûlée is such a fun dessert because you get to crack the top. I don't know why it's so fun, it just is. This crème brûlée is amazing because it not only tastes lovely, but also is no-bake! Don't you just love no-bake stuff? This recipe is made very similarly to curd, so it's very simple. It would be perfect to serve at a dinner party. This crème brûlée is also used as a frosting in the cupcake recipe on page 228. Is that even legal?

12 tablespoons (6 ounces/170 g) salted butter

4 large eggs

¾ cup (180 ml) canned full-fat coconut milk

½ cup plus 2 tablespoons (85 g) homemade maple sugar (page 364), divided (see Notes)

2 tablespoons raw honey

½ teaspoon vanilla extract

⅛ teaspoon fine-grain sea salt

SPECIAL EQUIPMENT

Candy thermometer

Kitchen torch

1. Brown the butter following the method described on page 360. Use a rubber spatula to transfer the browned butter (and all the brown bits at the bottom of the pan) to a medium-sized mixing bowl. Place the bowl in the freezer to harden the butter for 15 to 20 minutes.

2. In a large metal mixing bowl, combine the eggs, coconut milk, ½ cup (65 g) of the maple sugar, and honey. Place the bowl over a saucepan half filled with water set over medium heat. As the water starts to simmer, whisk the egg mixture constantly until it thickens and reaches 160°F (71°C) on a candy thermometer, 10 to 15 minutes. Remove from the heat and pour into a blender pitcher. Add the vanilla and salt, then blend on low, adding the cooled browned butter a few large spoonfuls at a time. After all the butter has been added, continue to blend until the mixture becomes light and creamy.

3. Divide the mixture evenly between two 7-ounce (210-ml) ramekins. Tap the ramekins on the counter to remove air bubbles, then cover with plastic wrap, pressing it directly on the surface. Place in the refrigerator for 1 hour to cool and set.

4. After the crème brûlée has cooled, divide the remaining 2 tablespoons of maple sugar equally between the two ramekins, sprinkling it evenly across the top. Using a kitchen torch, melt the sugar until it bubbles, becomes amber in color, and creates a caramelized shell over the surface.

Notes: *You have to use homemade maple sugar for this recipe. Store-bought maple sugar is too dry and will just burn when torched. Though homemade maple sugar feels dry to the touch, it retains some moisture, which makes it perfect for getting that beautiful caramelized top that is so fun to crack. If you don't want to make your own maple sugar, check Etsy; there you will find some amazing deals on homemade maple sugar sold directly by maple syrup producers.*

CHAPTER 9

EASY
as Pie

Old-Fashioned
FLAKY PIE CRUST

PREP TIME: 5 minutes
SETTING TIME: 10 to 15 minutes
COOK TIME: 10 minutes
READY IN: 25 minutes
YIELD: One 11-inch (28-cm) tart crust, one 9-inch (23-cm) pie or tart crust, one 8-inch (20-cm) bar crust, or four 4¾-inch (12-cm) tartlet crusts

I'm excited to give you the recipe for this pie crust for a few reasons. First and foremost, it uses lard, and not just any lard, but organic pastured leaf lard! Leaf lard is the crème de la crème of lard. Its subtle flavor makes it the most amazing ingredient for baking. It creates fantastic flake and texture in baked goods. This crust can be used for pies, tarts, quiches, and even pot pies. Not only does it sound fancy, but it's delicious. This is a crust your great-grandmother would have set on the windowsill to cool and would have been proud to call her own.

3 cups (275 g) sifted fine-ground blanched almond flour

½ teaspoon fine-grain sea salt

¼ cup (55 g) cold pastured leaf lard

4 tablespoons (2 ounces/56 g) cold unsalted butter, cubed, or ¼ cup (55 g) cold ghee

1 large egg

Tapioca flour or arrowroot flour, for dusting

Notes: To make this crust dairy-free, use ghee rather than butter.

I get my leaf lard from Fatworks; it's organic, pastured, and the highest quality out there!

Leftover dough can be used to create a pronounced crust rim as described in Step 3, rolled out between two sheets of parchment paper and used to create decorative crust designs or a lattice top, or used to make a 4½-inch (11.5-cm) mini pie or tart. It also freezes well.

If your oven has hot spots, like mine, you can do one of two things to get an even-colored crust: rotate the pie halfway through baking or bake it at 375°F (190°C). I've had successful results with this lower temperature.

Don't worry if your crust puffs up; it will deflate as it cools.

1 Put the almond flour and salt in the bowl of a large food processor. Pulse 5 times or until combined. Add the leaf lard, butter, and egg and process for 30 to 40 seconds or until completely smooth and combined, with no chunks remaining.

2 Lightly dust a sheet of parchment paper with tapioca flour. Transfer the dough to the parchment paper and pat into a mound. Dust some tapioca flour on top of the dough and continue to pat until the flour is worked into the dough mound and the dough becomes less sticky. The flour makes the dough easier to work with when pressing it into the pan or rolling it out to cut into shapes or crust designs.

3 If using an 11-inch (28-cm) tart pan or four 4¾-inch (12-cm) mini tart pans, press the entire amount of dough into the pan(s), about ¼ inch (6 mm) thick. If using a 9-inch (23-cm) pie or tart pan or an 8-inch (20-cm) square tart pan, cut away one-third of the dough and set aside. Evenly press the larger piece of dough into the pan, about ¼ inch (6 mm) thick. To create a pronounced rim or crust, as pictured, roll the remaining one-third of the dough into a long, thin rope, about ½ inch (1.25 cm) thick. Place evenly around the edge of the pan and pinch the sides into shape. (For other uses for the remaining dough, see Notes, opposite.) Place the crust in the freezer to chill and firm up for 10 to 15 minutes.

4 While the crust is chilling, adjust an oven rack to the middle position and preheat the oven to 425°F (218°C).

5 Remove the crust from the freezer. Use the tines of a fork to pierce the dough along the bottom and sides to allow steam to escape during baking.

6 To par-bake the crust: Bake for 7 to 8 minutes or until the crust is golden and dry to the touch. Let cool before filling and returning to the oven to finish baking. To prebake the crust: Use a crust shield to keep the top of the crust from browning too fast and potentially burning. Bake for 10 to 14 minutes or until the crust is browned and dry to the touch, rotating the pan halfway through baking if needed. Allow to cool before filling.

Fauxreo
CRUST

PREP TIME: 10 minutes

COOK TIME: 10 to 12 minutes

READY IN: 20 minutes

YIELD: One 11-inch (28-cm) tart crust, one 9-inch (23-cm) pie or tart crust, one 8-inch (20-cm) cake crust, or four 4¾-inch (12-cm) tartlet crusts

2 heaping cups (8½ ounces/240 g) raw pecan pieces

¼ cup (60 ml) pure maple syrup, dark

¼ cup (18 g) cacao powder or unsweetened cocoa powder

2 tablespoons coconut flour

2 tablespoons melted coconut oil

1 tablespoon smooth almond butter

⅛ teaspoon fine-grain sea salt

This is a Paleo take on the classic Oreo crust—a faux Oreo. Fauxreo, if you will. Clever, I know. Use this crust as a substitute in any recipe that calls for an Oreo crust. It's super easy to throw together and tastes incredible. It can be used raw or prebaked; it's delicious both ways!

1 If baking the crust, adjust an oven rack to the middle position and pre-heat the oven to 375°F (190°C).

2 Place all the ingredients in the bowl of a high-powered food processor. Process until crumbly and combined, scraping down the sides of the bowl as needed, about 30 seconds.

3 Press the crust evenly into one 11-inch (28-cm) tart pan, one 9-inch (23-cm) pie or tart pan, one 8-inch (20-cm) square tart pan, or four 4¾-inch (12-cm) mini tart pans, starting with the sides and working down to the middle.

4 To bake the crust: Poke around the bottom and sides with the tines of a fork to allow steam to escape during baking. Bake for 10 to 12 minutes or until lightly browned and dry to the touch. Allow to cool before filling.

Subs: Unsalted butter in place of the almond butter.

Graham
CRACKER CRUST

PREP TIME: 30 minutes
COOK TIME: 7 to 8 minutes
READY IN: 40 minutes
YIELD: One 11-inch (28-cm) tart crust, one 9-inch (23-cm) pie or tart crust, one 8-inch (20-cm) bar or cake crust, four 4¾-inch (12-cm) tartlet crusts, or 1 cup (115 g) graham cracker crumbles

Like Oreo crust, graham cracker crust is one of life's necessities. The thing that really brings this crust to life and makes it taste like the real deal is the date sugar. Who knew? This crust is so simple to throw together and even easier to work with. It rolls out and presses into pans so well. It will soon become a staple in all your graham cracker crust recipes.

2 cups (185 g) sifted fine-ground blanched almond flour

2 tablespoons arrowroot flour

2 tablespoons tapioca flour

1 teaspoon ground cinnamon

¼ teaspoon fine-grain sea salt

5 tablespoons (2½ ounces/70 g) cold salted butter, plus more for the pan(s)

¼ cup (30 g) date sugar

¼ cup (40 g) coconut sugar

3 tablespoons raw honey

1 teaspoon vanilla extract

1 Adjust an oven rack to the middle position and preheat the oven to 350°F (177°C). Grease one 11-inch (28-cm) tart pan, one 9-inch (23-cm) pie or tart pan, one 8-inch (20-cm) square tart pan, or four 4¾-inch (12-cm) mini tart pans; set aside. (If making this recipe to use as graham cracker crumbles, skip the step of greasing a pan and see Notes below.)

2 In a large mixing bowl, combine the flours, cinnamon, and salt. Stir together using a fork until mixed; set aside.

3 In a separate medium-sized mixing bowl, using a hand mixer set on medium-low speed, cream together the butter, sugars, honey, and vanilla until smooth.

4 Using a rubber spatula, scrape the butter mixture into the dry flour mixture and beat together on low speed until combined; the dough will appear dry and crumbly but will press together easily.

5 Transfer the dough to the prepared pan(s). Press it down around the bottom and then up the sides and onto the edges until covered. Poke around the bottom and sides with the tines of a fork to allow steam to escape during baking. Bake for 7 to 8 minutes or until lightly browned. Allow to cool before filling.

Notes: Don't worry if the crust rises during baking; it will go down as it cools. You can use your fingers to gently press it back into place.

If you're making graham cracker crumbles, you do not need to take the time to perfectly form the dough into a pan. You can pat or roll it out between two sheets of parchment paper until it's about 9 inches (23 cm) in diameter, or ¼ to ½ inch (3 to 6 mm) thick, then slide it onto a baking sheet, remove the top sheet of parchment, pop it in the oven, and bake as directed above.

Simple
CRUST

PREP TIME: 10 minutes

COOK TIME: 10 to 13 minutes

READY IN: 20 minutes

YIELD: One 11-inch (28-cm) tart crust, one 9-inch (23-cm) pie or tart crust, one 8-inch (20-cm) cake crust, or four 4¾-inch (12-cm) tartlet crusts

2 heaping cups (8½ ounces/240 g) raw pecan pieces

¼ cup (40 g) coconut flour

¼ cup (60 ml) pure maple syrup, dark

2 tablespoons melted coconut oil

2 tablespoons smooth almond butter

⅛ teaspoon fine-grain sea salt

This was the first crust recipe I ever made. It still tastes just as good to me now as it did back then. It's timeless. This crust can be enjoyed raw or baked, which makes it even better. Who doesn't love a tasty and versatile crust? Use this crust for anything from cheesecake to tarts; it'll keep you honest.

1 If planning to bake the crust: Adjust an oven rack to the middle position and preheat the oven to 375°F (190°C).

2 To make the crust: Place all the ingredients in the bowl of a high-powered food processor. Process until crumbly and combined, about 30 seconds, scraping down the sides of the bowl as needed.

3 Press the crust evenly into one 11-inch (28-cm) tart pan, one 9-inch (23-cm) pie or tart pan, one 8-inch (20-cm) square tart pan, or four 4¾-inch (12-cm) mini tart pans, starting with the sides and working down to the middle.

4 To bake the crust: Poke around the bottom and sides with the tines of a fork to allow steam to escape during baking. Bake for 10 to 13 minutes or until lightly browned and dry to the touch. Allow to cool before filling.

Subs: Unsalted butter in place of the almond butter.

Holiday
SPICED CRUST

PREP TIME: 10 minutes
COOK TIME: 10 to 13 minutes
READY IN: 20 minutes
YIELD: One 11-inch (28-cm) tart crust, one 9-inch (23-cm) pie or tart crust, or four 4¾-inch (12-cm) tartlet crusts

This crust is the same as the Simple Crust (page 172), but has some aromatic spices thrown in to bring it up to holiday standards. It pairs perfectly with any holiday-themed pie filling, whether it be pumpkin or eggnog, or a seasonal fall fruit like apples or pears. You name it, you've got it right here with this crust. Like the Simple Crust on which it is based, this crust can be used raw. Skip the baking if you want; it's delicious both ways!

2 heaping cups (8½ ounces/240 g) pecan pieces

¼ cup (40 g) coconut flour

¼ cup (60 ml) pure maple syrup, dark

2 tablespoons coconut oil, melted

2 tablespoons smooth almond butter

¼ teaspoon ground nutmeg

¼ teaspoon ground cloves

⅛ teaspoon fine-grain sea salt

1 If baking the crust: Adjust an oven rack to the middle position and pre-heat the oven to 375°F (190°C).

2 Place all the ingredients in the bowl of a high-powered food processor. Process until crumbly and combined, about 30 seconds, scraping down the sides of the bowl as needed.

3 Press the crust evenly into one 11-inch (28-cm) tart pan, one 9-inch (23-cm) pie or tart pan, one 8-inch (20-cm) square tart pan, or four 4¾-inch (12-cm) mini tart pans, starting with the sides and working down to the middle.

4 To bake the crust: Poke around the bottom and sides with the tines of a fork to allow steam to escape during baking. Bake for 10 to 13 minutes or until lightly browned and dry to the touch. Allow to cool before filling.

Subs: Unsalted butter in place of the almond butter.

PUMPKIN
PIE

PREP TIME: 25 minutes
COOK TIME: 50 to 55 minutes
READY IN: 1 hour 15 minutes
YIELD: One 9-inch (23-cm) pie

I consider myself a pumpkin pie connoisseur. I pity the fool who bakes a bland, tasteless pumpkin pie, unless that's your thing. Personally, I love a pumpkin pie with an attitude, some spice, and everything nice. This is my go-to recipe with special secret ingredients. I hope you love it as much as I do.

1 recipe Old-Fashioned Flaky Pie Crust dough (page 166)

FOR THE FILLING

1 can (15-ounce/425-g) pumpkin puree

4 large eggs

⅓ cup (80 ml) canned full-fat coconut milk

½ cup (65 g) maple sugar

3 tablespoons raw honey

1 tablespoon light molasses (not blackstrap)

2 teaspoons grated lemon zest

1¼ teaspoons pumpkin pie spice

1 teaspoon ground cinnamon

½ teaspoon fine-grain sea salt

½ teaspoon vanilla extract

¼ teaspoon ground cloves

⅛ teaspoon Chinese five spice

FOR SERVING

1 recipe Whipped Cream (page 372) or Whipped Coconut Cream (page 373)

1. Prepare the Old-Fashioned Flaky Pie Crust dough, following Steps 1 through 3 on page 166. Press two-thirds of the dough into a 9-inch (23-cm) pie pan. Roll the remaining dough into a long, thin rope, about ½ inch (1.25 cm) thick. Place the rope evenly around the edge of the pan and pinch the sides into shape. Chill and par-bake the crust following Steps 5 and 6 on page 166. While the crust is cooling, prepare the pie filling. (If filling and baking the pie right away, turn the oven down to 350°F/177°C.)

2. To make the filling: Put all the filling ingredients in the bowl of a large food processor. Process for 10 seconds, then scrape down the sides and process for another 30 to 40 seconds or until completely smooth and combined.

3. To bake the pie: Adjust an oven rack to the middle position and preheat the oven to 350°F (177°C). Pour the filling into the cooled, par-baked crust and use a rubber spatula to smooth the surface. Cover the crust edge with a crust shield or foil. Bake for 50 to 55 minutes or until firm and a toothpick inserted into the center comes out fairly clean.

4. While the pie is baking, prepare the whipped cream; store in the refrigerator until ready to use.

5. When the pie is done baking, let cool to room temperature, then garnish with whipped cream and serve. Store any leftovers in the refrigerator for up to 3 days.

Notes: *To make this pie dairy-free, use ghee rather than butter in the pie crust and use the Whipped Coconut Cream.*

The secret ingredients in my recipe are the molasses, lemon zest, and Chinese five spice. They add such a great flavor dimension to the pumpkin. Say goodbye to bland pumpkin pie forever!

In the photo, frozen cranberries are used as a garnish. If you would like to make your pie look festive, you can add these or sugar-rolled cranberries; just be sure to remove them before serving or eating, since they are for decorative purposes only.

MAKE AHEAD

OLD-FASHIONED FLAKY PIE CRUST—
1 DAY AHEAD: STORE COVERED

Mississippi
MUD PIE

PREP TIME: 1 hour
SETTING TIME: 2 hours
READY IN: 3 hours
YIELD: Two 4½-inch (11.5-cm) mini pies or one 8-inch (20-cm) pie

One of my favorite desserts to order at a restaurant is Mississippi Mud Pie. Mainly because I love both Oreos and coffee ice cream. And the combination of the two? Forget about it. Here is a great gluten-free alternative to enjoy anytime, anywhere, even in a plane, on a train, on a boat, or on a float—like it would make it that far without you eating it first.

1 recipe Coffee Ice Cream (page 344)

½ recipe Fauxreo Crust (page 168), raw or baked

1 recipe Ganache (pages 369 to 370), any type

½ cup (65 g) unsalted dry-roasted almond pieces, for garnish

MAKE AHEAD

FAUXREO CRUST—1 DAY AHEAD: STORE COVERED

1 Prepare the Coffee Ice Cream.

2 While the ice cream is churning, prepare the Fauxreo Crust. Press the crust evenly into two 4½-inch (11.5-cm) mini springform pans or one 8-inch (20-cm) springform pan, going up the sides, if desired. If baking the crust, follow the instructions in Step 4 on page 168. Let cool in the pan(s).

3 Once the ice cream is churned, use a spoon to transfer it evenly into the springform pan(s), on top of the crust. It's easiest to transfer when soft. Place in the freezer for 30 minutes or until firm.

4 Prepare the ganache and allow to cool slightly.

5 To remove the pie from the pan, run a knife under hot water for 10 seconds, then run the knife between the edge of the pan and the ice cream to release it from the sides. Another option is to let the pie thaw at room temperature for 5 to 10 minutes, letting the ice cream soften up.

6 To serve, pour ganache generously over each pie (or slice) and finish with a sprinkle of almond pieces. Store any leftovers covered in the freezer. Allow to thaw for 10 to 15 minutes before serving.

Notes: To make this pie dairy-free, use the Dairy-Free Ganache.

S'mores
PIE

PREP TIME: 50 minutes
COOK TIME: 10 minutes
SETTING TIME: 3 hours 40 minutes
READY IN: 4 hours 40 minutes
YIELD: One 9-inch (23-cm) pie

Sometimes you want s'mores, but you aren't camping. This is a serious problem that I've faced many times. That's why I took America's favorite camping pastime and shoved it all into a pie. Campfire not included.

1 recipe **Graham Cracker Crust (page 170)**

FOR THE CHOCOLATE MOUSSE LAYER

1 cup (7 ounces/200 g) chocolate chips

2 tablespoons salted butter

1 (13½-ounce/400-ml) can full-fat coconut milk

4 large egg whites

¼ cup plus 1 tablespoon (46 g) coconut sugar

1 teaspoon cream of tartar

¼ teaspoon fine-grain sea salt

1 teaspoon vanilla extract

1 recipe Marshmallow Crème, regular (page 366) or egg-free (page 368)

SPECIAL EQUIPMENT

Candy thermometer

Kitchen torch

MAKE AHEAD

GRAHAM CRACKER CRUST—1 DAY AHEAD;
STORE COVERED

1. Prepare the Graham Cracker Crust using a 9-inch (23-cm) pie pan. Let it cool while preparing the mousse layer.

2. Melt the chocolate chips and butter in double boiler over low heat or in a heatproof bowl set over a pan of gently simmering water. Stir frequently using a rubber spatula until completely melted and combined. Remove the chocolate mixture from the heat and set aside. Keep the water simmering to use in Step 5.

3. In a large heavy-bottomed saucepan, slowly bring the coconut milk to a gentle boil.

4. Meanwhile, using a hand mixer set on high speed, beat the egg whites, coconut sugar, cream of tartar, and salt in a heatproof mixing bowl. Beat until the mixture pales and thickens and soft peaks are about to form.

5. By this time the coconut milk should be ready. To temper the egg whites, slowly pour ½ cup (120 ml) of the hot coconut milk into the egg white mixture while whisking by hand, then beat in the remainder, pouring it in a steady stream. Set the bowl over the simmering water that was used to melt the chocolate. Cook the egg mixture by constantly hand-whisking until it becomes glossy and develops the consistency of thick soup, about 6 to 10 minutes, or until it reaches 160°F (71°C) on a candy thermometer.

6. Once the egg mixture is ready, remove it from the heat and whisk in the melted chocolate mixture and vanilla. Cover with plastic wrap, pressing it directly on the surface, and let cool in the refrigerator for 20 minutes. When cool, pour into the prepared crust and place back in the refrigerator while preparing the Marshmallow Crème.

7. Make the Marshmallow Crème, then use a rubber spatula to spread and swirl the crème evenly over the chocolate mousse layer. Place the pie in the refrigerator to set for at least 3 hours; overnight is best. Just before serving, toast the top of the Marshmallow Crème with a kitchen torch. Store any leftovers covered in the refrigerator for up to 3 days.

Notes: The chocolate mousse layer would be divine made with heavy cream. If you tolerate dairy well, find a nice organic, no-additive heavy cream and use it in place of the coconut milk. I would say that 1½ cups (350 ml) of heavy cream should do the trick!

Eggnog
CHIFFON PIE

PREP TIME: 25 minutes
COOK TIME: 10 minutes
SETTING TIME: 4 hours
READY IN: 4 hours 35 minutes
YIELD: One 11-inch (23-cm) pie

Chiffon anything sounds fancy. Sometimes I like being fancy. Mostly around Christmas, because I'm in a perpetually good mood and just want to bake nonstop. I made this pie a few Christmases ago and brought it to a party, where it was a huge hit. Plus, it has brandy in it. I don't know about you, but I can't make it through any family function without alcohol and lots of it. Just kidding (not really) . . . but seriously, the brandy gives this pie a truly authentic eggnog flavor. It's been a staple in my holiday baking ever since, and I had to include it here for you.

1 recipe Holiday Spiced Crust
(page 174), baked

FOR THE EGGNOG CHIFFON

1 (¼-ounce/7-g) packet (2½ teaspoons) unflavored gelatin, 225 bloom strength

½ cup (70 g) coconut sugar, divided

⅛ teaspoon fine-grain sea salt

½ cup (120 ml) water

3 large egg yolks, beaten

2 tablespoons rum or rum extract

2 tablespoons brandy (optional)

2 tablespoons raw honey

½ teaspoon ground nutmeg

⅛ teaspoon ground cloves

3 large egg whites

1 cup (240 ml) heavy cream

MAKE AHEAD
HOLIDAY SPICED CRUST—1 DAY AHEAD

1. Prepare the Holiday Spiced Crust using an 11-inch (23-cm) tart pan. Let it cool while preparing the filling.

2. In a medium-sized heavy-bottomed saucepan set over medium-high heat, combine the gelatin, ¼ cup (35 g) of the coconut sugar, and salt. Whisk until combined. Then stir in the water and egg yolks, whisking constantly, until the mixture comes to a gentle boil and has thickened slightly. Remove from the heat and pour through a fine-mesh sieve into a large mixing bowl. Stir in the rum, brandy (if using), honey, nutmeg, and cloves; set aside.

3. In a separate mixing bowl, use a hand mixer to beat the egg whites and the remaining ¼ cup (35 g) of coconut sugar until soft peaks begin to form; set aside.

4. Set the bowl containing the gelatin mixture over a larger bowl filled with water and ice. Stir until the mixture starts to firm up slightly, about 3 minutes, then immediately fold in the egg white mixture; set aside.

5. In a separate bowl, beat the heavy cream on high speed until soft peaks form. Then fold the whipped cream into the gelatin and egg mixture. Pour into the baked pie crust and refrigerate for at least 4 hours to set.

Notes: To make this pie dairy-free, use a hand mixer to whip the cream scooped off the tops of 2 (13½-ounce/400-ml) chilled cans of full-fat coconut milk until it's light and fluffy and resembles whipped cream.

This recipe can be made in either a pie pan or a tart pan, as pictured. To me, anything with the word chiffon in it is pie! If you use a standard 9-inch (23-cm) pie pan, just keep in mind that you may end up with extra filling.

Meyer Lemon
MERINGUE TARTLETS

These dairy-free Meyer lemon tartlets are perfect for any lemon lover, even those who can't tolerate eggs. Meyer lemons are great because they are sweeter than traditional lemons, so they don't make things overly tart. I mean, who wants an overly tart tart? Am I right or am I right? This tart is perfect for summer evenings or to delight afternoon guests.

PREP TIME: 20 minutes
COOK TIME: 10 to 14 minutes
SETTING TIME: 20 minutes
READY IN: 50 minutes
YIELD: Four 4¾-inch (12-cm) tartlets

1 recipe Simple Crust (page 172) or Old-Fashioned Flaky Pie Crust (page 166)

FOR THE DAIRY-FREE MEYER LEMON CURD

½ cup (120 ml) melted coconut butter

¼ cup plus 2 tablespoons (90 ml) fresh-squeezed Meyer lemon juice (2 to 3 lemons)

¼ cup (60 ml) light-colored raw honey

FOR THE TOPPING

1 recipe Italian Meringue (page 390) or Egg-Free Marshmallow Crème (page 368)

SPECIAL EQUIPMENT

Kitchen torch

MAKE AHEAD
PIE CRUST—1 DAY AHEAD

1. Prepare the Simple Crust, following Steps 1 and 2 on page 172, or the Old-Fashioned Flaky Pie Crust, following Steps 1 and 2 on page 166. Press the dough evenly into four 4¾-inch (12-cm) mini tart pans and bake according to the instructions in the crust recipe.

2. While the crusts are cooling, prepare the lemon curd: Place the coconut butter, lemon juice, and honey in a small mixing bowl. Use a spoon to stir together until combined, then transfer the curd into the cooled crusts. Refrigerate for about 20 minutes to firm and chill the curd.

3. Meanwhile, prepare the Italian Meringue or Egg-Free Marshmallow Crème for the topping. Transfer the meringue or crème to a piping bag fitted with a Wilton 2C or the desired tip and pipe a design. Another method is to use a rubber spatula to spread the meringue or crème across the tops of the tartlets. Toast the tops and edges of the meringue or crème using a kitchen torch and serve immediately. Store any leftover tartlets in the refrigerator for up to 1 day.

Notes: To make these tartlets egg-free, use the Egg-Free Marshmallow Crème for the topping.

Subs: Regular lemon juice in place of the Meyer lemon juice. Meyer lemons are less sour than regular lemons. If using regular lemon juice, taste the curd mixture, then add more honey if necessary.

Lemon Curd (page 388) in place of the Dairy-Free Meyer Lemon Curd.

Tuxedo TART

PREP TIME: 40 minutes
SETTING TIME: 4 hours
READY IN: 4 hours 40 minutes
YIELD: One 9-inch (23-cm) tart or four 4¾-inch (12-cm) tartlets

This recipe was inspired by my love for all things chocolate. Give me it all—white chocolate, dark chocolate, milk chocolate—and swirl it together so I can eat it. I also really enjoy making swirl patterns in desserts. Is that weird? Anyway, when I brought this tart to work for my co-workers to taste, they went crazy for it. I think any chocolate lover out there will do the same.

1 recipe Fauxreo Crust (page 168), raw or baked

1 recipe freshly made and still warm White Chocolate (page 140) or 1 cup (7 ounces/200 g) store-bought white chocolate chips or chopped white chocolate

¼ cup (60 ml) heavy cream

Double recipe Ganache (pages 369 to 370), any type

MAKE AHEAD

FAUXREO CRUST—1 DAY AHEAD

1 Prepare the Fauxreo Crust and press it into a 9-inch (23-cm) square or round tart pan or four 4¾-inch (12-cm) mini tart pans. If desired, bake according to the instructions in Step 4 on page 168.

2 While the crust is cooling (if baked), prepare the white chocolate. If using homemade, complete Step 1 on page 140, then, after adding the powdered milk and vanilla, drizzle the heavy cream into the white chocolate in a steady stream, while whisking, until completely combined; set aside. If using store-bought white chocolate, melt the white chocolate and heavy cream in a large heatproof bowl set over a pan of simmering water. Stir intermittently using a rubber spatula until the white chocolate and cream are completely melted and combined. Remove the bowl from the heat and set aside.

3 Make the ganache and let cool slightly, about 5 minutes. Pour the ganache into the cooled crust. By now the white chocolate will have cooled and thickened slightly and will have a texture similar to thin yogurt.

4 Add the white chocolate to the ganache a little at a time, using a butter knife to gently swirl the white chocolate into the ganache to create a design. Another method is to transfer the white chocolate to a resealable plastic bag, cut off a corner, and evenly pipe dots over the ganache filling, then use a toothpick to swirl the dots into a design. Place the finished tart(s) in the refrigerator to set for at least 4 hours or until the filling has firmed up.

Subs: Canned full-fat coconut milk in place of the heavy cream.

Blueberry
LEMON TARTLETS

PREP TIME: 40 minutes
SETTING TIME: 20 minutes
READY IN: 1 hour
YIELD: Four 4¾-inch (12-cm) tartlets

These tartlets aren't just a pretty face. They offer so much flavor, you'll need someone to pinch you just so you know that they're real. The idea for these tarts came from lemon-blueberry muffins. I wanted to take that concept and turn it into a tart. I also love blueberries; they are one of my favorite fruits. I especially love the tart ones. You know the ones that are a little lighter in color and almost sour when you bite into them? Oh man, those are my favorites. So these tarts are a little bit like that.

1 recipe Simple Crust (page 172), raw or baked

1 recipe Lemon Curd (page 388) or Dairy-Free Meyer Lemon Curd (page 184)

2 cups (12 ounces/340 g) blueberries

1 Prepare the Simple Crust and press it into four 4¾-inch (12-cm) mini tart pans. If desired, bake according to the instructions in Step 4 on page 172.

2 While the crusts are cooling (if baked), prepare the filling. Make the Lemon Curd and pour it evenly into the cooled crusts. Place in the refrigerator until the curd is cool and set, about 20 minutes.

3 Garnish each tart with about ½ cup (85 g) of blueberries.

MAKE AHEAD
SIMPLE CRUST—1 DAY AHEAD

Notes: *To make these tartlets dairy-free, use the Dairy-Free Meyer Lemon Curd.*

The tartlets pictured were lightly dusted with confectioners' sugar. For the same visual impact with no added sugar or flavor, you can use arrowroot or tapioca flour instead.

Browned Butter
CARAMEL BANANA TART

PREP TIME: 35 minutes
COOK TIME: 10 minutes
SETTING TIME: 1 hour
READY IN: 1 hour 45 minutes
YIELD: One 14 by 5-inch (35 by 12-cm) tart, one 9-inch (23-cm) tart, or four 4¾-inch (12-cm) tartlets

If a recipe has the words browned butter *anywhere in its title, I have to make it. Done and done. I'm obsessed with browned butter. It's such an easy way to add lots of flavor to simple dishes, making them irresistible. Before developing this recipe, I'd wanted to try out a browned butter caramel, but I wasn't sure what dish I would make it for. Then I started thinking of things that pair well with caramel, and bananas popped into my head. So I decided to make this tart with caramel and fried bananas. It turned out to be a really good idea. Taste for yourself.*

1 recipe Simple Crust (page 172) or Old-Fashioned Flaky Pie Crust (page 166)

Double recipe Browned Butter Salted Caramel Sauce (page 374)

8 bananas (1½ lbs/640 g)

3 tablespoons coconut oil, divided

MAKE AHEAD

PIE CRUST DOUGH—1 DAY AHEAD

1 Prepare the Simple Crust, following Steps 1 and 2 on page 172, or the Old-Fashioned Flaky Pie Crust, following Steps 1 and 2 on page 166. Press the dough evenly into a 14 by 5-inch (35 by 12-cm) rectangular tart pan, a 9-inch (23-cm) square or round tart pan, or four 4¾-inch (12-cm) mini tart pans. (*Note:* If using the Old-Fashioned Flaky Pie Crust and a 9-inch/23-cm pan, use just two-thirds of the dough.) Bake according to the instructions in the crust recipe.

2 While the crust is cooling, prepare the Browned Butter Salted Caramel Sauce, then set aside on the counter to cool.

3 While the caramel sauce cools, prepare the bananas: Slice the bananas into rounds of even thickness. Heat about 1 tablespoon of the coconut oil in a medium-sized skillet set over medium heat. Fry about one-third of the bananas in the skillet; once browned on the underside, use a spatula to gently flip the slices over and fry until they are browned and caramelized on both sides. Remove and repeat with the rest of the bananas and coconut oil. (It's best to fry the bananas in batches so as not to crowd them; they are easier to flip when there is more room in the pan.)

4 To assemble the tart: Layer the fried banana slices evenly across the cooled crust. Pour the caramel sauce over the bananas, tipping the pan as needed to coat the crust and banana slices evenly. Place in the refrigerator to set for 1 hour or until the caramel has thickened.

Notes: *This tart can be enjoyed warm or cool. Try throwing a scoop of ice cream on top for a messy, gooey à la mode version!*

Variation: **Salted Caramel Banana Tart.** *To save a step, you can make this tart with the Salted Caramel Sauce on page 374, which is made with plain (not browned) butter. Simply prepare a double batch of the Salted Caramel Sauce and follow the recipe above.*

Spiced MAPLE
PEAR TART

PREP TIME: 30 minutes
COOK TIME: 30 minutes
SETTING TIME: 2 hours
READY IN: 3 hours
YIELD: One 11-inch (28-cm) tart or four 4¾-inch (12-cm) tartlets

I saw this recipe in an issue of Better Homes and Gardens *magazine and knew immediately that I could Paleoize it. This tart tastes like autumn in your mouth. It would be a perfect addition to Thanksgiving dinner for those folks who aren't pumpkin pie fans.*

1 recipe Holiday Spiced Crust (page 174), baked

FOR THE PEARS

2 Bosc pears

1½ cups (350 ml) apple juice

⅓ cup (80 ml) water

⅓ cup (80 ml) pure maple syrup, dark

½ teaspoon vanilla extract

FOR THE FILLING

1 (13½-ounce/400-ml) can full-fat coconut milk

¼ cup (35 g) maple sugar

¼ cup (40 g) coconut sugar

¼ teaspoon fine-grain sea salt

¼ teaspoon ground cinnamon

⅛ teaspoon ginger powder

2 large eggs, beaten

4 tablespoons (2 ounces/56 g) cold salted butter

SPECIAL EQUIPMENT

Candy thermometer

MAKE AHEAD
HOLIDAY SPICED CRUST—1 DAY AHEAD

1 Prepare the Holiday Spiced Crust using an 11-inch (28-cm) tart pan or four 4¾-inch (12-cm) mini tart pans.

2 To prepare the pears: Peel the pears, cut them in half lengthwise, keeping the stems intact, and use a teaspoon to scoop out the seeds; set aside. In a large heavy-bottomed saucepan, combine the apple juice, water, maple syrup, and vanilla. Whisk together and bring to a boil over medium-high heat. Add the pear halves and cover. Lower the heat and simmer for 20 minutes. Then remove from the heat and transfer the pears and liquid to a medium-sized mixing bowl. Cover the bowl with plastic wrap and place in the refrigerator to soak for 2 hours.

3 To prepare the filling: Combine the coconut milk, sugars, salt, cinnamon, ginger, and eggs in a large heatproof mixing bowl. Place the bowl over a saucepan half filled with water set over medium heat. As the water starts to simmer, stir the filling mixture constantly using a whisk until it thickens and reaches 160°F (71°C), about 10 minutes. Remove from the heat and transfer to a blender pitcher. Add the butter, then blend on low until smooth and creamy. Pour into the prepared crust, cover with plastic wrap, and place in the refrigerator to chill and firm up for at least 1 hour.

4 When ready to serve, remove the pears from the poaching liquid and gently slice them almost to the top to create a fan effect. Remove the plastic wrap from the tart(s). If making four mini tarts, place a sliced pear half in a fan design in the center of each tart. If making one larger tart, arrange the stem ends of the pear halves in the center of the tart and fan out the pear halves across the top to create a circle. Using a spoon, drizzle some of the remaining poaching liquid across the top for added effect. Eat the tart within a few hours if possible. It will keep longer, but the filling may cause the crust to become very soft in the middle.

Strawberry
MERINGUE TARTLETS

PREP TIME: 45 minutes
SETTING TIME: 20 minutes
READY IN: 1 hour 5 minutes
YIELD: Four 4¾-inch (12-cm) tartlets

1 recipe Simple Crust (page 172), baked, or Old-Fashioned Flaky Pie Crust (page 166)

Double recipe Strawberry Sauce (page 378)

1 recipe Italian Meringue (page 390)

SPECIAL EQUIPMENT
Kitchen torch

MAKE AHEAD
PIE CRUST—1 DAY AHEAD

This recipe is an updated version of an old classic. Lemon meringue tarts are the usual go-to. I wanted to take that idea and update it. These strawberry tarts are perfect for strawberry season, but taste great at any time of year.

1 Prepare the Simple Crust or Old-Fashioned Flaky Pie Crust using four 4¾-inch (12-cm) mini tart pans.

2 While the crusts are cooling, prepare the Strawberry Sauce.

3 Once the sauce has cooled to room temperature, pour the sauce evenly into each crust. Place in the refrigerator so that the sauce can cool further and set, about 20 minutes.

4 Meanwhile, prepare the Italian Meringue.

5 Use a large spoon to place a big dollop of meringue on top of the strawberry sauce. Toast the top of the meringue using a kitchen torch. These tartlets are best eaten the day they are made, but will keep in the refrigerator for up to 1 day if necessary.

CHAPTER 10

Let them EAT Cake

Prelude to
A CAKE

Hey there, cake maker! This introduction is for you. Before you dive into this chapter and start flipping through the photos of elaborately decorated cakes, I need to set the record straight. I don't want you jumping to the conclusion that these recipes are only for ambitious or advanced cake makers. Far from it. In this chapter I will give you the tools you need to make each cake recipe your own! If you don't want to make a fancy multilayer cake and just need a simple single-layer cake, or you couldn't care less about how pretty it looks, well, I'm here to make sure that your needs are met. On the other hand, if you want to make fancy cakes for special occasions or just work on getting better at your cake-making skills, you are fairly represented here as well. I'm like a cake politician. I'm here to represent the people and give them what they want. Let them eat cake!

Here are some key things to keep in mind when working from this chapter:

» *Most of these* cake recipes are made using a large 11-cup (2.6-liter) food processor rather than a bowl and a hand mixer, which is more common. The reason is simple: Using a food processor is faster, requires less work on your part, and yields consistent results. I'm not trying to reinvent the wheel here; I'm just trying to make cake making an easier and more enjoyable experience. If you don't own a large food processor, check Costco, which sells a great Cuisinart one for about $100. Another option is a large-capacity blender. If your only option is to make the cake batter the traditional way, with a bowl and a hand mixer, I understand. I've included instructions for using a bowl and a hand mixer at the end of the cake recipes that can be made this way.

» *Most of the recipes* for cake batter will make two 6-inch (15-cm) cake layers, one 8-inch (20-cm) cake layer, or 12 cupcakes. If that's all you need, frost away and you're good to go! The batter for the two-layer, 8-inch (20-cm) cakes and three-layer cakes will need to be made and baked in separate batches due to the capacity of the large food processors found in most home kitchens. A double batch or even one-and-a-half batches just won't fit.

» *I find that* a two-layer, 6-inch (15-cm) cake tends to serve six people nicely; a single-layer, 8-inch (20-cm) cake, ten people; and a batch of cupcakes, well, twelve people, unless of course someone, like yours truly, wants more than one.

» *I recommend having* at least two of the same-size cake pans for making layer cakes. That way, while one cake layer is baking, you can be getting the next batch ready. Then, if you have a multilayer cake, you can work on a rotation system. Cakes bake most evenly on the middle rack of the oven, so I recommend baking no more than the number of cakes that can fit comfortably on one rack. The typical home oven can fit four 6-inch (15-cm) cakes, three 8-inch (20-cm) cakes, or two 9-inch (23-cm) cakes side by side (cakes any larger should be baked one at a time). It should be noted, however, that it's not ideal to make a batch of batter well ahead of time. I advise against this because the liquid in the batter will start to activate the baking soda, and if the cake isn't baked soon enough after the batter is made, the leavening properties will weaken and the cake may not rise properly. This is another reason why the rotation system works so well.

» *One pro tip* I learned a while back is not only to grease the cake pans but also to line the bottoms of the pans with parchment paper, whether you're using pans with a regular or a nonstick finish. This two-step process prevents any cake from sticking to the pan, and as a result helps immensely with removal. Specialty cooking or baking stores sell precut parchment paper in various sizes for this exact purpose. If you're using regular (not springform) cake pans, these precut sheets are a great time-saver. For springform pans, however, the parchment paper doesn't have to be perfectly round; it just has to be large enough to cover the base of the pan. I simply tear off a piece about the size of my pan and place it on the bottom of the pan (with the ring removed). Then I secure the ring to the base and let the edges stick out. Easy!

» *Speaking of pans* and easy removal, I hands-down prefer cake pans with removable bottoms, such as springform pans, and preferably with a nonstick finish. It makes cake removal a breeze. As added insurance, I recommend greasing the sides and bottom of the pan, even when parchment paper is used and the pan has a nonstick finish: First, I line the bottom of the pan with parchment, then I grease the paper and the sides of the pan. When making cakes with white flour, you usually don't grease the sides of the pan so that the layers can rise higher, but when using grain-free flour, I don't find this to be an issue. No one likes a cake with chunks torn out of it because it stuck to the pan. Stop eating my cake, you over-hungry pan!

Note: All the cakes in this chapter can be made in regular (not springform) cake pans, but using regular pans can make the cakes trickier to remove, even if the pans are well greased and lined with parchment paper. Why add stress to your life? Pick up a set of springform pans! I use pans with a dark finish; if you use light-colored aluminum pans, you may need to add additional baking time.

» *It's best to* let the cake cool in the pan for about 15 minutes or until the pan is cool to the touch. This gives the cake time to settle. Then run a knife along the inside edge of the pan to loosen any cake that may have stuck to the side while baking. (*Note:* If you're using a cake pan with a nonstick finish, it's best to use a plastic knife for this task to avoid scratching the surface.) Then remove the cake, keeping it on the parchment paper, and let it cool completely before frosting. Leaving cakes or cupcakes in the pan to cool completely can cause condensation to form, leading to soggy cake.

» *Before frosting a cake,* use a serrated knife to cut off any uneven spots on the top of a cake layer that may make it difficult for another layer to sit evenly and securely on top of it. This is usually done only for the bottom and middle layers; it doesn't really affect the top layer since that layer is completely frosted and is not supporting another layer. Note that the step of removing uneven edges prior to frosting isn't done in the case of naked cakes, since you want to keep the layers exposed. It should also be noted that while the bottom layer is placed right side up, the following cake layer should be placed upside down, and so forth. This ensures that the sides are even and consistent as the cake increases in height, and provides stability.

» *On classic cake decorating,* a circle is piped around the top edge of each layer to act as a dam, and then filling or frosting is spread across the inside of the dam. This is done so that the filling or frosting is placed evenly and doesn't spill out over the edges when another layer is set on top of it. Any frosting that does seep out can be incorporated into the frosting used to coat the sides of the cake.

» *For a more* polished look, you can first apply what's called a *crumb coat*. It's the equivalent of putting on a primer coat of paint. You put a light layer of frosting on the cake to remove or seal in any crumbs, then refrigerate the cake for an hour before applying the final coat of frosting; this gives you a smoother frosting surface.

» *When using* an offset spatula to frost a cake, it's best to work on a rotating cake stand (or cake turntable, as it's also known). This helps you apply the frosting quickly and evenly since you can rotate the cake in any direction you need. It also helps you get a nice even surface when smoothing out the frosting. When applying the frosting, start at the top and work your way down the sides to the bottom. To frost the top of the cake, grab a large dollop of frosting with the spatula and place it in the center, then spread it toward the edges of the cake, using the flat bottom of the spatula to smooth it out across the surface. For the sides, place a large dollop of frosting, then use the spatula at an upright angle, with the bottom placed against the side of the cake. Spread the frosting, while slowly spinning the stand, without lifting the spatula from the surface. Try not to touch the cake when spreading frosting, or crumbs may get into it; this is why I recommend applying a crumb coat first. For cupcakes, there's no need to get fancy; just spread a large dollop of frosting across the surface like you would butter on bread, until you've reached the desired thickness.

» *I always recommend* making more frosting than you think you'll need. It's better to have too much frosting than not enough. Who wants to have to stop in the middle of decorating a cake to make more frosting? I've given recommended amounts, but some folks are more heavy-handed than others.

» *The nice thing* about cake making is that you can do a lot of the work ahead of time, which makes the task seem less daunting. If you are making a cake for a special occasion, make the layers the day before. All the cakes in this chapter can be left out at room temperature, uncovered. (You could probably stretch it to two days, but cake tastes best when it's fresh.) Then, the next day, you can use your available time to assemble, frost, and decorate the cake. Above all, make it your own!

Cake
FROSTING TECHNIQUES

Frosting cakes and cupcakes is one of those tasks that seems really intimidating until you actually do it. It's like anything else in life: practice makes perfect. Some people are going to get the hang of it right away, and others may struggle at first. That's the nature of the frosting beast, but I'm here to tell you in all honesty that it's not as hard as it looks.

When it comes to frosting, I've learned a few tricks through lots of practice and trial-and-error. If you don't feel confident in your frosting abilities, these tricks will help you get the basics down. And remember that frosting cakes and cupcakes can be daunting even when you know what you're doing. Every time I frost a cake, I get a nervous pit in my stomach. But as Julia Child said, "The only real stumbling block is fear of failure. In cooking you've got to have a what-the-hell attitude." I repeat that to myself right before I decorate cakes because sometimes you just need to get in there and frost with reckless abandon. (It never hurts to go in with informed reckless abandon, though.)

CHOOSE EASY-TO-USE PIPING BAGS

I prefer 16-inch (40.5-cm) disposable piping bags. Wilton makes great ones that come in a pack of twelve for only $3. I prefer these for a couple of reasons: First, they are disposable, which means one less thing to wash; and second, I find that the larger bags are easier to work with in general. You can fit a whole batch of frosting in one bag without it seeping out the back and getting all over the place. Piping bags don't come with holes precut to fit the decorating tips. They come this way so that you can cut the appropriate size to accommodate your decorating tip, whether it is large or small.

Another disposable option is parchment bags. These come in sheets that you fold and tape together to form a bag. They tend to come in large-quantity packs that are very inexpensive. The benefit of parchment bags is that you can easily fold the bag tighter or looser to accommodate the amount of frosting you're using. These are what you'll likely find in a retail bakery.

A third option is reusable canvas decorating bags. Canvas bags don't come with holes precut, either, so if you decide to go this route and you plan on using both small and large decorating tips, you may need a few bags. I recommend that you try out the different options to see which you prefer.

In a pinch, you can take a gallon-size resealable plastic freezer bag, snip off a small section of the corner, and drop the piping tip inside the bag to fit securely in the cut corner. Then fill and use just like a decorating bag. This works great for quick drizzle application too, no piping tip needed.

HOW TO CUT THE RIGHT SIZE OPENING IN THE PIPING BAG AND INSERT THE PIPING TIP

To determine the correct size hole to create at the tip of your piping bag (or resealable plastic bag), set the tip against the bottom pointed part of the bag, then cut the bag tip across, even to the size of the piping tip. Too big a hole and the piping tip will fall right through. It's better to cut less than you think you need to and go from there, because you can always cut off more as needed. You want the tip to fit snugly inside the bag with only the end of the tip sticking out. Drop in your piping tip and push it down into the piping bag, leaving the end of the tip exposed. Be sure to press down tightly enough that the tip fits in the bag securely. Some people use a coupler, which is a two-part device that is used to change decorating tips without having to change the bag. Different-sized couplers are sold to fit different-sized tips.

USE FRESHLY MADE FROSTING WHENEVER POSSIBLE

In general, frosting works best when freshly made. This is particularly true of buttercreams. In the recipes I've included helpful storage tips, but whenever possible, I recommend icing a cake soon after making the frosting.

HOW TO FILL THE PIPING BAG

When filling the piping bag with frosting, I find that it's best to place the bag, tip end down, in a tall glass. This way the tip rests on the bottom of the glass and the sides of the glass support the bag, allowing it to be held open so that frosting can easily be transferred into the bag without making a mess. It's easiest to use a rubber spatula for this task because you can scrape the frosting

use enough pressure, then the frosting may not come out at all. I have the most success piping fancy designs with buttercreams; they are the perfect texture and consistency for piping designs. I prefer to use thicker frostings, like cream cheese frostings, when I'm not piping designs, but rather am covering a cake with frosting using an offset spatula. I tend to take this approach when I know that I will be using fresh flowers or something else as the main decoration focus. (See the White Cake on pages 210 to 213 and the Caramel Maple Fig Cake on pages 232 to 235 for examples.) This is by no means a rule that I stick to 100 percent of the time, though; in fact, I used a cheese-based frosting to pipe designs on the Blackberry Elderflower Cake on pages 222 and 223 and the Holiday Spice Cake on pages 274 to 277. Play around with different types of frosting to see which you prefer to use for different applications.

PRACTICE MAKES PERFECT (BUT IMPERFECT IS OKAY)

If you have a big-ticket item that you need to frost for a special occasion, practice a few times first so that you will feel more confident when the big frosting moment arrives. You can teach yourself a lot by just laying out a blank sheet of parchment paper and piping designs. Your hand will start to learn the motions and find just the right amount of pressure. Practicing will also help you figure out where on the piping bag to place your hands so that it feels comfortable and functional. Practicing is also great to do because you can see beforehand how each piping tip differs in its application of frosting and its unique design. The most important thing to remember is that people are going to eat your cake, regardless of what it looks like; if it's not perfect, you're probably the only one who will notice. Have you ever declined to eat a slice of cake or a cupcake because the frosting wasn't perfect? Me neither.

IF ALL ELSE FAILS, SEEK OUT LIVE ACTION

I don't know about you, but I'm a visual person. I need to see something with my own two eyes before I can fully understand it. Thank goodness we live in the age of YouTube and have the ability to find anything we need on the Internet! If you are curious about how to apply frosting using a specific technique, check YouTube; it has great cake decorating tutorials that can really come in handy. Once you have the method down, take some time and practice. Again, frosting cakes is one of those things that you'll only get better at with practice and confidence.

out of the bowl and just plop it into the bag. Another simple way to transfer frosting into the piping bag is to turn the prepared bag partly inside out, place your hand inside (which is actually the outside of the bag), and use it as a glove to scoop the frosting out of the bowl. Then turn the bag back out and voilà! (You people who have dogs know what I'm talking about here: I'm sure you've used this method while picking up after your pet. Kind of a gross comparison, but same idea!)

HOW TO HOLD THE BAG

If there is any excess bag at the top, fold it down to remove air and compress the frosting inside the bag. Using your non-dominant hand, hold the filled bag at the top; use your dominant hand underneath to apply pressure and guide the piping bag. Again, this is what works best for me; if it feels uncomfortable to you, try switching positions. This is similar to holding a guitar or skateboarding; sometimes a certain way just feels more comfortable regardless of which is your dominant side.

APPLY THE RIGHT AMOUNT OF PRESSURE

When it comes to piping frosting, it's important to use the right amount of pressure. Press too hard and you risk having the frosting come out too quickly and splatting all over your cake. On the flip side, if you don't

1.

2.

3.

4.

Decorating tips are like television shows; everyone has a favorite. They are such personal items that I think you need to decide for yourself which tips to choose. Throughout this book I've used a variety of decorating tips for different occasions. I will go over those tips and how to use them here so that you can become more familiar with them, if you aren't already.

WILTON 1M—ROSE TIP

This is the tip that I used to frost the Almond Cake on pages 214 to 217 and the Chocolate Cupcakes on pages 226 and 227. To use it, tilt the piping bag slightly to the side and hold the tip approximately ½ inch above the surface of the cake. Starting in the center, pipe in a tight circle, then continue to swirl around the initial circle, with the edges touching, almost on top of each other. When the desired rose size is reached or you've reached the edge of the cake, pull up toward you—this will let any additional frosting blend in with the edge and not stick straight up.

WILTON 1A—SMALL ROUND TIP

This is a great tip for piping frosting onto cupcakes. It gives a neat swirled look, similar to a soft-serve ice cream cone. I used this tip to frost the Hot Fudge Sundae Cupcakes on pages 224 and 225. To use it, hold the piping bag at a 90-degree angle, with the tip approximately ½ inch above the cupcake surface. Pipe a thick circle around the edge of the cupcake. Pipe another one similar in thickness but a little smaller, on top of the first circle, then repeat with a final, even smaller circle, or with a dollop. To pipe a dollop, hold the tip ½ inch above the second piped circle and squeeze the bag to release frosting until the circle below is halfway covered. Pull up quickly to stop the flow of frosting.

WILTON 2C—DROP FLOWER TIP

This is my favorite tip to use for piping meringue. I used it for the Meyer Lemon Meringue Tartlets on pages 184 and 185. This tip creates a unique flowerlike lined design that looks neat when you toast it with a kitchen torch. To use it, hold the bag at a 90-degree angle, with the tip about ¼ inch above or even lightly resting on the dessert surface. Apply pressure until you've reached the desired dollop size, then pull up quickly to stop the flow of frosting and leave a pointed tip. Pipe evenly spaced dollops around the edge of the dessert, then pipe another circle inside the first one and so on until you've reached the center of the dessert and no space remains.

ATECO 808—LARGE ROUND TIP

This tip is similar to the Wilton 1A small round tip, but—you guessed it—it's larger! It is one of my favorite tips to use when I want just a huge dollop of frosting on top of a cupcake. I love using this tip with alternative frostings like Whipped Cream (page 372), Marshmallow Crème (pages 366 to 368), and meringue-based frostings (such as the Italian Meringue on page 390). I used it to frost the S'mores Cupcakes on pages 246 and 247 and the Chocolate-Covered Strawberry Cupcakes on pages 262 and 263. To use this tip, hold the piping bag at a 90-degree angle, with the tip lightly touching the cupcake surface. Squeeze the bag firmly to release frosting, pulling the bag up slowly as the frosting spreads across the cupcake, until you've reached the edge. Then pull quickly to the side of the cupcake and back toward you to stop the flow of frosting. This will help the frosting tail (the last bit of frosting that makes it out) blend in with the sides instead of sticking straight up.

I also used this tip to pipe the dots in between the Holiday Spice Cake layers on pages 274 to 277 and to pipe the dots on outside of the Strawberry Cheesecake Cake on pages 236 and 237. Start by piping large dots (dollops) of frosting evenly around the sides of the cake. You can also do this on the top of the cake if you prefer, or you can use an offset spatula to spread the frosting across. After you've evenly piped dots around the sides of the cake, use the tip of an offset spatula or the back of a spoon to gently drag half of each dot toward you. This makes a neat-looking pattern that is simple to create and is sure to impress everyone.

ATECO 847—LARGE CLOSED STAR TIP

This is my absolute favorite tip for making gorgeous, fancy-looking cupcakes. I used it on the "Reese's" Cupcakes on pages 230 and 231, the Salted Caramel Cupcakes on pages 242 and 243, and the Eggnog Cupcakes on pages 272 and 273. To use this tip, hold the piping bag at a 45-degree angle, with the tip about ¼ inch above or even lightly resting on the surface of the cupcake. Starting in the center of the cupcake, begin to pipe frosting in a circle, working outward toward the edge of the cupcake but not quite reaching it; you want some cake to be visible on the sides. This layer is going to act as a base for the rest of the frosting. Then continue to pipe, gently starting to pull up and piping frosting on top of the first layer back toward the center so that it swirls its way up to the top, getting smaller and smaller. Pull up quickly to stop the flow of frosting and leave a pointed tip.

ATECO 867—LARGE DROP FLOWER TIP

I used this tip to frost the beautiful flowerlike dollops between the layers of the Blackberry Elderflower Cake on pages 222 and 223. It is basically a larger version of the Wilton 2C, meaning that your dollops will be substantially larger. For comparison, check out the Meyer Lemon Meringue Tartlets on pages 184 and 185, which were piped with the smaller 2C tip. To use the Ateco 867 tip, hold the piping bag at a 90-degree angle, with the tip about ¼ inch above or even lightly resting on the surface of the cake. Apply pressure until you've reached the desired dollop size, then pull up quickly to stop the flow of frosting and leave a pointed tip. Pipe evenly spaced dollops around the edge of the cake, then place another circle of dollops inside that circle and so on until you've reached the center and no space remains.

Note:

The cake pictured is the Death by Chocolate Cake (page 238) made with Vanilla Buttercream (page 394) and cooled Ganache (pages 369 to 370) poured on top.

Classic
YELLOW CAKE

PREP TIME: 15 minutes

COOK TIME: 20 to 35 minutes

READY IN: 55 minutes

YIELD: One 2-layer, 6-inch (15-cm) cake or one single-layer, 8-inch (20-cm) cake (to make the 3-layer cake shown in the photos, see Variations)

I love love love love yellow cake with chocolate frosting. That's four loves I just typed. I would type more, but I think you get the picture. One of the things I missed most when going grain-free was classic yellow cake; it's such a simple pleasure. There is absolutely nothing fancy about yellow cake; it's just delicious. I guess sometimes that's all you need. This cake would be great to take to a gluten-free birthday party, especially when made as a triple-layer cake! Candles not included.

FOR THE CAKE

2 cups (185 g) sifted fine-ground blanched almond flour

¼ cup (35 g) tapioca flour

2 tablespoons coconut flour

¼ cup (35 g) maple sugar

2 tablespoons coconut sugar

½ teaspoon baking soda

½ teaspoon fine-grain sea salt

4 large egg whites, room temperature

½ teaspoon cream of tartar

¼ cup (55 g) palm shortening, plus more for the pan(s)

4 tablespoons (2 ounces/56 g) unsalted butter, softened

2 large egg yolks (from separated eggs, above)

½ cup (120 ml) half-and-half

½ cup (120 ml) sour cream

¼ cup (60 ml) light-colored raw honey, melted

2 teaspoons vanilla extract

FOR THE FROSTING

1 recipe Chocolate Buttercream (page 396)

MAKE AHEAD
CAKE LAYERS—1 DAY AHEAD

1. Adjust an oven rack to the middle position and preheat the oven to 350°F (177°C). Line the bottoms of two 6-inch (15-cm) or one 8-inch (20-cm) springform cake pan(s) with parchment paper, then grease the paper and sides of the pan liberally with palm shortening; set aside.

2. In the bowl of a large food processor, combine the flours, sugars, baking soda, and salt. Pulse 30 times or until combined.

3. In a separate medium-sized mixing bowl, combine the egg whites and cream of tartar. Beat using a hand mixer set on high until the egg whites are very foamy and soft peaks are about to form; set aside.

4. Add the palm shortening, butter, egg yolks, half-and-half, sour cream, honey, and vanilla to the bowl of the food processor, followed by the beaten egg whites. Process until combined. Scrape down the sides as needed and process for another 30 seconds until a smooth and creamy cake batter has formed.

5. Pour the batter into the prepared cake pan(s) and use a rubber spatula to help scrape all the batter into the pan(s). Bake for 30 to 35 minutes or until a toothpick inserted into the center of the cake comes out clean.

6. Remove from the oven and let cool in the pan(s) for 15 minutes. To remove the cake from the pan, run a knife around the edge between the cake and the pan, until they no longer touch. Remove the cake from the pan and let cool completely.

7. Once the cake is completely cool, prepare the Chocolate Buttercream.

8. To assemble: If making a single-layer, 8-inch (20-cm) cake, place the cake on a cake plate and use an offset spatula to cover the top and sides with the frosting. If making a two-layer cake, place the first layer on a cake plate and use a serrated knife to cut away any uneven spots on the top of the cake. Pipe a dam of frosting around the edge of the cake to keep the frosting from seeping over the edges once it's placed. Then place a large dollop of frosting in the center of the cake and use an offset spatula to spread it across until it reaches the dam edge. Place the second cake layer on top, upside down. Then spread the remaining frosting over both layers, up the sides and across the top. Garnish as desired (see page 60 for decorating ideas). Store the cake at room temperature in an airtight container or wrapped well in plastic for up to 2 days.

Notes: To make the cake batter with a hand mixer: Put the flours, sugars, baking soda, and salt in a large mixing bowl. Stir together using a fork until combined. Put the egg whites and cream of tartar in a separate medium-sized mixing bowl. Beat using a hand mixer set on high speed until the eggs are very foamy and soft peaks are about to form; set aside. In another bowl, combine the palm shortening, butter, egg yolks, heavy cream, sour cream, honey, and vanilla. Beat on medium speed until combined. Transfer the palm shortening mixture to the dry ingredients, add the beaten egg whites, and then beat together on medium-low speed until combined. Transfer to the greased and parchment-lined cake pan(s) and bake as directed.

If using a light-colored aluminum pan, you may need to add additional baking time.

Subs: Sour cream gives this cake a buttermilk taste. Ironically, when I tested it with actual buttermilk, it didn't taste so great.

To make a dairy-free version of this cake, use ghee in place of the butter and full-fat coconut milk in place of the heavy cream, and omit the sour cream.

Variations:

Classic Yellow Cupcakes. *Line a standard 12-cup muffin pan with paper liners. Make the cake batter, following Steps 2 through 4, opposite. Use a spoon to transfer the batter into the lined cups, filling each three-quarters full. Bake for 23 to 27 minutes or until a toothpick comes out clean. Let cool in the pan for 10 minutes, then remove from the pan to cool completely. Finish with the frosting, using a pastry bag and tip (or a resealable plastic bag with a corner cut off) or a small offset spatula. Store at room temperature in an airtight container or wrapped well in plastic for up to 2 days.*

Triple-Layer Classic Yellow Cake (pictured on next page). *As soon as you stack three cake layers, you get something that has "celebration" written all over it, making it perfect for a birthday or any festive get-together. To make a triple-layer, 8-inch (20-cm) cake, as shown in the photos, you will need to make three single batches of the cake batter and a double batch of the frosting. For maximum efficiency, you will need three 8-inch (20-cm) cake pans; having three on hand will allow you to prepare the second layer while the first is baking and the third layer while the second is baking. If working with only one pan, prepare one layer at time. While the first layer is cooling, start preparing the second batch of batter. After all three cake layers are baked and are cooling, prepare a double batch of the Chocolate Buttercream. To assemble and frost the cake, follow the directions for a two-layer cake in Step 8, opposite, piping a dam of frosting on the first two layers and placing the third cake layer right side up. Serves 10 to 12.*

White CAKE

PREP TIME: 15 minutes
COOK TIME: 30 to 35 minutes
READY IN: 45 minutes
YIELD: One 2-layer, 6-inch (15-cm) cake or one single-layer, 8-inch (20-cm) cake (to make the tiered cake shown in the photos, see Variations)

FOR THE CAKE

2 cups (185 g) sifted fine-ground blanched almond flour

¼ cup (35 g) tapioca flour

2 tablespoons coconut flour

¼ cup (40 g) coconut sugar

2 tablespoons maple sugar

½ teaspoon baking soda

½ teaspoon fine-grain sea salt

4 large egg whites, room temperature

½ teaspoon cream of tartar

½ cup (115 g) palm shortening, plus more for the pan(s)

½ cup (120 ml) canned full-fat coconut milk

¼ cup (60 ml) light-colored raw honey, melted

2 teaspoons vanilla extract

⅛ teaspoon almond extract

FOR THE FROSTING

1 recipe Swiss Meringue Buttercream (page 392), Cream Cheese Frosting (page 398), or Chocolate Buttercream (page 396)

MAKE AHEAD
CAKE LAYERS—1 DAY AHEAD

Baking a cake just became a piece of cake thanks to this recipe. Pun totally intended. This white cake recipe is so incredibly versatile, it's going to become a staple in your grain-free kitchen. Not only can you use it to make cakes, but it's also a great base for cupcakes, muffins, and quick breads. Oh, the possibilities!

1. Adjust an oven rack to the middle position and preheat the oven to 350°F (177°C). Line the bottoms of two 6-inch (15-cm) or one 8-inch (20-cm) springform cake pan(s) with parchment paper, then grease the paper and sides of the pan(s) liberally with palm shortening; set aside.

2. In the bowl of a large food processor, combine the flours, sugars, baking soda, and salt. Pulse 30 times or until combined.

3. In a separate medium-sized mixing bowl, combine the egg whites and cream of tartar. Beat using a hand mixer set on high speed until the eggs are very foamy and soft peaks are about to form; set aside.

4. Add the palm shortening, coconut milk, honey, vanilla, and almond extract to the bowl of the food processor, followed by the beaten egg whites. Process until combined. Scrape down the sides as needed and process for another 30 seconds, until a smooth and creamy cake batter has formed.

5. Pour the batter into the prepared cake pan(s) and use a rubber spatula to help scrape all the batter into the pan(s). Bake for 30 to 35 minutes or until a toothpick inserted into the center of the cake comes out clean.

6. Remove from the oven and let cool in the pan(s) for 15 minutes. To remove the cake from the pan, run a knife around the edge between the cake and the pan, until they no longer touch. Remove from the pan and let cool completely.

7. Once the cake is completely cool, prepare the frosting.

8. To assemble: If making a single-layer, 8-inch (20-cm) cake, place the cake on a cake plate and use an offset spatula to cover the top and sides with the frosting. If making a two-layer cake, place the first layer on a cake plate and use a serrated knife to cut away any uneven spots on the top of the cake. Pipe a dam of frosting around the edge of the cake to keep the frosting from seeping over the edges once it's placed. Then place a large dollop of frosting in the center of the cake and use an offset spatula to spread it across the center of the cake until it reaches the dam edge. Place the second cake layer on top, upside down, then spread the frosting over both layers, up the sides and across the top. Garnish as desired. If Cream Cheese Frosting was used, store the cake in the refrigerator for up to 2 days. If buttercream was used, store the cake at room temperature in an airtight container or wrapped well in plastic for up to 2 days.

Notes: *The cake is dairy-free, but the frosting options are not. For a dairy-free dessert, try Strawberry Lemonade Meringue Frosting (page 382) or Dairy-Free Eggnog Meringue Frosting (page 412).*

Technically this recipe isn't white in the sense of a traditional white cake. Those cakes are made using white flour and white sugar, which give a lovely white color. This is more like a tan cake because the almond flour and maple sugar give it a slight tint.

To make the cake batter with a hand mixer: Put the flours, sugars, baking soda, and salt in a large mixing bowl. Stir together using a fork until combined. Put the egg whites and cream of tartar in a separate medium-sized mixing bowl. Beat using a hand mixer set on high speed until the eggs are very foamy and soft peaks are about to form; set aside. In another separate bowl, combine the palm shortening, coconut milk, honey, vanilla, and almond extract. Beat on medium speed until combined. Transfer the palm shortening mixture to the dry ingredients, add the beaten egg whites, and then beat on medium-low speed until combined. Transfer to the greased and parchment-lined cake pan(s) and bake as directed.

If using a light-colored aluminum pan, you may need to add additional baking time.

Variations:

White Cupcakes. *Adjust an oven rack to the middle position and preheat the oven to 350°F (177°C). Line a standard 12-cup muffin pan with paper liners. Make the cake batter, following Steps 2 through 4, opposite. Use a spoon to transfer the batter into the lined cups, filling each about three-quarters full. Bake for 20 to 25 minutes or until a toothpick comes out clean. Let cool in the pan for 10 minutes, then remove to cool completely. Finish with the desired frosting. If Cream Cheese Frosting was used, store the cupcakes in the refrigerator for up to 2 days. If buttercream was used, store the cupcakes at room temperature in an airtight container or wrapped well in plastic for up to 2 days.*

Tiered White Cake (pictured on next page). *The cake shown in the photos is made up of four 8-inch (20-cm) layers on the bottom and four 6-inch (15-cm) layers on the top. I realize that this is a lot for the average home cook to tackle, but it's always good to have a fabulous cake recipe in your arsenal should an occasion demanding it ever arise. It's also great for those who want to take their baking to the next level. Because a double batch of batter won't fit in a large food processor, each of the four larger cake layers needs to be prepared individually, requiring a total of six batches of batter to make all the layers (including the four smaller layers). To save time when making the 8-inch (20-cm) layers, use two pans: While one layer is baking, you can clean out the food processor, prepare the next layer, and continue to rotate them out. For the four 6-inch (15-cm) layers, make two single batches of cake batter, following the same rotation method, but bake two layers at a time. Let all the layers cool completely before frosting. Make two double batches of the frosting; this quantity should yield enough frosting to pipe in between the layers and cover the cake. (Note: If using Swiss Meringue Buttercream, you will need to use an extra-large heatproof bowl for the double boiler setup since a double batch of this frosting calls for 10 egg whites.) This will also depend on how heavy-handed you are when frosting. It's always smart to have extra ingredients on hand in case you need more frosting. To assemble the cake, follow the guidelines for a two-layer cake in Step 8, opposite, repeating the process until all the layers are stacked and frosted. Serves 12.*

Almond CAKE

PREP TIME: 15 minutes
COOK TIME: 30 minutes
READY IN: 1 hour
YIELD: One 2-layer, 6-inch (15-cm) cake (pictured) or one single-layer, 8-inch (20-cm) cake

I recently became acquainted with almond extract. It always sounded so old-timey to me, like an ingredient your grandma would have used in her famous fruitcake or something—not an ingredient used in some hip, cool, delicious cake. Well, what the heck do I know? Almond extract is amazing! It gives such flavor to cakes and breads, and there is something so pleasant and familiar about it. Seriously, go grab a bottle and get to work. I'll put a gold star on your Paleo baking chart this week.

FOR THE CAKE

2 cups (185 g) sifted fine-ground blanched almond flour

¼ cup (35 g) tapioca flour

2 tablespoons coconut flour

¼ cup (35 g) maple sugar

2 tablespoons coconut sugar

½ teaspoon baking soda

½ teaspoon fine-grain sea salt

4 large egg whites, room temperature

½ teaspoon cream of tartar

½ cup (115 g) palm shortening, plus more for the pan(s)

½ cup (120 ml) half-and-half

½ cup (120 ml) sour cream

¼ cup (60 ml) light-colored raw honey, melted

2 teaspoons vanilla extract

1 teaspoon almond extract

FOR THE FROSTING

1 recipe Swiss Meringue Buttercream (page 392)*

* *If decorating the cake with the fancy piped designs shown in the photos, make a double recipe of the buttercream.*

MAKE AHEAD
CAKE LAYERS—1 DAY AHEAD

1. Adjust an oven rack to the middle position and preheat the oven to 350°F (177°C). Line the bottoms of two 6-inch (15-cm) or one 8-inch (20-cm) springform cake pan(s) with parchment paper, then grease the paper and sides of the pan(s) liberally with palm shortening; set aside.

2. Put the flours, sugars, baking soda, and salt in the bowl of a large food processor. Pulse 30 times or until combined.

3. In a separate medium-sized mixing bowl, combine the egg whites and cream of tartar. Beat using a hand mixer set on high speed until the eggs are very foamy and soft peaks are about to form; set aside.

4. Add the palm shortening, half-and-half, sour cream, honey, vanilla, and almond extract to the bowl of the food processor, followed by the beaten egg whites. Process until combined. Scrape down the sides as needed and process for another 30 seconds, until a smooth and creamy batter has formed.

5. Pour the batter into the prepared cake pan(s) and use a rubber spatula to help scrape all the batter into the pan(s). Bake for 27 to 30 minutes or until a toothpick inserted into the center of the cake comes out clean.

6. Remove from the oven and let cool in the pan(s) for 15 minutes, then run a knife between the cake edge and pan to loosen the cake. Remove and let cool completely.

7. Once the cake has cooled completely, prepare the Swiss Meringue Buttercream.

8. To assemble: If making a single-layer, 8-inch (20-cm) cake, place the cake on a cake plate and use an offset spatula to cover the top and sides with the frosting. If making a two-layer cake, as pictured, place a cake layer on a cake plate and use a serrated knife to cut away any uneven spots on the top of the cake. Pipe a dam of frosting around the edge of the cake to keep the frosting from seeping over the edges once it's placed. Place a dollop of frosting in the center of the cake and use an offset spatula to spread it across the cake until it reaches the dam edge. Place the second cake layer on top, upside down, then spread the frosting over both layers, up the sides and across the top. Garnish as desired (see page 60 for ideas). To create the piped design pictured, see Notes, opposite. Store the cake at room temperature in an airtight container or wrapped well in plastic for up to 2 days.

Notes: To create the frosting decoration shown in the photos, follow the instructions for using the Wilton 1M rose tip in the Decorating Tips section on page 203.

To make the cake batter with a hand mixer: Put the flours, sugars, baking soda, and salt in a large mixing bowl. Stir together using a fork until combined. Put the egg whites and cream of tartar in a separate medium-sized mixing bowl. Beat using a hand mixer set on high speed until the eggs are very foamy and soft peaks are about to form; set aside. In separate bowl, combine the palm shortening, half-and-half, sour cream, honey, vanilla, and almond extract. Beat on medium speed until combined. Transfer the palm shortening mixture to the dry ingredients, add the beaten egg whites, and then beat together on medium-low speed until combined. Transfer to the greased and parchment-lined cake pan(s) and bake as directed.

If using a light-colored aluminum pan, you may need to add additional baking time.

Subs: ½ cup (120 ml) of canned full-fat coconut milk in place of the half-and-half and sour cream.

Heavy cream in place of the half-and-half.

Variation: **Almond Cupcakes.** Adjust an oven rack to the middle position and preheat the oven to 350°F (177°C). Line a standard 12-cup muffin pan with paper liners. Make the cake batter, following Steps 2 through 4, opposite. Use a spoon to transfer the batter into the lined cups, filling each about three-quarters full. Bake for 20 to 25 minutes or until a toothpick comes out clean. Let cool in the pan for 10 minutes, then remove to cool completely. Finish with the desired frosting. Store the cupcakes at room temperature in an airtight container or wrapped well in plastic for up to 2 days.

Limoncello
POUND CAKE

PREP TIME: 15 minutes
COOK TIME: 30 to 35 minutes
READY IN: 45 minutes
YIELD: One 2-layer, 6-inch (15-cm) cake or one single-layer, 8-inch (20-cm) cake (to make the layer cake shown in the photos, see Variations)

FOR THE CAKE

2 cups (185 g) sifted fine-ground blanched almond flour

¼ cup (35 g) tapioca flour

2 tablespoons coconut flour

¼ cup (35 g) maple sugar

2 tablespoons coconut sugar

½ teaspoon baking soda

½ teaspoon fine-grain sea salt

4 large egg whites, room temperature

½ teaspoon cream of tartar

½ cup (115 g) palm shortening, plus more for the pan(s)

½ cup (120 ml) canned full-fat coconut milk

¼ cup (60 ml) light-colored raw honey, melted

3 tablespoons fresh-squeezed lemon juice

2 teaspoons grated lemon zest

1 teaspoon vanilla extract

1 teaspoon lemon extract

FOR THE FILLING (OPTIONAL; FOR LAYER CAKE)

1 recipe Lemon Curd (page 388) or Dairy-Free Meyer Lemon Curd (page 184)

FOR THE GLAZE/FROSTING

1 recipe Lemon Glaze (page 406), Lemon Cream Cheese Frosting (page 408), or Lemon Meringue Buttercream (page 404)

I adore Limoncello. Whenever I indulge in it, I imagine myself in the south of Italy, the wind blowing through my hair, watching the sunset over the ocean with a hunky Italian guy . . . wait, where am I? Oh, excuse me, I got lost for a minute! I also love cake, so why not combine the two? This one is for lemon lovers only! No actual Limoncello was harmed in the making of this cake; it just tastes that way.

1 Adjust an oven rack to the middle position and preheat the oven to 350°F (177°C). Line two 6-inch (15-cm) or one 8-inch (20-cm) springform cake pan(s) with parchment paper, then grease the paper and sides of the pan(s) lightly with palm shortening; set aside.

2 In the bowl of a large food processor, combine the flours, sugars, baking soda, and salt. Pulse 30 times or until combined.

3 In a separate medium-sized mixing bowl, combine the egg whites and cream of tartar. Beat using a hand mixer set on high speed until the eggs are very foamy and soft peaks are about to form; set aside.

4 Add the palm shortening, coconut milk, honey, lemon juice, zest, vanilla, and lemon extract to the bowl of the food processor, followed by the beaten egg whites. Process to combine, then scrape down the sides and process for another 30 seconds, until a smooth and creamy cake batter has formed.

5 Pour the batter into the prepared cake pan(s) and use a rubber spatula to help scrape all the batter into the pan(s). Bake for 30 to 35 minutes or until a toothpick inserted into the center of the cake comes out clean.

6 Remove the cake(s) from the oven and let cool in the pan(s) for 15 minutes. Then run a knife around the edge between the cake and the pan, until they no longer touch, and remove from the pan(s) to cool completely.

7 Once the cake has completely cooled, prepare the filling (if making a layer cake) and the glaze or frosting.

8 To assemble: If making a single-layer, 8-inch (20-cm) cake, place the cake on a cake plate and drizzle with the glaze, or use an offset spatula to cover the top and sides with the frosting. If making a two-layer cake, place a cake layer on a cake plate. Use a serrated knife to cut away any uneven spots on the top of the cake. If using frosting, pipe a dam of frosting around the edge of the cake to keep the curd from seeping over the edges once it's poured. Pour the curd into the center of the cake and spread using an offset spatula or a rubber spatula until it reaches the dam edge. Set the second cake layer on top. Then spread the remaining frosting over both layers, up the sides and across the top. If using glaze, instead of creating a dam, just let the curd drip down the sides. Then pour the glaze over the top and let it drip down as well. Garnish as desired (see page 60 for ideas). If buttercream or glaze was used, store the cake at room temperature in an airtight container or wrapped well in plastic for up to 2 days. If cream cheese frosting was used, store the cake in the refrigerator for up to 2 days.

Notes: The cake pictured was made using Lemon Curd for the filling and Lemon Glaze drizzled on top.

To make this cake dairy-free, use the Dairy-Free Meyer Lemon Curd for the filling between the layers, and use the Lemon Glaze.

If you want to use Limoncello in the cake, add ¼ cup (60 ml) and reduce the amount of coconut milk to ¼ cup (60 ml). Then taste and add lemon juice as needed, 1 tablespoon at a time. To use Limoncello in the curd or frosting, use 1 tablespoon in place of 1 tablespoon of the lemon juice.

To make the cake batter using a hand mixer: Put the flours, sugars, baking soda, and salt in a large mixing bowl. Stir together using a fork until combined. In a separate medium-sized mixing bowl, put the egg whites and cream of tartar. Beat using a hand mixer set on high speed until the eggs are very foamy and soft peaks are about to form; set aside. In another bowl, combine the palm shortening, coconut milk, honey, lemon juice, zest, vanilla, and lemon extract. Beat on medium speed until combined. Transfer the coconut milk mixture to the dry ingredients, add the beaten egg whites, and then beat together on medium-low speed until combined. Transfer to the greased and parchment-lined cake pan(s) and bake as directed.

If using a light-colored aluminum pan, you may need to add additional baking time.

Variations:

Lemon Butter Cake. *Reduce the amount of palm shortening to ¼ cup (55 g) and add 4 tablespoons (2 ounces/56 g) of butter in Step 4.*

Limoncello Cupcakes. *Adjust an oven rack to the middle position and preheat the oven to 350°F (177°C). Line a 12-cup muffin pan with paper liners. Make the cake batter, following Steps 2 through 4, opposite. Use a spoon to transfer the batter into the lined cups, filling each about three-quarters full. Bake for 20 to 25 minutes or until a toothpick comes out clean. Let cool in the pan for 10 minutes, then remove to cool completely. Finish with the desired frosting. Store the cupcakes in a cool, dry place (or in the refrigerator if cream cheese frosting was used) for up to 2 days.*

Limoncello Pound Cake (pictured on next page). *To make the two-layer, 8-inch (20-cm) cake pictured, you will need to make two single batches of the cake batter. (A double batch of the batter will not fit in a large food processor.) To make the cake, follow the instructions above, but line and grease two 8-inch (20-cm) springform cake pans as described in Step 1. Make the batter for the first layer and bake and cool it as instructed in Steps 5 and 6. While the first layer is baking, make the batter for the second layer and pour it into the second prepared cake pan so that it can be popped into the oven as soon as the first cake layer is done baking. To assemble the cake, follow the instructions in Step 8 for layering, filling, and frosting or glazing a two-layer cake. Serves 8 to 10.*

BLACKBERRY
ELDERFLOWER CAKE

PREP TIME: 15 minutes
COOK TIME: 60 to 70 minutes
READY IN: 1 hour 15 minutes
YIELD: One 3-layer, 6-inch (15-cm) cake

This cake was inspired by a recipe from my favorite blogger, Linda Lomelino. Her work inspires me to become a better baker and food photographer on the daily, so of course I had to make my own version of one of her cakes. I'm obsessed with elderflower-flavored anything. It felt only natural to use blackberries; they are not only beautiful to look at, but have a great flavor that pairs so well with elderflower. This cake is my pride and joy. I want to hold its hand, teach it to ride a bike, and read it bedtime stories. And no chocolate is involved—can you believe it?

Palm shortening, for the pans

1 recipe plus ½ recipe Almond Cake batter (page 214; see Notes)

1 recipe Elderflower Mascarpone Frosting (page 400)

¾ cup (6 ounces/170 g) fresh blackberries, divided

Notes: To make the layers for this cake, it's necessary to make one full batch of the batter and one half batch. The 1½ batches required won't fit in a large food processor. For maximum efficiency, you will need three 6-inch (15-cm) cake pans. If you do not own three pans in this size, you will need to let the pans cool completely before baking the third layer.

If you wish to completely cover the three cake layers rather than pipe on the frosting to make the naked cake shown, you will need to make a double batch of the frosting.

To make a 2-layer, 6-inch (15-cm) cake or a single-layer, 8-inch (20-cm) cake, make a single batch of the cake batter. One recipe of the frosting will be enough to cover the cake.

Subs: Strawberries for the blackberries.

1. Adjust an oven rack to the middle position and preheat the oven to 350°F (177°C). Line the bottoms of three 6-inch (15-cm) springform cake pans with parchment paper, then grease the paper and sides of the pans with palm shortening; set aside.

2. Prepare a single batch of the Almond Cake batter, completing Steps 2 and 3 on page 214. Pour the batter evenly into two of the prepared cake pans and use a rubber spatula to help scrape all the batter into the pans. Bake for 30 to 35 minutes or until a toothpick inserted into the center of the cake comes out clean. Remove from the oven and let cool in the pans while you make the half recipe of batter, about 15 minutes. To remove the cakes from the pans, run a knife around the edge between the cake and the pan, until they no longer touch. Remove from the pans and let cool completely.

3. Pour the half recipe of cake batter evenly into the third prepared cake pan and use a rubber spatula to help scrape all the batter into the pan. Bake for 30 to 35 minutes or until a toothpick inserted into the center of the cake comes out clean. Remove from the oven and let cool for about 15 minutes, then remove from the pan, following the instructions in Step 2, and let cool completely.

4. Once all three cake layers are completely cool, prepare the Elderflower Mascarpone Frosting and transfer it to a piping bag or resealable plastic bag with a corner snipped off, fitted with an Ateco 867 or similar large drop flower tip.

5. To assemble: Cut ½ cup of the blackberries in half lengthwise. Reserve the remaining whole blackberries for garnishing the top of the cake. Place one of the cake layers on a cake plate. Pipe frosting on top of the cake, then top with the halved blackberries. Place the second cake layer on top and repeat the process. Place the third layer on top of the second layer and garnish with frosting, with a mound of whole blackberries in the center. Store any leftover cake in the refrigerator for up to 1 day; be sure to enjoy it by the next day.

MAKE AHEAD
CAKE LAYERS—1 DAY AHEAD

Hot Fudge
SUNDAE CUPCAKES

PREP TIME: 35 minutes
COOK TIME: 20 to 25 minutes
READY IN: 55 minutes
YIELD: 1 dozen cupcakes

I got the idea for these cupcakes from a friend of mine who randomly comes up with wacky dessert ideas. One time he said, "You know what would be so good right now? Cupcakes that are like a hot fudge sundae." I then grabbed a notepad and said, "What other ideas do you have?" It's been a great collaboration so far.

1 recipe Chocolate Cupcakes (page 226)

1 recipe Swiss Meringue Buttercream (page 392) or Cream Cheese Frosting (page 398)

1 recipe Ganache (pages 369 to 370), any type, or Chocolate Shell Coating (page 376)

12 cherries, for garnish

MAKE AHEAD
CHOCOLATE CUPCAKES—1 DAY AHEAD

1 Prepare the Chocolate Cupcakes.

2 Once the cupcakes have cooled, prepare the frosting. Transfer to a piping bag fitted with the desired tip (the frosting can also be applied with a small offset spatula). Place in the refrigerator until needed, about 10 minutes; any longer and the buttercream may harden too much. If this happens, just let it sit at room temperature until softened.

3 Prepare the ganache. Let cool slightly, then transfer to a piping bag or to a resealable plastic bag with a corner cut off.

4 To assemble: Frost each cupcake, then squeeze some ganache over the top and let it drip down the sides of the frosting. Garnish with a cherry. If using the Cream Cheese Frosting, store the cupcakes in the refrigerator for up to 2 days. If using the Swiss Meringue Buttercream, store at room temperature in an airtight container or wrapped well in plastic for up to 2 days.

Chocolate
CUPCAKES

PREP TIME: 20 minutes
COOK TIME: 20 to 25 minutes
READY IN: 45 minutes
YIELD: 1 dozen cupcakes

These cupcakes are so close to the real thing, you'd swear that they ARE the real thing. In fact, they may even be better. They have so much flavor and the texture is so on point, you'd never know the difference. This is my go-to Paleo dessert to make for any celebration or birthday. These cupcakes make everyone happy!

1 cup (92 g) sifted fine-ground blanched almond flour

1 tablespoon coconut sugar

½ teaspoon baking soda

½ teaspoon fine-grain sea salt

⅛ teaspoon ground cinnamon

1 cup (7 ounces/200 g) chocolate chips

½ cup (120 ml) canned full-fat coconut milk, room temperature

¼ cup (55 g) palm shortening

2 large eggs

½ teaspoon vanilla extract

1 recipe Chocolate Buttercream (page 396)

MAKE AHEAD

CHOCOLATE CUPCAKES—1 DAY AHEAD

1. Adjust an oven rack to the middle position and preheat the oven to 350°F (177°C). Line a 12-cup muffin pan with paper liners; set aside.

2. In a medium-sized bowl, combine the almond flour, coconut sugar, baking soda, salt, and cinnamon. Stir together using a fork until combined; set aside.

3. Melt the chocolate chips and coconut milk in a double boiler over low heat or in a large heatproof bowl set over a pan of gently simmering water. Stir intermittently using a rubber spatula until the chocolate is completely melted and combined with the coconut milk. Then add the palm shortening and stir it into the chocolate mixture as it melts, until completely combined. Remove from the heat and let cool slightly.

4. Stir the eggs and vanilla into the melted chocolate mixture. If you used a double boiler rather than a large mixing bowl set over a pan of water to melt the chocolate, transfer the melted chocolate and egg mixture to a large mixing bowl.

5. Gently fold the dry ingredients into the melted chocolate mixture and stir using a rubber spatula or whisk until just combined. Overmixing could cause the middles of the cupcakes to sink.

6. Use a small (1-tablespoon) cookie scoop or a large spoon to transfer the batter into the cupcake liners, filling each about two-thirds full. Bake for 20 to 25 minutes or until a toothpick comes out clean. Let cool in the pan for 10 minutes, then remove from the pan to cool completely before frosting.

7. Prepare the Chocolate Buttercream, then pipe it onto the cupcakes using a piping bag fitted with the desired tip (a Wilton 1M tip was used to frost the cupcakes pictured; the frosting can also be applied with a small offset spatula). Store at room temperature in an airtight container or wrapped well in plastic for up to 2 days.

Notes: The cupcakes are dairy-free, but the Chocolate Buttercream is not. For a dairy-free option, try topping the cupcakes with Marshmallow Crème (page 366).

Crème Brûlée
CUPCAKES

PREP TIME: 45 minutes
COOK TIME: 25 minutes
READY IN: 1 hour 10 minutes
YIELD: 1 dozen cupcakes

I'm sorry, did you see this? No, seriously, did you see this? It's crème brûlée on a freaking cupcake, as the frosting. I actually came across this idea when I Googled the ingredients for crème brûlée. Yes, I Googled. Then I had to figure out how to Paleoize it for your eating pleasure. My favorite part is caramelizing the sugar on top; you get to use a kitchen torch and feel all profesh and stuff. And then, when that caramelized sugar cracks under a spoon . . . there are few greater things in life.

1 recipe Classic Yellow Cupcakes (page 207) or White Cupcakes (page 211)

1 recipe Caramel Crème Brûlée (page 162), minus the 2 tablespoons of maple sugar used in Step 4

¼ cup (35 g) homemade maple sugar

SPECIAL EQUIPMENT
Kitchen torch

MAKE AHEAD
CUPCAKES—1 DAY AHEAD

1. Make the cupcakes.

2. While the cupcakes are baking, prepare the Caramel Crème Brûlée, following Steps 1 and 2 on page 162. Transfer to a small bowl and place in the refrigerator for 30 minutes or until set. After the cupcakes have cooled, transfer the crème brûlée to a piping bag or resealable plastic bag with a corner cut off, fitted with a large round tip.

3. To assemble: Pipe the crème brûlée on top of each cupcake. Sprinkle maple sugar across the crème brûlée, then use a kitchen torch to melt the sugar until it bubbles, becomes amber in color, and creates a caramelized shell over the surface. Store the cupcakes in the refrigerator for up to 1 day.

Notes: *For this recipe, you have to use homemade maple sugar on top. Store-bought maple sugar is too dry and will burn when torched. Though homemade maple sugar feels dry to the touch, it retains some moisture, which makes it perfect for getting that beautiful caramelized top that is so fun to crack. If you don't want to make your own maple sugar, check Etsy; there you will find some amazing deals on homemade maple sugar sold directly by maple syrup producers.*

"Reese's" CUPCAKES

PREP TIME: 25 minutes
COOK TIME: 20 to 25 minutes
READY IN: 45 minutes
YIELD: 1 dozen cupcakes

1 recipe Chocolate Cupcakes (page 226)

1 recipe Almond Butter Center (page 362)

FOR GARNISH (OPTIONAL)

3 Almond Butter Cups (page 146) or store-bought nut butter cups

MAKE AHEAD

CHOCOLATE CUPCAKES—1 DAY AHEAD

If you use peanut butter in place of almond butter in this recipe, I won't tell anyone. Either way, these cupcakes are sure to be a hit.

1 Prepare the cupcakes, following Steps 1 through 6 on page 226.

2 Once the cupcakes have cooled completely, prepare the Almond Butter Center. Transfer to a piping bag fitted with the desired tip (the frosting can also be applied with a small offset spatula). If using Almond Butter Cups for garnish, cut them into fourths.

3 To assemble: Frost each cupcake, then garnish with a fourth of an Almond Butter Cup, if using. Store at room temperature in an airtight container or wrapped well in plastic for up to 2 days.

Notes: If you decide to use peanut butter cups instead of Almond Butter Cups in this recipe, Justin's brand makes delicious ones without a ton of crap that you don't want. Sun Cups is a brand of sunflower seed butter cups that you could use as well. The Almond Butter Center could be made with peanut butter too.

Caramel Maple FIG CAKE

PREP TIME: 30 minutes
COOK TIME: 30 to 35 minutes
READY IN: 1 hour
YIELD: One 2-layer, 6-inch (15-cm) cake or one single-layer, 8-inch (20-cm) cake (to make the 4-layer cake shown in the photos, see Variations)

This jaw-dropping cake was inspired by a recipe I saw online. The figs were so beautiful that I had to make a version of my own! I think figs are such statement pieces and are so fun to decorate with. Colorful fruits make the best cake decorations.

1 recipe Salted Caramel Sauce (page 374), for the layers

FOR THE BATTER

2 cups (185 g) sifted fine-ground blanched almond flour

¼ cup (35 g) tapioca flour

2 tablespoons coconut flour

½ cup (65 g) maple sugar

½ teaspoon baking soda

½ teaspoon fine-grain sea salt

⅛ teaspoon ground cinnamon

4 large egg whites, room temperature

½ teaspoon cream of tartar

½ cup (115 g) palm shortening, plus more for the pan(s)

½ cup (120 ml) canned full-fat coconut milk

¼ cup (60 ml) light-colored raw honey, melted

1 teaspoon almond extract

1 teaspoon vanilla extract

FOR THE FROSTING

1 recipe Vanilla Buttercream (page 394), Cream Cheese Frosting (page 398), or Mascarpone and Goat Cheese Frosting (page 402)

FOR GARNISH

2 figs, quartered

Handful of fresh blackberries and blueberries (optional)

Fresh flowers (optional; see page 60 for tips)

1. Adjust an oven rack to the middle position and preheat the oven to 350°F (177°C). Line the bottoms of two 6-inch (15-cm) or one 8-inch (20-cm) springform cake pan(s) with parchment paper, then grease the paper and sides of the pan(s) liberally with palm shortening; set aside.

2. Prepare the Salted Caramel Sauce and place in the refrigerator to cool while preparing the cake layer(s). The caramel is easier to spread when cold.

3. In the bowl of a large food processor, combine the flours, maple sugar, baking soda, salt, and cinnamon. Pulse 30 times or until combined.

4. In a separate medium-sized mixing bowl, combine the egg whites and cream of tartar. Beat using a hand mixer set on high speed until the eggs are very foamy and soft peaks are about to form; set aside.

5. Add the palm shortening, coconut milk, honey, almond extract, and vanilla to the bowl of the food processor, followed by the beaten egg whites. Process until combined. Scrape down the sides as needed and process for another 30 seconds, until a smooth and creamy cake batter has formed.

6. Pour the batter into the prepared cake pan(s) and use a rubber spatula to help scrape all the batter into the pan(s). Bake for 30 to 35 minutes or until a toothpick inserted into the center of the cake comes out clean. Let cool in the pan(s) for 15 minutes, then run a knife along the edge between the cake and the pan to loosen the cake from the sides. Remove and let cool completely.

7. Once the cake is completely cool, prepare the frosting.

8. To assemble: If making a single-layer, 8-inch (20-cm) cake, place the cake on a cake plate and use an offset spatula to spread a layer of caramel sauce across the top. Then spread a layer of frosting on top of the caramel, completely covering the caramel and the sides of the cake. If making a two-layer cake, place the first cake layer on a cake plate and use a serrated knife to cut away any uneven spots on the top of the cake. Use an offset spatula to spread a layer of caramel sauce across the top of the cake. Then spread a layer of frosting over the caramel. Place the second cake layer upside down on top of the first layer and cover the top and sides of the cake with the remaining frosting. Use plastic or wooden dowels to secure

the cake and keep the layers from sliding (these are helpful because the caramel tends to spread as it comes back up to room temperature). Garnish the top of the cake with quartered figs and berries or fresh flowers or both, if desired. If using a cheese-based frosting, store the cake in the refrigerator for up to 2 days. If using buttercream, store the cake at room temperature in an airtight container or wrapped well in plastic for up to 2 days.

Notes: *To make the cake batter using a hand mixer: Put the flours, maple sugar, baking soda, salt, and cinnamon in a large mixing bowl. Stir together using a fork until combined. Put the egg whites and cream of tartar in a separate medium-sized mixing bowl. Beat using a hand mixer set on high speed until the eggs are very foamy and soft peaks are about to form; set aside. In separate bowl, combine the palm shortening, coconut milk, honey, almond extract, and vanilla. Beat on medium speed until combined. Transfer the palm shortening mixture to the dry ingredients, add the beaten egg whites, and then beat together on medium-low speed until combined. Transfer to the greased and parchment-lined cake pan(s) and bake as directed.*

Variations:

Caramel Maple Fig Cupcakes. *Adjust an oven rack to the middle position and preheat the oven to 350°F (177°C). Line a 12-cup muffin pan with paper liners. Use a spoon to transfer the batter into the lined cups, filling each about three-quarters full. Bake for 20 to 25 minutes or until a toothpick comes out clean. Let cool in the pan for 10 minutes, then remove to cool completely. Pipe or spread the frosting on top, then drizzle the caramel sauce on top of the frosting. Garnish with fig slices, berries, or flowers.*

Four-Layer Caramel Maple Fig Cake (pictured on next page). *To make the four-layer cake shown in the photos, line the bottoms of four 6-inch (15-cm) springform cake pans with parchment paper, then grease the paper and sides of the pans liberally with palm shortening; set aside. (If you have only two springform cake pans in this size, you can still make the cake; you will simply need to wait to make the second batch of batter until you've removed the first two cake layers from the oven, as explained below.)*

Prepare a double batch of the Salted Caramel Sauce and place in the refrigerator to cool while preparing the cake layers.

To make the cake layers, prepare one batch of batter at a time, following Steps 3 through 5, opposite. Bake the two cake layers, following Step 6. If you have four 6-inch (15-cm) springform cake pans, you can begin the second batch of batter while the first two cakes are baking and pop the second set of cakes in the oven as soon as the first two are removed. If you have only two pans, begin the second batch of batter after you've removed the first two cakes from the oven. While the second set of cake layers is cooling, make the frosting. To assemble the cake, follow the instructions for assembling a two-layer cake in Step 8, repeating the process for the third and fourth cake layers. Serves 8 to 10.

MAKE AHEAD

CAKE LAYERS—1 DAY AHEAD

Strawberry
CHEESECAKE CAKE

PREP TIME: 1 hour
COOK TIME: 1½ hours
READY IN: 2½ hours
YIELD: One 3-layer, 8-inch (20-cm) cake

1 recipe Graham Cracker Crust dough (page 170) or Simple Crust dough (page 172)

3 recipes Classic Yellow Cake (page 206) or White Cake (page 210) (see Notes)

Triple recipe Strawberry Cream Cheese Frosting (page 380) or Strawberry Lemonade Meringue Frosting (page 382)

MAKE AHEAD
CAKE LAYERS—1 DAY AHEAD

Notes: Because no more than a single batch of batter will fit in a large food processor at once, it's necessary to make the layers for this cake one at a time. To save time, use three identical pans if you have them; while one layer is baking, you can prepare the next one and rotate them out, popping the next layer in the oven as soon as the previous one is removed. If you have only two pans in this size, you will need to wait to make the batter for the second layer until after you've removed the first cake layer from the oven, and do the same with the third layer.

This is such a fun and incredibly delicious cake! It's as if a regular cake ate a strawberry cheesecake and then they had a baby. That doesn't make any sense, but you're smart, you get it.

1 Adjust an oven rack to the middle position and preheat the oven to 350°F (177°C). Line the bottoms of three 8-inch (20-cm) springform cake pans with parchment paper, then grease the paper and sides of the pans liberally with palm shortening; set aside.

2 Prepare the dough for the Graham Cracker Crust, following Steps 2 through 4 on page 170, or the Simple Crust, following Step 2 on page 172. Press the crust into the bottom of one of the prepared pans. Set the pan in the freezer to chill while you prepare the cake batter.

3 Make three individual batches of cake batter, one at a time, following Steps 2 through 4 in the cake recipe (see Notes for guidance on how best to stagger the making and baking of the three layers). Pour the first batch of batter into the chilled pan with the crust, using a rubber spatula to help scrape all the batter into the pan, and bake for 30 to 35 minutes or until a toothpick inserted into the center of the cake comes out clean.

4 Remove from the oven and let cool in the pan for 15 minutes. To remove the cake from the pan, run a knife around the edge between the cake and the pan, until they no longer touch. Remove from the pan and let cool completely.

5 Bake and cool the remaining two cake layers in the other two prepared cake pans as described above.

6 Once all three cake layers are completely cool, prepare a triple batch of the frosting.

7 To assemble: Place the cake layer with the crust on a cake plate. Use a serrated knife to cut away any uneven spots on the top of the cake. Pipe a dam of frosting around the edge of cake; this will keep the frosting from seeping over the edges once the second layer is placed. Place a dollop of frosting in the center of the cake and use an offset spatula to spread it across the cake until it reaches the dam edge. Set the second cake layer on top, pipe a dam of frosting around the edge, place a dollop of frosting in the center, and then use the spatula to spread the frosting across to the dam edge. Set the third cake layer on top, then frost the top and sides of all three layers, until completely covered. Store the cake in the refrigerator for up to 3 days.

Death by CHOCOLATE CAKE

PREP TIME: 20 minutes
COOK TIME: 40 to 50 minutes
READY IN: 1 hour
YIELD: One 2-layer, 6-inch (15-cm) cake or one single-layer, 8-inch (20-cm) cake (to make the 4-layer cake shown in the photos, see Variation)

Chocolate lovers only need apply. I'm pretty sure the title of this recipe gives everything away. If you've been reading closely, you know by now that I pretty much live for chocolate. It's my favorite of all the desserts in the land. So I needed a cake that would do my love for chocolate justice—that I could chocolate overdose on. Mission accomplished. I hope you enjoy this beauty as much as I do. I can't wait to see how much more chocolate depraved you make it.

FOR THE CAKE

2 cups (185 g) sifted fine-ground blanched almond flour

2 tablespoons coconut sugar

1 teaspoon baking soda

1 teaspoon fine-grain sea salt

¼ teaspoon ground cinnamon

2 cups (14 ounces/400 g) semisweet chocolate chips

1 cup (240 ml) canned full-fat coconut milk, room temperature

½ cup (115 g) palm shortening, plus more for the pan(s)

1 teaspoon vanilla extract

4 large eggs

FOR THE LAYERS AND GARNISH

1 recipe Ganache (pages 369 to 370), any type, divided

FOR THE FROSTING

1 recipe Chocolate Buttercream (page 396)

FOR GARNISH (OPTIONAL)

1 cup (7 ounces/200 g) chocolate chips

MAKE AHEAD
CAKE LAYERS—1 DAY AHEAD

1. Adjust an oven rack to the middle position and preheat the oven to 350°F (177°C). Line the bottoms of two 6-inch (15-cm) or one 8-inch (20-cm) springform cake pan(s) with parchment paper, then grease the paper and sides of the pan(s) liberally with palm shortening; set aside.

2. In a medium-sized bowl, combine the almond flour, coconut sugar, baking soda, salt, and cinnamon and stir together using a fork until mixed. Set aside.

3. Melt the 2 cups (400 g) of chocolate chips and coconut milk in a double boiler over low heat or in a large heatproof bowl set over a pan of gently simmering water. Stir together until smooth and combined. Then add the palm shortening and stir it into the mixture as it melts, until completely combined. Remove from the heat and let cool slightly.

4. Using a rubber spatula, stir the vanilla and eggs into the melted chocolate mixture. If you used a double boiler rather than a large mixing bowl set over a pan of water to melt the chocolate, transfer the melted chocolate and egg mixture to a large mixing bowl.

5. Gently fold the dry ingredients into the melted chocolate mixture using a rubber spatula or whisk until just combined. Overmixing could cause the middle of the cake to sink.

6. Transfer the batter to the prepared cake pan(s) and use a rubber spatula to help scrape all the batter into the pan(s). Bake for 47 to 50 minutes for an 8-inch (20-cm) cake or 40 to 45 minutes for two 6-inch (15-cm) cakes, or until a toothpick inserted into the center comes out clean. Let cool in the pan(s) for 15 minutes. To remove the cake from the pan, run a knife around the edge between the cake and the pan, until they no longer touch. Remove the cake from the pan and let cool completely.

7. Once the cake is completely cool, prepare the ganache and Chocolate Buttercream. Let the ganache cool slightly, then transfer two-thirds of it to a piping bag or to a resealable plastic bag with a corner cut off.

8 To assemble: If making a single-layer, 8-inch (20-cm) cake, place the cake on a cake plate and use an offset spatula to frost the top and sides with the buttercream. Drizzle the ganache on top and sprinkle with the chocolate chips. If making a two-layer cake, place a cake layer on a cake plate and use a serrated knife to cut away any uneven spots on the top of the cake. Pipe a dam of ganache around the edge of the cake to keep the frosting from seeping over the edges. Place a large dollop of ganache in the center of the cake and use an offset spatula to spread it across until it reaches the dam edge. Place the second cake layer upside down on top of the first layer. Spread the buttercream over the top and sides of the cake. Pouring the remaining one-third of the ganache over the top and garnish with the chocolate chips. (The ganache may need to be gently reheated if it has cooled too much.) Store the cake at room temperature in an airtight container or wrapped well in plastic for up to 2 days.

Notes: If using a light-colored aluminum pan, you may need to add additional baking time.

*Variation: **Four-Layer Death by Chocolate Cake (pictured on next page).** The cake shown in the photos was made with four 8-inch (20-cm) layers. To make the layers for this cake, prepare two single batches of batter and then bake two cake layers at a time. A double batch of batter would be hard to fit in a bowl. To save time, use four identical pans; while one set of cakes is baking, you can prepare the second set and then rotate them into the oven when the first set is done.*

When the second set of cakes is baked, out of the oven, and completely cool, prepare a triple batch of the ganache and a double batch of the Chocolate Buttercream. Let the ganache cool slightly and transfer two-thirds of it to a piping bag or to a resealable plastic bag with a corner cut off.

To assemble, follow the guidelines for a two-layer cake in Step 8, repeating the process until all the layers are stacked and frosted. Garnish with 1 (12-ounce/340-g) bag of chocolate chips. Serves 10 to 12.

Salted
CARAMEL CUPCAKES

PREP TIME: 25 minutes
COOK TIME: 23 to 25 minutes
READY IN: 50 minutes
YIELD: 1 dozen cupcakes

Salted caramel is one of the best things in life. If I see salted caramel anything, I have to have it. These cupcakes are the cure for any salted caramel crisis you may be going through. I love this recipe because it's easy to whip up, and you can get really creative with different cake pairings. The Classic Yellow Cake (page 206) and the Chocolate Cupcakes (page 226) would also be great options. It almost sounds like we are wedding cake tasting or something. Did someone say cake tasting? I want to go!

1 recipe White Cupcakes (page 211)

FOR THE SALTED CARAMEL FROSTING

1 recipe Salted Caramel Sauce (page 374)

16 tablespoons (8 ounces/225 g) unsalted butter, room temperature

FOR GARNISH (OPTIONAL)

Coarse or flake sea salt

MAKE AHEAD
WHITE CUPCAKES—1 DAY AHEAD

1 Prepare the White Cupcakes.

2 Once the cupcakes have cooled, prepare the frosting: Begin by making the Salted Caramel Sauce, then remove from the heat and let cool to room temperature.

3 Once the caramel sauce is cool, put the butter in a mixing bowl and beat with a hand mixer set on low speed. As the butter continues to soften, gradually increase the mixer speed to high until the butter is light and fluffy. With the mixer on, add all but about 2 tablespoons of the caramel sauce to the butter in three additions, beating well after each addition, until combined. Set the pan with the reserved caramel sauce aside.

4 To assemble: Transfer the frosting to a piping bag fitted with the desired tip (an Ateco 847 was used for the cupcakes pictured; the cupcakes can also be frosted with a small offset spatula). Pipe the frosting on top of the cupcakes, then drizzle some of the reserved caramel sauce over the top. Garnish each cupcake with a small pinch of salt, if desired. Store at room temperature in an airtight container or wrapped well in plastic for up to 2 days.

No-Bake Strawberry CHEESECAKE JARS

PREP TIME: 15 minutes
SETTING TIME: 6 hours
READY IN: 6 hours 15 minutes
YIELD: 4 servings

I like single-serving desserts. They keep me in check. Instead of eating an entire cheesecake, I can eat just one of these guys and I'm totally content. Not only that, but how fun is it to eat stuff out of cute little jars? It makes me feel so fancy.

1 recipe Graham Cracker Crust (page 170) or 1 cup (230 g) store-bought gluten-free graham cracker crumbs (see Notes)

1 recipe Strawberry Sauce (page 378)

FOR THE FILLING

1 heaping cup (170 g) raw cashew pieces, soaked in water for at least 4 hours or preferably overnight

¼ cup (60 ml) melted coconut oil

2 tablespoons canned full-fat coconut milk

2 tablespoons pure maple syrup, dark

2 teaspoons vanilla extract

½ cup (90 g) peeled and diced zucchini

2 tablespoons coconut sugar

⅛ teaspoon fine-grain sea salt

1 to 3 tablespoons fresh-squeezed lemon juice

SPECIAL EQUIPMENT

Four 8-ounce (240-ml) wide-mouth mason jars

1   If using store-bought gluten-free graham cracker crumbs, skip ahead to Step 2; otherwise, prepare the Graham Cracker Crust and set aside to cool. Once cool, crumble the crust by hand or using a fork.

2   Prepare the Strawberry Sauce and store in the refrigerator until ready to use.

3   To make the filling: Drain the soaked cashew pieces and place them in a blender; process until the cashews are somewhat broken down. Add the coconut oil, coconut milk, maple syrup, and vanilla and blend until smooth. Then add the zucchini, coconut sugar, salt, and 1 tablespoon of lemon juice and blend again until a smooth and creamy batter has formed. Taste the mixture and add more lemon juice, 1 tablespoon at a time, as needed; the flavor should be lightly lemony but not overdone. Blend one more time to combine the additional juice, if added.

4   Divide the graham cracker crumbs among four 8-ounce (240-ml) wide-mouth mason jars, reserving some crumbs for garnish. Then pour the cheesecake filling evenly into the jars, leaving about an inch of space at the top for the Strawberry Sauce. Place the jars in the freezer to set for at least 2 hours.

5   Remove the jars from the freezer 15 minutes prior to serving to allow them to thaw. Use a big spoon to top each jar with a large dollop of the Strawberry Sauce, then sprinkle the reserved graham cracker crumbs on top for garnish. Store in the freezer for up to 2 weeks. Let thaw for 15 minutes before eating.

Notes: The Kinnikinnick brand is my go-to for store-bought gluten-free graham cracker crumbs.

Subs: 2 tablespoons of unsweetened vanilla almond milk or cashew milk in place of the coconut milk.

S'mores CUPCAKES

PREP TIME: 30 minutes
COOK TIME: 20 minutes
READY IN: 1 hour
YIELD: 18 cupcakes

The idea for these cupcakes came to me in my pre-Paleo days—the days when cute little cupcake shops started popping up everywhere, selling all kinds of flirty flavors. I thought to myself, "How delicious would it be if there was a s'mores cupcake?" It would have a graham cracker bottom, a chocolate cake center, and then a toasted marshmallow topping for the frosting. Follow your dreams; they may lead to cupcakes.

1 recipe Graham Cracker Crust dough (page 170)

1 recipe Chocolate Cupcake batter (page 226)

1 recipe Marshmallow Crème, regular (page 366) or egg-free (page 368)

SPECIAL EQUIPMENT
Kitchen torch

MAKE AHEAD
CHOCOLATE CUPCAKE BATTER—
1 DAY AHEAD

1. Line a 12-cup muffin pan with paper liners. Prepare the dough for the Graham Cracker Crust, following Steps 2 through 4 on page 170. Press the crust evenly into the cupcake liners, about one-quarter of the way up or ¼ inch (6 mm) thick. Set the leftover dough aside. Place the muffin pan in the freezer to chill the crusts while preparing the cupcake batter, or for at least 15 minutes.

2. Adjust an oven rack to the middle position and preheat the oven to 350°F (177°C). Prepare the batter for the Chocolate Cupcakes, following Steps 2 through 5 on page 226. Use a cookie scoop or large spoon to transfer the batter into the cupcake liners, on top of the Graham Cracker Crust, filling each about two-thirds full; the cupcakes will rise slightly when baking. Bake for 20 minutes or until a toothpick comes out clean. Let cool in the pan for about 10 minutes, then remove from the pan to cool completely. Repeat the process with the remaining crust dough and batter.

3. Once the second batch has cooled, prepare the Marshmallow Crème, then transfer the crème to a piping bag fitted with the desired tip (an Ateco 808 tip was used to frost the cupcakes pictured; the cupcakes can also be frosted with a small offset spatula). Pipe the crème onto the cupcakes, then toast the tops and edges of the crème using a kitchen torch. Store at room temperature in an airtight container or wrapped well in plastic for up to 2 days.

Notes: You want to chill the crusts first because they bake quicker than the cupcakes. By having the crusts at a colder temperature, they will bake at a slower rate, matching that of the cupcakes. An quicker alternative is to use Kinnikinnick Gluten-Free Graham Style Crumbs. Use the recipe on the back of the box and you'll be good to go!

You will notice that the yield is 18 as opposed to the standard dozen. This is due to the fact that the cupcakes have a graham cracker bottom. Therefore, you are using less batter per cupcake, leaving you with enough ingredients for 6 additional cupcakes. Who is going to complain about more cupcakes? Not me!

I prefer to use the egg white–based Marshmallow Crème for this recipe because I find that it toasts better and gives more of a classic s'mores look and taste.

Chocolate Dream
CHEESECAKE

PREP TIME: 15 minutes
SETTING TIME: 8 hours
READY IN: 8 hours 15 minutes
YIELD: One 8-inch (20-cm) cheesecake

If I've taught you anything by now, you know that chocolate makes everything better. Especially cheesecake. This recipe is great for chocoholics and cheesecake aficionados. It's super easy to make and tastes just like the real stuff; you won't feel like you're missing a thing.

1 recipe Fauxreo Crust dough (page 168)

FOR THE FILLING

2 cups (310 g) raw cashew pieces, soaked in water for at least 4 hours or preferably overnight

¼ cup (60 ml) melted coconut oil

¼ cup (60 ml) canned full-fat coconut milk

¼ cup (60 ml) pure maple syrup, dark

2 teaspoons vanilla extract

1 cup (185 g) peeled and diced zucchini

½ cup (35 g) cacao powder or unsweetened cocoa powder

¼ cup (40 g) coconut sugar

¼ teaspoon fine-grain sea salt

1 to 3 tablespoons fresh-squeezed lemon juice, or to taste

FOR GARNISH (OPTIONAL)

Unsweetened cocoa powder

¼ cup (50 g) chocolate chips, for drizzling

2 tablespoons chopped chocolate

2 tablespoons chopped pistachios

MAKE AHEAD
FAUXREO CRUST—
1 WEEK AHEAD: KEEP FROZEN
UNTIL READY TO USE

1 Line an 8-inch (20-cm) springform cake pan with parchment paper; set aside.

2 Prepare the dough for the Fauxreo Crust, following Step 2 on page 168. Press the dough into the prepared pan and place in the freezer to set.

3 To make the filling: Drain the soaked cashews and put them in a blender; process until the cashews are somewhat broken down. Add the coconut oil, coconut milk, maple syrup, and vanilla and blend until smooth. Then add the zucchini, cocoa powder, coconut sugar, salt, and 1 tablespoon of lemon juice and blend again until a smooth and creamy batter has formed. Taste the mixture and add more lemon juice, 1 tablespoon at a time, as needed; the flavor should be lightly lemony but not overdone. Blend one more time to combine the additional juice, if added.

4 Remove the crust from the freezer and pour the cheesecake filling evenly into it. Place back in the freezer to set for at least 4 hours.

5 Remove the cheesecake from the freezer 20 minutes prior to serving to allow it to thaw. Remove the thawed cheesecake from the pan. Melt the chocolate chips in a microwave-safe bowl. Sprinkle cocoa powder over the top (if using), use a spoon to drizzle with melted chocolate (if using), and garnish as desired. Store in the freezer for up to 2 weeks. Let thaw for 15 minutes before eating.

Notes: To make this cheesecake dairy-free, use the Dairy-Free Ganache.

Depending on the type of lemon you use, the flavor could be stronger or weaker. That's why I recommending adding and tasting as you go to get the perfect flavor. It may take more or less of the recommended amount.

Subs: Unsweetened vanilla almond milk in place of the coconut milk.

Key Lime
CHEESECAKE CUPS

PREP TIME: 15 minutes
SETTING TIME: 6 hours
READY IN: 6 hours 15 minutes
YIELD: 1 dozen cheesecake cups

Put the lime in the coconut . . . or cheesecake, if you will. These cheesecake cups are a must-make for any Key lime pie fan out there. They are completely dairy-free and no-bake, and they include hidden veggies. Who doesn't like hidden veggies? The zucchini makes all the difference and adds a smooth, velvety texture that can't be beat.

½ recipe Simple Crust dough
(page 172)

FOR THE FILLING

1 heaping cup (170 g) raw cashew pieces, soaked in water for at least 4 hours or preferably overnight

¼ cup (60 ml) melted coconut oil

2 tablespoons canned full-fat coconut milk

2 tablespoons pure maple syrup, dark

1 teaspoon vanilla extract

½ cup (90 g) peeled and diced zucchini

2 tablespoons coconut sugar

⅛ teaspoon fine-grain sea salt

2 tablespoons fresh-squeezed lemon juice, plus more if needed

2 tablespoons fresh-squeezed lime juice, plus more if needed

2 teaspoons grated lime zest

1 recipe Whipped Cream (page 372) or Whipped Coconut Cream (page 373), for serving

12 thin lime wedges, for garnish

SPECIAL EQUIPMENT

12 standard-size silicone baking cups or foil liners

1 Line a 12-cup muffin pan with silicone baking cups or foil liners.

2 Prepare a half recipe of the Simple Crust dough, following Step 2 on page 172. Press the dough into the lined cups, making each crust about ¼ inch (6 mm) thick; place in the freezer to set while preparing the cheesecake filling.

3 To make the filling: Drain the soaked cashew pieces and put them in a blender; process until the cashews are somewhat broken down. Add the coconut oil, coconut milk, maple syrup, and vanilla and blend until smooth. Then add the zucchini, coconut sugar, salt, lemon juice, lime juice, and zest. Blend again until a smooth and creamy batter has formed. Taste the mixture and add a little more lemon and lime juice if needed; the flavor should be lightly citrusy but not overdone. Blend one more time to combine the additional juice, if added.

4 Pour the cheesecake filling evenly into the crust-lined cups, filling each about three-quarters full. Place the muffin pan in the freezer to set for 2 to 4 hours or until firm.

5 Remove the pan from the freezer 15 minutes prior to serving to give the cheesecake cups time to thaw. While waiting for them to thaw, prepare the whipped cream. Leave the cheesecakes in their baking cups or carefully remove them if desired. Either pipe or use a spoon to top each cheesecake cup with a large dollop of whipped cream, then garnish with a lime wedge. The ungarnished cheesecake cups can be stored in the freezer for up to 2 weeks. Let thaw for 15 minutes and garnish just before serving.

Notes: To make these cups dairy-free, use the Whipped Coconut Cream.

Depending on the types of lemons and limes you use, the flavor could be stronger or weaker. That's why I recommending adding and tasting as you go to get the perfect flavor. It may take more or less than the recommended amount.

Subs: 2 tablespoons of unsweetened vanilla almond milk or cashew milk in place of the coconut milk.

ROCKY ROAD
CUPCAKES

PREP TIME: 45 minutes
COOK TIME: 20 to 25 minutes
READY IN: 1 hour 5 minutes
YIELD: 1 dozen cupcakes

These might be my favorite cupcakes. They are so fun to make and even more fun to eat. Chocolate cake, chocolate buttercream, and a marshmallow top—what's not to love? Don't forget about the chopped almond garnish, either. All these flavors were just meant to be together. They're the four best friends that anyone could have.

1 recipe Chocolate Cupcakes (page 226)

1 recipe Chocolate Buttercream (page 396)

1 recipe Marshmallow Crème, regular (page 366) or egg-free (page 368)

4 ounces (115 g) unsalted dry-roasted almond pieces, for garnish

MAKE AHEAD
CHOCOLATE CUPCAKES—1 DAY AHEAD

1 Prepare the Chocolate Cupcakes, following Steps 1 through 6 on page 226.

2 While the cupcakes cool, prepare the Chocolate Buttercream. Transfer the frosting to a piping bag fitted with the desired tip (a Wilton 1A is best; the cupcakes can also be frosted with a small offset spatula). Pipe the buttercream in a circle around each cupcake, starting at the edge and leaving the center unfrosted.

3 Prepare the Marshmallow Crème. Immediately transfer it to a piping bag fitted with the desired tip (a Wilton 1A or 1C is best). Note that the Egg-Free Marshmallow Crème will thicken as it sits and eventually will become firm and difficult to pipe; therefore, make sure to work quickly if using this crème. Pipe the Marshmallow Crème into the unfrosted center area of each cupcake. Garnish with a sprinkle of almond pieces. Store at room temperature in an airtight container or wrapped well in plastic for up to 2 days.

Notes: If you didn't let the chocolate cool enough before adding it to the buttercream, the warm chocolate will soften the butter, and the frosting may need to be refrigerated to firm up and then beaten again before using.

Molten Chocolate
LAVA CAKE

PREP TIME: 20 minutes
SETTING TIME: 30 minutes
COOK TIME: 15 to 18 minutes
READY IN: 1 hour 5 minutes
YIELD: 4 servings

Rumor has it that molten chocolate lava cakes were actually a catering disaster. The dessert for the event was supposed to be individual chocolate cakes, but someone accidentally took them out of the oven too early, and when they served them to the dinner guests, they weren't cooked all the way through in the middle. So the chef just rolled with it and told the guests that they were "Chocolate Lava Cakes." Genius. And that's how the greatest dessert ever was born.

5 tablespoons (2½ ounces/70 g) salted butter, plus more for the ramekins

1 cup (7 ounces/200 g) semisweet chocolate chips

2 tablespoons fine-ground blanched almond flour

1 heaping tablespoon cacao powder or unsweetened cocoa powder

⅛ teaspoon fine-grain sea salt

2 large eggs

2 large egg yolks

3 tablespoons coconut sugar

¼ teaspoon vanilla extract

Hot water for the baking dish

FOR GARNISH (OPTIONAL)

Cacao powder or unsweetened cocoa powder

Arrowroot flour or tapioca flour, for dusting (to resemble powdered sugar)

Fresh raspberries

1. Grease four 7-ounce (210-ml) ramekins liberally with butter; set aside. Melt the butter and chocolate chips in a double boiler over low heat or in a heatproof bowl set over a pan of gently simmering water. Stir frequently, using a rubber spatula, until completely melted and combined. Remove from the heat and let sit until the bowl is relatively cool to the touch. While the chocolate is cooling, prepare the other ingredients.

2. In a small mixing bowl, combine the almond flour, cacao powder, and salt. Use a fork to stir together until well combined; set aside.

3. In a large mixing bowl, whisk together the eggs, egg yolks, coconut sugar, and vanilla until frothy. Use a rubber spatula to transfer and fold the chocolate into the egg and sugar mixture. Then sift in the almond flour mixture and whisk until combined.

4. Pour the batter evenly into the ramekins. Tap lightly on the counter to remove air bubbles. Refrigerate uncovered for 30 minutes to set.

5. After about 15 minutes, adjust an oven rack to the middle position and preheat the oven to 425°F (218°C). Place the ramekins in a 13 by 9-inch (33 by 23-cm) baking dish. Carefully pour hot water (tap or boiled) into the baking dish and around the ramekins until it reaches halfway up the sides of the ramekins. Bake for 15 to 18 minutes or until the edges look finished but the middles appear undone. Remove the ramekins from the baking dish and let cool for at least 10 minutes.

6. To serve: Slide a butter knife around the edge of a ramekin to pull the cake away from the sides, then turn it upside down over a plate and tap the bottom firmly until the cake slides out. Garnish with sifted cacao powder, raspberries, or any other desired toppings. Repeat with the remaining cakes. Store any leftovers, ungarnished, in the refrigerator for up to 1 day, then reheat in the microwave for 30 seconds before garnishing and eating.

MAKE AHEAD

CAKE BATTER—1 WEEK AHEAD: STORE COVERED IN RAMEKINS. THEN BAKE AS DESCRIBED

Salted Caramel
CHEESECAKE BITES

PREP TIME: 15 minutes
SETTING TIME: 6 hours
READY IN: 6 hours 15 minutes
YIELD: 2 dozen bites

I've included this recipe because . . . caramel. This recipe was previously published on my blog and the response was overwhelming! People LOVE this recipe. Their biggest complaint? They can't get the caramel to the cheesecake fast enough; they end up eating it all first. These are so my people.

½ recipe Simple Crust dough (page 172)

1 recipe Salted Caramel Sauce (page 374)

FOR THE FILLING

1 heaping cup (170 g) raw cashew pieces, soaked in water for at least 4 hours or preferably overnight

¼ cup (60 ml) melted coconut oil

2 tablespoons canned full-fat coconut milk

2 tablespoons pure maple syrup, dark

2 teaspoons vanilla extract

½ cup (90 g) peeled and diced zucchini

2 tablespoons coconut sugar

⅛ teaspoon fine-grain sea salt

2 tablespoons fresh-squeezed lemon juice, plus more if needed

FOR GARNISH

2 teaspoons coarsely ground sea salt or sea salt flakes, for garnish

SPECIAL EQUIPMENT

12 mini silicone baking cups or foil liners

1. Line a mini (24-cup) muffin pan with silicone baking cups or foil liners; set aside.

2. Prepare a half recipe of the Simple Crust and press the dough into each cupcake liner, about ¼ inch (6 mm) high. Place in the freezer to set.

3. Prepare the Salted Caramel Sauce and place in the refrigerator until ready to use.

4. To make the filling: Drain the soaked cashew pieces and put them in a blender; process until the cashews are somewhat broken down. Add the coconut oil, coconut milk, maple syrup, and vanilla and blend until smooth. Then add the zucchini, coconut sugar, salt, and 2 tablespoons of lemon juice and blend until a smooth and creamy batter has formed. Taste and add a little more lemon juice if needed; the flavor should be lightly lemony but not overdone. Blend one more time to combine the additional lemon juice, if added.

5. Remove the crusts from the freezer and pour the cheesecake filling evenly into the liners, leaving about ¼ inch of space at the top for the caramel. Place back in the freezer to set for at least 2 hours.

6. Remove the mini cheesecakes from the freezer 15 minutes prior to serving to allow them to thaw. Transfer the caramel sauce to a piping bag or to a resealable plastic bag with a corner cut off. Squeeze a dollop of caramel on top of each cheesecake bite, then garnish with a sprinkle of sea salt. Store in the freezer for up to 2 weeks. Let thaw for 15 minutes before serving.

Notes: To make these cheesecake bites dairy-free, use ghee rather than butter in the Salted Caramel Sauce.

Depending on the type of lemon you use, the flavor could be stronger or weaker. That's why I recommending tasting to determine if more is needed to get the perfect flavor.

Subs: Unsweetened vanilla almond milk or unsweetened cashew milk in place of the coconut milk.

MAKE AHEAD

SIMPLE CRUST—1 DAY AHEAD: STORE COVERED AT ROOM TEMPERATURE

SALTED CARAMEL SAUCE—3 DAYS AHEAD: STORE IN THE REFRIGERATOR

"Reese's" CHEESECAKE

PREP TIME: 15 minutes
SETTING TIME: 8 hours
READY IN: 8 hours 15 minutes
YIELD: One 8-inch (20-cm) cheesecake

My favorite candy of all time is Reese's Peanut Butter Cups. Favorite as in, if the zombie apocalypse were to occur, I would be like Woody Harrelson and his Twinkies in Zombieland, searching everywhere for just one Reese's Peanut Butter Cup. Mmm . . . Reese's. Anyway, believe it or not, Reese's aren't Paleo. Not even remotely. I know, total bummer, but fret not, I've got you covered. This recipe is a game-changer: By the last bite you won't even remember what a Reese's Cup is, let alone miss it.

1 recipe Fauxreo Crust dough (page 168)

FOR THE FILLING

2 cups (310 g) raw cashew pieces, soaked in water for at least 4 hours or preferably overnight

¼ cup (60 ml) melted coconut oil

¼ cup (60 ml) canned full-fat coconut milk

¼ cup (60 ml) pure maple syrup, dark

1 tablespoon vanilla extract

1 cup (185 g) peeled and diced zucchini

½ cup (115 g) smooth almond butter

¼ cup (40 g) coconut sugar

¼ teaspoon fine-grain sea salt

1 to 3 tablespoons fresh-squeezed lemon juice

TOPPINGS

1 recipe Ganache (pages 369 to 370), any type

6 Almond Butter Cups (page 146) or store-bought nut butter or sunflower seed butter cups, coarsely chopped

1 Line an 8-inch (20-cm) springform cake pan with parchment paper; set aside.

2 Prepare the dough for the Fauxreo Crust, following Step 2 on page 168. Press the dough into the prepared cake pan. Place in the freezer to set.

3 To make the filling: Drain the soaked cashew pieces and put them in a blender; process until the cashews are somewhat broken down. Add the coconut oil, coconut milk, maple syrup, and vanilla and blend until smooth. Then add the zucchini, almond butter, coconut sugar, salt, and 1 tablespoon of lemon juice and blend again until a smooth and creamy batter has formed. Taste and add more lemon juice, 1 tablespoon at a time, as needed; the flavor should be lightly lemony but not overdone. Blend one more time to combine the additional lemon juice, if added.

4 Remove the crust from the freezer and pour the cheesecake batter evenly into the pan. Place back in the freezer to set for at least 4 hours.

5 Remove the cheesecake from the freezer 20 minutes prior to serving. Prepare the ganache and let cool to barely warm or room temperature but still pourable; if poured while still hot, it may melt the cheesecake as well as the almond butter cup garnish. Once the ganache has cooled, remove the cheesecake from the pan and pour the ganache over the top, letting it drip down the sides, then garnish with the crushed Almond Butter Cups. Another option is to reserve some ganache and transfer it to a resealable plastic bag, cut off a corner, and drizzle the ganache over the Almond Butter Cups (as pictured). Serve immediately. Store leftovers in the freezer for up to 2 weeks; allow to thaw for 15 to 20 minutes before serving.

Notes: *To make this cheesecake dairy-free, use the Dairy-Free Ganache.*

My favorite almond butter on planet Earth is smooth Barney Butter. You can find it in most health food stores, like Whole Foods and Sprouts.

Depending on the type of lemon you use, the lemon flavor could be stronger or weaker. That's why I recommending adding and tasting as you go to get it perfect.

Subs: *Unsweetened vanilla almond milk in place of the coconut milk.*

Bourbon Butter
PECAN CUPCAKES

PREP TIME: 35 minutes
COOK TIME: 20 to 25 minutes
READY IN: 55 minutes
YIELD: 1 dozen cupcakes

I love adult cupcakes—you know, the boozy ones. These cupcakes are kind of like that, but with only a hint of the good stuff in the frosting. I'm also a huge fan of butter pecan anything, because, well, it's incredibly delicious. I like alcohol too, but that's another story for another time.

1 recipe Chocolate Cupcakes (page 226)

FOR THE FROSTING

17 tablespoons (8½ ounces/240 g) unsalted butter, divided

½ cup (60 g) raw pecan pieces

12 raw pecan halves

2½ teaspoons vanilla extract, divided

¼ cup (40 g) coconut sugar

¼ teaspoon ground cinnamon

⅛ teaspoon fine-grain sea salt

½ cup (65 g) maple sugar

2 tablespoons bourbon

MAKE AHEAD
CHOCOLATE CUPCAKES—1 DAY AHEAD

1. Make the Chocolate Cupcakes, following Steps 1 through 6 on page 226. Once the cupcakes have cooled, prepare the frosting.

2. To make the frosting: Melt 1 tablespoon of the butter in a skillet set over medium heat. Add the pecan pieces and halves and use a spatula to move them around the pan, coating them in the melted butter. Then add ½ teaspoon of the vanilla and stir. Continue to cook the pecans until lightly toasted, about 5 to 7 minutes, stirring occasionally. Meanwhile, combine the coconut sugar, cinnamon, and salt in a small mixing bowl and stir together using a fork. When the pecans are done, toss them in the coconut sugar mixture until evenly coated. Transfer the coated pecans to a metal sieve, tapping the edges to remove any excess sugar. Then pick out the pecan halves for garnish and place the pecan pieces back in the bowl until ready to use.

3. In a mixing bowl, beat the remaining 1 cup (16 tablespoons/225 g) of butter and maple sugar together with a hand mixer set on low speed, gradually increasing the speed, until smooth and combined. Then beat in the bourbon and the remaining 2 teaspoons of vanilla until combined. Using a rubber spatula, stir the toasted pecan pieces and coconut sugar mixture into the butter mixture until combined.

4. To assemble: Use an ice cream scoop or large cookie scoop to place the frosting on top of each cupcake, then garnish with a pecan half. Store at room temperature in an airtight container or wrapped well in plastic for up to 2 days.

Notes: *If you don't have bourbon on hand, you can use plain ol' whiskey instead; it will work just fine.*

Chocolate-Covered
STRAWBERRY CUPCAKES

PREP TIME: 35 minutes
COOK TIME: 20 to 25 minutes
READY IN: 55 minutes
YIELD: 1 dozen cupcakes

Valentine's Day cupcakes, anyone? These are great whether you have a sig other or not. I mean, look at them; they have chocolate-covered strawberries on top. You can hold them close, make a toast, and celebrate your love for them. Or you can make them for your single friends on Valentine's Day. That would be the nice thing to do. Just don't eat them all first, because that would be mean.

1 recipe Chocolate Cupcakes (page 226)

1 recipe Strawberry Cream Cheese Frosting (page 380) or Strawberry Lemonade Meringue Frosting (page 382)

FOR THE CHOCOLATE-COVERED STRAWBERRIES

1 (3-ounce/85-g) dark chocolate bar (63% to 85% cacao), chopped or broken into pieces, for dipping

¼ cup (1¾ ounces/50 g) milk chocolate chips, for drizzling (optional)

12 large fresh strawberries with stems

MAKE AHEAD
CHOCOLATE CUPCAKES—1 DAY AHEAD
CHOCOLATE-COVERED
STRAWBERRIES—1 DAY AHEAD

1. Prepare the Chocolate Cupcakes, following Steps 1 through 6 on page 226.

2. Once the cupcakes have cooled, prepare the frosting.

3. To make the chocolate-covered strawberries: Melt the dark chocolate in a double boiler over low heat or in a heatproof bowl set over a pan of gently simmering water. Stir frequently, using a rubber spatula, until the chocolate is completely melted and smooth. Remove from the heat. Repeat the process with the milk chocolate chips, if using. Let cool slightly so that the chocolate is still warm enough to pipe smoothly, but not hot. Then transfer the milk chocolate to a piping bag or resealable plastic bag with a corner cut off.

4. Lay out a sheet of parchment paper. Holding each strawberry by the stem, dip it into the melted chocolate, lift to let the excess chocolate drip back into the bowl, and then place on the parchment paper to set. Let harden slightly, then drizzle the milk chocolate over the dark, if desired. Place the chocolate-covered strawberries in the refrigerator for 10 minutes to harden completely.

5. To assemble: Transfer the frosting to a piping bag fitted with the desired tip (such as a Wilton 1A) and pipe it onto the cupcakes, or frost each cupcake by hand using a small offset spatula. Then place a chocolate-covered strawberry on top of each frosted cupcake. Store in the refrigerator for up to 2 days.

Notes: To make these cupcakes dairy-free, use the Strawberry Lemonade Meringue Frosting and omit the milk chocolate chips.

Another frosting option would be to beat ½ cup of Strawberry Sauce (page 378) or store-bought no-sugar-added strawberry fruit spread into the Vanilla Buttercream (page 394).

RED, WHITE, AND
BLUEBERRY CUPCAKES

PREP TIME: 25 minutes
COOK TIME: 25 minutes
READY IN: 50 minutes
YIELD: 1 dozen cupcakes

One of my favorite holidays to bake for, oddly enough, is the Fourth of July. You can get so creative with the red, white, and blue theme and make so many great things. From tarts to pies to cupcakes, you can use blueberries paired with any red fruit, like raspberries, strawberries, or cherries. So many possibilities. Don't you just love possibilities?

1 recipe Classic Yellow Cupcakes (page 207) or White Cupcakes (page 211)

1 recipe Whipped Cream (page 372) or Whipped Coconut Cream (page 373)

FOR GARNISH

½ cup (3 ounces/85 g) fresh blueberries

½ cup (3 ounces/85 g) fresh raspberries

1 Prepare the cupcakes.

2 One the cupcakes have cooled, prepare the whipped cream. Transfer to a piping bag fitted with the desired tip.

3 To assemble: Frost each cupcake with the whipped cream, then garnish with blueberries and raspberries. Store in the refrigerator for up to 2 days.

Notes: To make these dairy-free, use the White Cupcakes and top them with Whipped Coconut Cream.

MAKE AHEAD
CUPCAKES—1 DAY AHEAD

Spooky
HALLOWEEN CAKE

PREP TIME: 20 minutes
COOK TIME: 30 to 50 minutes
READY IN: 50 minutes
YIELD: One 2-layer, 6-inch (15-cm) cake or one single-layer, 8-inch (20-cm) cake (to make the tiered cake shown in the photos, see Variation)

I love making holiday-inspired cakes because you can get so creative with props and presentation. I imagined this cake when I went into a craft store and walked by the Halloween scrapbooking section. I immediately got the idea to use scrapbooking supplies to decorate a cake and then use natural red food coloring for an even spookier effect. Muahahahahahahaha (evil Halloween laugh). This cake would be great for a Halloween party for kids and adults alike!

FOR THE CHOCOLATE CAKE

2 cups (185 g) sifted fine-grain blanched almond flour

2 tablespoons coconut sugar

1 teaspoon baking soda

1 teaspoon fine-grain sea salt

¼ teaspoon ground cinnamon

2 cups (14 ounces/400 g) semisweet chocolate chips

1 cup (240 ml) canned full-fat coconut milk

½ cup (115 g) palm shortening, plus more for greasing

1 teaspoon vanilla extract

4 large eggs

FOR THE FROSTING

1 recipe Cream Cheese Frosting (page 398), Mascarpone and Goat Cheese Frosting (page 402), or Vanilla Buttercream (page 394)

1 Adjust an oven rack to the middle position and preheat the oven to 350°F (177°C). Line the bottoms of two 6-inch (15-cm) or one 8-inch (20-cm) springform cake pan(s) with parchment paper, then grease the paper and sides of the pan(s) liberally with palm shortening; set aside.

2 In a medium-sized bowl, combine the almond flour, coconut sugar, baking soda, salt, and cinnamon and stir together using a fork until mixed; set aside.

3 Melt the chocolate chips and coconut milk in a double boiler over low heat or in a large heatproof bowl set over a pan of gently simmering water. Stir intermittently, using a rubber spatula, until the chocolate is completely melted and combined with the coconut milk. Remove from the heat.

4 Using a rubber spatula, stir in the palm shortening. Then stir the vanilla and eggs into the melted chocolate mixture. If you used a double boiler rather than a mixing bowl set over a pan of water to melt the chocolate, transfer the melted chocolate and egg mixture to a large mixing bowl.

5 Using the rubber spatula, gently fold the dry ingredients into the melted chocolate mixture until just combined. Overmixing could cause the middle of the cake to sink.

6 Transfer the batter to the prepared cake pan(s) and use a rubber spatula to help scrape all the batter into the pan(s). Bake for 45 to 50 minutes for an 8-inch (20-cm) cake or 30 minutes for two 6-inch (15-cm) cakes, or until a toothpick inserted into the center comes out clean. Let cool in the pan(s) for 15 minutes, then run a knife along the edge of the pan to loosen the cake. Remove and let cool completely before assembling and frosting.

7 Once the cake has cooled completely, prepare the frosting. If making a two-layer cake, place one-third of the frosting in a piping bag fitted with the desired tip.

8 To assemble: If making a single-layer cake, place the cake on a cake plate and use an offset spatula to cover the top and sides with the frosting. If making a two-layer cake, place the first cake layer on a cake plate and use a serrated knife to cut away any uneven spots on the top of the cake. Pipe a dam of frosting around the edge of the cake to keep the frosting from seeping over the edge. Then place a large dollop of frosting in the center of the cake and use an offset spatula to spread it across until it reaches the dam edge. Place the second cake layer upside down on top of the first layer, then spread the remaining frosting over the top and sides of both layers. Garnish as desired (see page 60 for decorating ideas). Store in the refrigerator for up to 2 days.

Notes: If using a light-colored aluminum pan, you may need to add additional baking time.

Variation: **Halloween Party Cake (pictured on next page).** *This cake shown in the photos consists of three 8-inch (20-cm) layers and two 6-inch (15-cm) layers. You will need to make four individual batches of batter. (I suggest doing it this way because a double batch may be hard to fit in a bowl.) To save time when making the larger layers, use two pans: While one layer is baking, you can prepare the next one and then rotate them out. For the smaller cake layers on top, make a single batch of batter and bake the two cakes at the same time. When they come out of the oven, make a double batch of the frosting. To assemble the cake, follow the guidelines in Steps 7 and 8 for a two-layer cake, repeating the process until all the layers are stacked and frosted.*

PEPPERMINT
MOCHA CUPCAKES

PREP TIME: 20 minutes
COOK TIME: 20 minutes
READY IN: 40 minutes
YIELD: 1 dozen cupcakes

I don't think there are enough peppermint mocha–flavored things in life. So these happened. I love Starbucks Peppermint Mochas around the holidays, and I also love cupcakes around the holidays, so, I mean, really, what's not to love here?

FOR THE CUPCAKES

1 cup (92 g) sifted fine-ground blanched almond flour

2 tablespoons instant espresso powder

1 tablespoon coconut sugar

½ teaspoon baking soda

½ teaspoon fine-grain sea salt

⅛ teaspoon ground cinnamon

1 (2.8-ounce/80-g) dark mint chocolate bar, chopped or broken into pieces

¾ cup (5¼ ounces/150 g) chocolate chips

½ cup (120 ml) canned full-fat coconut milk

¼ cup (55 g) palm shortening

½ teaspoon vanilla extract

¼ teaspoon peppermint extract

2 large eggs

FOR THE FROSTING

1 recipe Chocolate Buttercream (page 396)

¼ teaspoon peppermint extract

FOR GARNISH

2 tablespoons unsweetened shredded coconut

1 Adjust an oven rack to the middle position and preheat the oven to 350°F (177°C). Line a 12-cup muffin pan with paper liners; set aside.

2 In a medium-sized mixing bowl, combine the almond flour, espresso powder, coconut sugar, baking soda, salt, and cinnamon and stir together using a fork until combined; set aside.

3 Melt the chocolate and coconut milk in a double boiler over low heat or in a large heatproof bowl set over a pan of gently simmering water. Stir intermittently, using a rubber spatula, until the chocolate is completely melted and combined with the coconut milk. Remove from the heat and let cool slightly.

4 Using the rubber spatula, stir the palm shortening into the melted chocolate mixture. Then stir in the vanilla, peppermint extract, and eggs. If you used a double boiler rather than a mixing bowl set over a pan of water to melt the chocolate, transfer the melted chocolate and egg mixture to a large mixing bowl.

5 Fold the dry ingredients into the melted chocolate mixture and stir using a rubber spatula or whisk until completely combined.

6 Use a cookie scoop or large spoon to transfer the batter into the cupcake liners, filling them about two-thirds full (they will rise slightly when baking). Bake for 20 minutes or until a toothpick comes out clean. Let cool in the pan for 10 minutes, then remove from the pan to cool completely.

7 Once the cupcakes have cooled, make the Chocolate Buttercream, adding the peppermint extract when the vanilla is added. Transfer the frosting to a piping bag fitted with the desired tip and pipe it onto the cupcakes (the cupcakes can also be frosted with a small offset spatula). Garnish with the shredded coconut. Store at room temperature in an air-tight container or wrapped well in plastic for up to 2 days.

MAKE AHEAD
CHOCOLATE CUPCAKES—1 DAY AHEAD

Eggnog
CUPCAKES

PREP TIME: 15 minutes
COOK TIME: 23 to 25 minutes
READY IN: 40 minutes
YIELD: 1 dozen cupcakes

Eggnog is to my December what pumpkin is to my September. The second it hits December 1, pour me a huge glass and let the holiday cheer commence. I want eggnog-flavored everything. In fact, I even get eggnog snobby about which kind I buy because I prefer the taste of certain brands. One time my friend was coming to visit and I made him pack my favorite brand of eggnog in his suitcase and bring it to me when he visited, because they don't sell it where I live. The closest store to him was out, so he had to go to three other stores to find it. He doesn't visit during eggnog season anymore, but what a great friend! Long story short, if you love eggnog as much as I do, these cupcakes won't let you down.

FOR THE CUPCAKES

2 cups (185 g) sifted fine-ground blanched almond flour

¼ cup (35 g) tapioca flour

2 tablespoons coconut flour

¼ cup (35 g) maple sugar

2 tablespoons coconut sugar

½ teaspoon baking soda

½ teaspoon fine-grain sea salt

½ teaspoon ground nutmeg

½ teaspoon ground cinnamon

4 large egg whites, room temperature

½ teaspoon cream of tartar

¾ cup (180 ml) regular or dairy-free eggnog

½ cup (115 g) palm shortening

¼ cup (60 ml) light-colored raw honey

2 teaspoons vanilla extract

FOR THE FROSTING

1 recipe Eggnog Bliss Meringue Buttercream (page 410), Dairy-Free Eggnog Meringue Frosting (page 412), or Eggnog Cream Cheese Frosting (page 414)

1. Adjust an oven rack to the middle position and preheat the oven to 350°F (177°C). Line a 12-cup muffin pan with paper liners; set aside.

2. In the bowl of a large food processor, combine the flours, sugars, baking soda, salt, nutmeg, and cinnamon. Pulse 30 times or until combined. In a separate medium-sized mixing bowl, combine the egg whites and cream of tartar. Beat using a hand mixer set on high speed until soft peaks form; set aside.

3. Add the eggnog, palm shortening, honey, and vanilla to the bowl of the food processor, followed by the beaten egg whites. Process until combined. Scrape down the sides as needed and process for another 30 seconds, or until a smooth and creamy cake batter has formed.

4. Use a large spoon to transfer the batter into the cupcake liners, filling each about three-quarters full. Bake for 23 to 25 minutes or until a toothpick comes out clean. Let cool in the pan for 10 minutes, then remove from the pan to cool completely.

5. Once the cupcakes have cooled, make the desired frosting. Transfer to a piping bag fitted with the desired tip and pipe the frosting onto the cupcakes (the cupcakes can also be frosted with a small offset spatula). If using a cheese-based frosting, store the cupcakes in the refrigerator for up to 2 days. If using a buttercream, store at room temperature in an airtight container or wrapped well in plastic for up to 2 days.

Notes: To make these dairy-free, use dairy-free eggnog in the cupcake batter and the Dairy-Free Eggnog Meringue Frosting.

My favorite dairy-free eggnog is Califia Farms Almond Milk Holiday Nog. You can find it at most health food stores, like Whole Foods and Sprouts. If using regular eggnog, go for a high-quality organic or grass-fed version.

MAKE AHEAD
CUPCAKES—1 DAY AHEAD

Holiday
SPICE CAKE

PREP TIME: 20 minutes
COOK TIME: 30 to 35 minutes
READY IN: 50 minutes
YIELD: One 2-layer, 6-inch (15-cm) cake or one single-layer, 8-inch (20-cm) cake (to make the 3-layer cake shown in the photo, see Variations)

Admittedly I'm not the most creative when it comes to nut-free baked goods. Since grain-free flour options are so limited, I find it hard to step out of my almond flour comfort zone. It's like when you forget your phone at home and have to go the entire day without it. You may as well be missing a limb. That's how I feel when I bake without nut flours. This recipe was inspired by my friend Laura, who baked me some Paleo gingersnap cupcakes over the holidays. She had never Paleo baked in her life and managed to do it without almond flour. What an inspiration! I got in the kitchen and made this cake, and it came out incredible.

FOR THE CAKE (SEE NOTES)

½ cup (80 g) packed coconut flour

¼ cup (40 g) coconut sugar

2 tablespoons tapioca flour

1 teaspoon ground cinnamon

1 teaspoon ginger powder

½ teaspoon baking soda

¼ teaspoon fine-grain sea salt

¼ teaspoon ground allspice

¼ teaspoon ground cloves

½ cup (120 ml) canned coconut milk, full fat

½ cup (120 ml) pure maple syrup, any type

¼ cup (55 g) palm shortening, ghee, or unsalted butter, softened, plus more for greasing

2 teaspoons fresh-squeezed lemon juice

2 teaspoons grated fresh ginger root

1 teaspoon grated lemon zest

1 teaspoon vanilla extract

5 large eggs

FOR THE FROSTING

1 recipe Mascarpone and Goat Cheese Frosting (page 402), Eggnog Bliss Meringue Buttercream (page 410), Dairy-Free Eggnog Meringue Frosting (page 412), or Eggnog Cream Cheese Frosting (page 414)

FOR GARNISH

12 frozen cranberries

1. Adjust an oven rack to the middle position and preheat the oven to 350°F (177°C). Line the bottoms of two 6-inch (15-cm) or one 8-inch (20-cm) springform cake pan(s) with parchment paper, then grease the paper and sides of the pan(s) liberally with palm shortening; set aside.

2. In the bowl of a large food processor, combine the coconut flour, coconut sugar, tapioca flour, cinnamon, ginger powder, baking soda, salt, allspice, and cloves. Pulse 30 times or until combined.

3. Add the coconut milk, maple syrup, palm shortening, lemon juice, grated ginger, zest, vanilla, and eggs to the bowl of the food processor. Process until combined. Scrape down the sides as needed and process for another 30 to 40 seconds until a smooth liquid cake batter has formed.

4. Pour the batter into the prepared cake pan(s) and use a rubber spatula to help scrape all the batter into the pan(s). Bake for 30 to 35 minutes or until a toothpick inserted into the center of the cake comes out clean.

5. Remove from the oven and let cool in the pan(s) for 15 minutes. To remove the cake from the pan, run a knife around the edge between the cake and the pan, until they no longer touch. Remove the cake(s) from the pan(s) and let cool completely.

6. Once the cake is completely cool, prepare the frosting.

7. To assemble: If making a single-layer, 8-inch (20-cm) cake, place the cake on a cake plate and use an offset spatula to cover the top and sides with the frosting. Garnish the top with frozen cranberries. If making a two-layer cake, transfer the frosting to a piping bag fitted with the desired tip (such as a Wilton 1A). Place the first layer on a cake plate and pipe dollops of frosting in a circle around the cake, starting at the edge and moving to the center. Place the second cake layer on top and repeat, then garnish with frozen cranberries. If using a cheese-based frosting, store the cake in the refrigerator for up to 2 days. If using buttercream, store the cake at room temperature in an airtight container or wrapped well in plastic for up to 2 days.

Notes: To make this cake dairy-free, use palm shortening or ghee in the cake layers and the Dairy-Free Eggnog Meringue Frosting to frost the cake.

To make the batter using a hand mixer: In a large mixing bowl, put the coconut flour, coconut sugar, tapioca flour, cinnamon, ginger, baking soda, salt, allspice, and cloves. Stir together using a fork until combined. In a separate medium-sized mixing bowl, put the coconut milk, maple syrup, palm shortening, lemon juice, grated ginger, zest, vanilla, and eggs. Beat together with a hand mixer set on medium speed until combined. Transfer the wet ingredients to the dry, then beat together on medium-low speed until combined. Transfer to the greased and parchment-lined cake pan(s) and bake as directed.

If using a light-colored aluminum pan, you may need to add additional baking time.

Variations:

Holiday Spice Cupcakes. Adjust an oven rack to the middle position and preheat the oven to 350°F (177°C). Line a standard 12-cup muffin pan with paper liners. Make the cake batter, following Steps 2 and 3, opposite. Use a spoon to transfer the batter into the lined cups, filling each about three-quarters full. Bake for 20 to 25 minutes, until a toothpick comes out clean. Let cool in the pan for 10 minutes, then remove to cool completely. Finish with the desired frosting and place a frozen cranberry on top of each cupcake for garnish.

Three-Layer Holiday Spice Cake (pictured on page 277). To make the cake shown in the photo, you will need to make one full batch of batter and one half batch. One full batch is enough for two 6-inch (15-cm) layers. To save time, use three identical pans: While the first two layers are baking, you can prepare the half batch of batter for the third layer. When making the half batch, use 3 eggs. After removing the last cake layer from the oven, make the frosting. To assemble, follow the guidelines in Step 7 for a two-layer cake, repeating the process until all three layers are stacked and frosted.

CHAPTER 11

That's the WAY the COOKIE crumbles

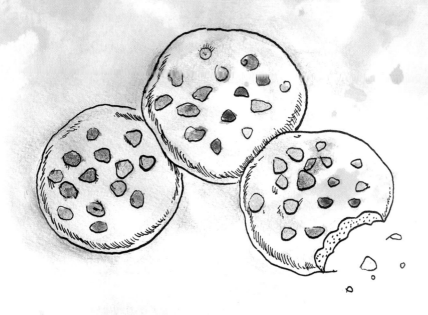

Chocolate
FUDGE COOKIES

PREP TIME: 15 minutes
RESTING TIME: 15 to 20 minutes
COOK TIME (PER BATCH): 10 minutes
READY IN: 40 minutes
YIELD: 20 cookies

These are my favorite chocolate cookies in the whole wide world (besides Oreos, but I digress). This recipe is so easy and delicious; it's my go-to when I need chocolate in cookie form. These cookies would be great to take to a potluck or work event, or even a holiday cookie exchange. No one will ever know that they are gluten- and refined sugar–free!

1½ cups (10½ ounces/300 g) dark chocolate chips (63% to 85% cacao), divided

2 tablespoons unsalted butter, ghee, or melted coconut oil

¾ cup (70 g) sifted fine-ground blanched almond flour

½ cup (75 g) coconut sugar

¼ cup (20 g) packed cacao powder or unsweetened cocoa powder

½ teaspoon baking soda

¼ teaspoon fine-grain sea salt

2 large eggs, room temperature

1 teaspoon vanilla extract

Notes: *To make these cookies dairy-free, use ghee or coconut oil rather than butter.*

Variation: **Mint Chocolate Fudge Cookies.** *Want to take these cookies to the next level? Add ¼ teaspoon of peppermint extract and substitute two 3-ounce (85-g) dark mint chocolate bars for 1 cup (200 g) of the chocolate chips. My favorite mint chocolate bars are from Alter Eco.*

1. Melt 1 cup (200 g) of the chocolate chips and the butter in a double boiler over low heat or in a heatproof bowl set over a pan of gently simmering water. Stir frequently, using a rubber spatula, until completely melted and combined. Remove from the heat and let cool for about 5 to 7 minutes, until the bowl is relatively cool to the touch.

2. Meanwhile, put the almond flour, coconut sugar, cacao powder, baking soda, and salt in a medium-sized mixing bowl. Stir together well using a fork; set aside.

3. Use a rubber spatula to mix the eggs and vanilla into the cooled chocolate mixture. Then use the spatula to scrape the chocolate mixture into the almond flour mixture. With a hand mixer set on low speed, beat until well combined. The dough should be cool enough to add the remaining ½ cup (3½ ounces/100 g) of chocolate chips without melting them. If not, place the bowl in the freezer for 5 minutes. Add the remaining chocolate chips and beat on low until combined.

4. Chill the dough uncovered in the freezer for 15 to 20 minutes or until firm. While the dough is chilling, adjust an oven rack to the middle position and preheat the oven to 350°F (177°C). Line two baking sheets with parchment paper or nonstick baking mats; set aside. (*Note:* If working with only one baking sheet, allow it to cool completely between batches.)

5. Grab some dough and roll it into a 1-inch (2.5-cm) ball. Place on a lined baking sheet and use your fingertips to smooth out the edges. Repeat with the rest of the dough, spacing the cookies 2 inches (5 cm) apart, about 10 cookies per sheet. If using only one baking sheet, refrigerate the remaining dough until ready to bake.

6. Bake each sheet separately for 10 minutes or until a toothpick comes out clean when inserted into the middle of a cookie. Remove the parchment paper or baking mat from the baking sheet and let the cookies cool. Store covered at room temperature for up to 3 days.

EGG FREE

Browned Butter
SNICKERDOODLES

PREP TIME: 25 minutes
RESTING TIME: 1 hour
COOK TIME (PER BATCH): 11 to 12 minutes
READY IN: 1 hour 35 minutes
YIELD: 30 cookies

You have snickerdoodles, and then you have Browned Butter Snickerdoodles. Browned butter is unlike anything else out there. Its sophisticated flavor really takes a recipe to the next level. These snickerdoodles are a perfect example of how browned butter can kick things up a notch.

12 tablespoons (6 ounces/170 g) salted butter

2 cups (185 g) sifted fine-ground blanched almond flour

¼ cup (40 g) coconut flour

1½ teaspoons baking soda

1 teaspoon cream of tartar

1 teaspoon ground cinnamon

¼ teaspoon fine-grain sea salt

1 cup (135 g) sifted maple sugar

2 large eggs, room temperature

1 teaspoon vanilla extract

FOR ROLLING

3 tablespoons maple sugar

2 teaspoons ground cinnamon

Notes: You really want to let the cookie dough rest and chill. Here's why: 1) Resting will let the flavors settle into each other before baking, 2) chilling the dough will make it firm enough to roll into balls and then through the sugar and cinnamon, and 3) if you don't chill the dough to firm it up, the cookies will spread too much when baking.

1 Brown the butter following the method described on page 360; let cool. Meanwhile, prepare the other ingredients.

2 In a large mixing bowl, combine the flours, baking soda, cream of tartar, cinnamon, and salt. Stir together using a fork until well combined; set aside. Put the maple sugar in a separate medium-sized mixing bowl.

3 Once the butter has cooled, use a rubber spatula to transfer it to the maple sugar bowl. Use the spatula to scrape in the browned bits as well. Beat the butter and sugar together with a hand mixer set on low speed until combined, about 1 minute. Add the eggs one at a time, mixing well after each addition, then add the vanilla. Increase the mixer speed to high and continue to beat until smooth bubbles appear on the surface, about 1 minute.

4 Use the rubber spatula to transfer the egg mixture to the flour mixture. Beat on low until thoroughly combined. Scrape down the sides of the bowl and cover with plastic wrap, pressing it directly on the surface of the dough. Place in the freezer to chill for 1 hour.

5 After about 45 minutes, adjust an oven rack to the middle position and preheat the oven to 350°F (177°C). Line three baking sheets with parchment paper or nonstick baking mats; set aside. [Note: Because the yield is large, you will need to bake the cookies in three rotations; if working with only one or two baking sheets, allow the pan(s) to cool completely between batches and keep the dough chilled between batches.]

6 Prepare the rolling ingredients by putting the 3 tablespoons of maple sugar in a small bowl and the 2 teaspoons of cinnamon in another small bowl.

7 Once the dough is chilled, grab some dough and roll it between your palms to form a 1-inch (2.5-cm) ball. Lightly roll each ball in the maple sugar and then quickly but gently through the cinnamon. Place each finished ball on a prepared baking sheet, spacing them about 2 inches (5 cm) apart, or 9 to 12 cookies per sheet.

8 Bake each sheet separately for 11 to 12 minutes or until the edges of the cookies are lightly browned. Once the cookies are done, remove the parchment paper or baking mat from the baking sheet and let the cookies cool. Store covered at room temperature for up to 3 days.

DAIRY FREE

Simple Chocolate
CHIP COOKIES

PREP TIME: 20 minutes
COOK TIME: 7 to 10 minutes
READY IN: 30 minutes
YIELD: 18 cookies

Some might say that it's impossible to make a great batch of chocolate chip cookies without butter. I disagree. These cookies are completely dairy-free and one of the easiest cookie recipes to make.

2 cups (185 g) sifted fine-ground blanched almond flour

1 teaspoon baking soda

½ teaspoon fine-grain sea salt

⅓ cup (80 ml) raw honey

¼ cup (60 ml) melted coconut oil

1 teaspoon vanilla extract

1 large egg, room temperature

1 cup (7 ounces/200 g) chocolate chips

1 Adjust an oven rack to the middle position and preheat the oven to 350°F (177°C). Line two baking sheets with parchment paper or nonstick baking mats; set aside. (*Note:* If you're working with only one baking sheet, allow it to cool completely between batches.)

2 In a large mixing bowl, combine the almond flour, baking soda, and salt. Stir together using a fork until well combined.

3 In a separate medium-sized bowl, combine the honey, coconut oil, vanilla, and egg. Beat with a hand mixer set on low speed until smooth. Add the honey mixture to the flour mixture and beat on low until combined. Stir in the chocolate chips.

4 Use a small cookie scoop to transfer the dough evenly onto the prepared baking sheets, spacing the cookies about 2 inches (5 cm) apart, about 9 per sheet. If using only one baking sheet, refrigerate the remaining dough until ready to bake.

5 Bake each sheet separately for 7 to 10 minutes or until the tops and edges of the cookies are lightly browned. Remove the parchment or baking mat from the baking sheet and let the cookies cool slightly before using a spatula to transfer them to a cooling rack. Store covered at room temperature for up to 3 days.

Notes: Make the cookie dough now and bake later! Wrap the dough in plastic wrap, shape it into a log, and then throw it in the freezer. When the cookie urge strikes, remove the dough from the freezer and let stand for 5 to 10 minutes, then cut into ¾-inch (2-cm)-thick slices. Bake a few cookies at a time or the entire batch.

Shortbread
COOKIES

PREP TIME: 45 minutes
RESTING TIME: 30 minutes
COOK TIME (PER BATCH): 7 to 10 minutes
READY IN: 1 hour 20 minutes
YIELD: 3 dozen cookies

When I was a kid, I could always count on my grandma for three things: gum, loose change, and shortbread cookies in a tin container. Remember the ones with the paper liners that came in all different shapes? Why would a shortbread cookie be shaped like a pretzel? Logic doesn't apply here, I guess, only deliciousness. My shortbread cookie recipe came about when I was experimenting with cashew meal in baking. When I tried a cookie, I was surprised by how much it tasted like shortbread.

6 tablespoons (3 ounces/85 g) salted butter

2 cups (310 g) raw cashew pieces

3 tablespoons coconut flour

2 tablespoons maple sugar

½ teaspoon fine-grain sea salt

⅛ teaspoon ground cinnamon

¼ cup (60 ml) raw honey

½ teaspoon vanilla extract

1 large egg white, room temperature

1. Brown the butter following the method described on page 360; let cool completely. Meanwhile, prepare the other ingredients.

2. Put the cashews in the bowl of a high-powered food processor and process until they turn to meal. Scrape down the bowl and process for another 5 minutes or so, stopping to scrape down as needed, until the nut oils start to release and the cashew meal turns into a thick dough ball or a doughlike consistency. Add the coconut flour, maple sugar, salt, and cinnamon and process again until combined.

3. In a separate large bowl, combine the honey and vanilla. Then, using a rubber spatula, add the cooled browned butter, scraping in the browned bits at the bottom of the saucepan as well. Mix together with a hand mixer set on low speed, then beat in the egg white and continue to mix until combined. Transfer the cashew dough to the butter mixture and beat on medium-low until smooth ripples start to form and the dough no longer appears chunky. Be careful not to overmix; doing so may cause the butter to separate. Cover with plastic wrap, pressing it directly onto the surface of the dough, and place in the freezer to firm up for 30 minutes.

4. After about 20 minutes, adjust an oven rack to the top position and preheat the oven to 350°F (177°C). Line three baking sheets, preferably light-colored aluminum ones, with parchment paper or nonstick baking mats; set aside. [*Note:* Because the yield is large, you will need to bake the cookies in three rotations; if working with only one or two baking sheets, allow the pan(s) to cool completely between batches and keep the dough chilled between batches.]

5. Divide the dough in half and place one portion in the refrigerator. Place the other half of the dough on a sheet of parchment paper, set another sheet of parchment on top, and roll out the dough to about ⅝ inch (1.5 cm) thick. Use a Wilton size D round cookie cutter or 1½-inch (4-cm) round cookie cutter to cut out the cookies. Remove the extra dough and transfer the cookies to a lined baking sheet, spaced about 1 inch (2.5 cm) apart, or 12 to 16 cookies per sheet; the cookies will not spread as they bake. Use a fingertip to smooth out the edges of the cookies, which can become rough during the cutting process. Gather up the dough scraps and repeat the process until all the dough has been used.

6 Bake each sheet separately for 7 to 10 minutes or until the bottoms of the cookies start to brown. Remove the parchment paper or baking mat from the baking sheet and let the cookies cool completely. Repeat the rolling, cutting, and baking process with the remaining refrigerated dough. Store covered at room temperature for up to 3 days.

Notes: If the butter breaks from the dough, the cause could be overmixing the dough or the butter being too warm when it was introduced to the other ingredients. This is why I recommend cooling the butter completely. Let it cool on the counter; don't try to rush the process by placing it in the refrigerator or freezer. The dough doesn't work well if the butter hardens.

If the butter does separate, you can still save the dough: Just chill it until the butter starts to become firm again and then, using a hand mixer, beat on low until the butter is incorporated into the dough. Chill again until the dough becomes firm enough to roll.

The dough will be hard when you remove it from the freezer. Use your fingertips to press in and grab the dough; once you break the top layer, the rest will be easier to grab. The dough works best when cold; it will roll and cut very easily. If your dough is being stubborn, try letting it chill longer.

The bottoms of these cookies tend to brown very quickly, so if possible, use a very light-colored aluminum baking sheet to prevent the bottoms from browning too much. That's why the top oven rack is suggested for baking.

ALMOND BUTTER PATTIES

PREP TIME: 45 minutes
RESTING TIME: 30 minutes
COOK TIME: 20 to 30 minutes
SETTING TIME: 30 minutes
READY IN: 2 hours 5 minutes
YIELD: 3 dozen cookies

**1 recipe Shortbread Cookie dough
(page 286)**

**1 recipe Almond Butter Center
(page 362)**

**1 recipe Chocolate Shell Coating
(page 376)**

MAKE AHEAD
SHORTBREAD COOKIES—1 DAY AHEAD

These cookies are based on another Girl Scout cookie favorite, only made with almond butter instead of peanut butter. These will be a "must-make" during Girl Scout cookie season to keep you sane. Trust me.

1 Prepare the Shortbread Cookie dough, following Steps 1 through 3 on page 286. While the dough is chilling, prepare the Almond Butter Center. Refrigerate the Almond Butter Center for 10 to 15 minutes to thicken if needed.

2 Roll, cut out, and bake the Shortbread Cookies, following Steps 4 through 6 on pages 286 and 287. Leave the cooled cookies on the parchment paper and transfer them back onto the two baking sheets for assembly; set aside.

3 Prepare the Chocolate Shell Coating and let cool slightly. By this time the Almond Butter Center should be ready. While the chocolate is cooling, spoon a small dollop of the Almond Butter Center onto the top of each cookie and use a knife to spread it in a circular motion until it reaches the edge and is about ¼ inch (6 mm) thick. Place the cookie back on one of the lined baking sheets, repeating the process until no plain cookies remain.

4 To coat the cookies: Hold a cookie by its sides and lower it into the Chocolate Shell Coating, almond butter side down. Use a candy-dipping fork or a plastic fork with the two middle prongs broken off to gently turn the cookie over and move it around in the chocolate until the cookie and almond butter are completely coated. With the almond butter facing up, use the fork to remove the cookie by its bottom from the chocolate bowl and let any excess chocolate drain back into the bowl. Place the dipped cookie back on the lined baking sheet to set. Repeat with the rest of the cookies. Once all the cookies have been dipped, place the baking sheet in the refrigerator for 30 minutes to harden the chocolate. Store the cookies covered in the refrigerator for up to 3 days.

EGG FREE*

Paleo
MOONPIES

PREP TIME: 50 minutes
COOK TIME: 15 minutes
SETTING TIME: 1 hour 15 minutes
READY IN: 2 hours 20 minutes
YIELD: 6 MoonPies

Quick—when was the last time you had a MoonPie? It's been forever, right? I know! When I asked myself this same question, I couldn't remember the last time I had one. They are one of my favorite things in life. So obviously I had to create my own recipe. Problem solved, crisis averted.

1 recipe Graham Cracker Crust dough (page 170)

1 recipe Marshmallow Crème, egg-free (page 368) or regular (page 366)

1 recipe Chocolate Shell Coating (page 376)

MAKE AHEAD

PALEO MOONPIE COOKIES (MADE WITH GRAHAM CRACKER CRUST DOUGH)—1 DAY AHEAD

Notes: I prefer the Egg-Free Marshmallow Crème for this recipe because its texture is most similar to that of a real MoonPie. Use it to make this recipe egg-free. Don't let it sit too long or it will start to firm up. If it gets too firm, beat it on low speed until it resembles crème again. Also, make sure that your chocolate isn't too warm, or it may melt the marshmallow.

You can use this recipe to make bars by layering everything in an 8-inch (20-cm) glass baking dish. You can also change your cookie size or shape by using a different cookie cutter. Don't want a whole Paleo MoonPie sandwich? Make Paleo Mallomars using the same process, but leave the top cookie off!

1. Preheat the oven to 350°F (177°C). Line two baking sheets with parchment paper or nonstick baking mats; set aside. (*Note:* If working with only one baking sheet, allow it to cool completely between batches.)

2. Prepare the Graham Cracker Crust dough following Steps 2 through 4 on page 170. Transfer the dough to one of the lined baking sheets and press into a mound. Place a sheet of parchment paper on top and roll it out to ¼ inch (6 mm) thick. Use a 2¾-inch (7-cm) circular cookie cutter, or Wilton size A, to cut 6 cookies, about ½ inch (1.25 cm) apart (they will spread slightly while baking). Pull away the dough scraps, leaving the cookies on the sheet. Roll out the dough scraps on the second baking sheet and repeat the process, cutting out 6 additional cookies. Bake each sheet separately for 7 to 8 minutes, until the cookies appear dry and the edges are golden brown. Remove the parchment paper from the baking sheet and let the cookies cool.

3. While the cookies are cooling, prepare the Marshmallow Crème.

4. To assemble: Turn a cookie over so the bottom is facing up. Using a large spoon, place a big dollop of Marshmallow Crème on the cookie bottom. This works best if the dollop is taller rather than wider so it has room to spread when sandwiched. Top the crème with a second cookie and gently press down until the crème reaches the edge. Place the cookie sandwich on a parchment-lined baking sheet. Repeat the process with the remaining cookies and Marshmallow Crème. Place in the refrigerator to chill for at least 15 minutes.

5. Prepare the Chocolate Shell Coating and allow to cool. It should be pourable, but not so hot that it melts the Marshmallow Crème.

6. Place a chilled sandwich in the bowl of melted chocolate. Using a candy-dipping fork or a plastic fork with the two middle prongs broken off, turn the sandwich upside down and coat the sides until completely covered. Use the fork to remove the sandwich from the chocolate, letting any excess chocolate drain back into the bowl. Place back on the parchment-lined baking sheet and repeat the process with the remaining sandwiches. Once all the sandwiches are dipped in chocolate, place the baking sheet in the refrigerator to chill for 30 minutes to 1 hour. Store in the fridge until ready to serve. Keep any leftovers covered in the fridge for up to 3 days.

Strawberries AND CREAM COOKIES

PREP TIME: 25 minutes
RESTING TIME: 1 hour
COOK TIME (PER BATCH): 12 to 15 minutes
READY IN: 1 hour 35 minutes
YIELD: 20 cookies

These cookies would be perfect for Valentine's Day! Not only because they are red and white, and therefore the official colors of Valentine's Day, but also because they are delicious and made with love. Awww . . .

12 tablespoons (6 ounces/170 g) salted butter

2 cups (185 g) sifted fine-ground blanched almond flour

¼ cup (40 g) coconut flour

1½ teaspoons baking soda

1 teaspoon cream of tartar

¼ teaspoon fine-grain sea salt

1 cup (135 g) sifted maple sugar

2 large eggs, room temperature

1 teaspoon vanilla extract

1 cup (6 ounces/180 g) chopped white chocolate or white chocolate chips

½ cup (100 g) dried strawberries, chopped

1. Brown the butter following the method described on page 360; let cool. Meanwhile, prepare the other ingredients.

2. In a large mixing bowl, combine the flours, baking soda, cream of tartar, and salt. Stir together using a fork until well combined; set aside. Put the maple sugar in a separate medium-sized mixing bowl.

3. Once the butter has cooled, use a rubber spatula to transfer it into the maple sugar bowl, scraping in the browned bits from the bottom of the pan as well. With a hand mixer set on low speed, beat the butter and sugar together until combined, about 1 minute. Add the eggs one at a time, mixing well after each addition, then add the vanilla. Increase the mixer speed to high and continue to beat until smooth bubbles appear on the surface, about 1 minute.

4. Transfer the egg mixture to the flour mixture, then beat on low speed until thoroughly combined. Mix in the white chocolate and dried strawberries by hand. Scrape down the sides of the bowl and cover with plastic wrap, pressing it directly on the surface of the dough. Place in the freezer to chill for 1 hour.

5. After about 45 minutes, adjust an oven rack to the middle position and preheat the oven to 350°F (177°C). Line three baking sheets with parchment paper or nonstick baking mats; set aside. [*Note:* Because the yield is large and these cookies spread when baked, you will need to bake the cookies in three rotations; if working with only one or two baking sheets, allow the pan(s) to cool completely between batches and keep the dough chilled between batches.]

6. Once the dough is chilled, grab some dough and roll it between your palms to form a 2-inch (5-cm) ball. Place the dough balls on the prepared baking sheets, spaced about 2 inches (5 cm) apart, or 6 to 8 cookies per sheet. Bake each sheet separately for 12 to 15 minutes or until the cookies are lightly browned on the bottoms and edges. Remove the parchment paper or baking mat from the baking sheet and let the cookies cool. Store covered at room temperature for up to 3 days.

Notes: Be sure to use regular dried strawberries with no sugar added, not freeze-dried ones. Steve's PaleoGoods sells the best dried strawberries on the planet; I highly recommend them. Another fun option is to use dried peaches and make peaches and cream cookies.

Devil's Food
COOKIES

I used to love the fat-free packaged version of these cookies in the 1990s. I also used to love 90210 in the '90s. Things change.

❧

PREP TIME: 1 hour
RESTING TIME: 10 minutes
COOK TIME: 20 minutes
SETTING TIME: 30 minutes
READY IN: 2 hours
YIELD: 18 cookies

1 recipe Chocolate Fudge Cookie dough (page 280)
1 recipe Marshmallow Crème, egg-free (page 368) or regular (page 366)
1 recipe Chocolate Shell Coating (page 376)

MAKE AHEAD
CHOCOLATE FUDGE COOKIES—
1 DAY AHEAD

1 Prepare the Chocolate Fudge Cookie dough, but omit the ½ cup (3½ ounces/100 g) of chocolate chips added in Step 3 on page 280. Adjust an oven rack to the middle position and preheat the oven to 350°F (177°C). Line two baking sheets with parchment paper or nonstick baking mats; set aside. (*Note:* If working with only one baking sheet, allow it to cool completely between batches.)

2 Chill the dough in the refrigerator for 10 minutes. Then use a small cookie scoop to transfer the dough evenly onto the prepared baking sheets, spacing the cookies about 2 inches (5 cm) apart, or 9 per sheet. Use your fingertips to lightly press down and slightly flatten the top of each cookie. If using only one baking sheet, refrigerate the remaining dough until ready to bake.

3 Bake each sheet separately for 10 minutes or until a toothpick comes out clean when inserted into the middle of a cookie. Let the cookies cool completely on the baking sheet. While the cookies are cooling, make the Marshmallow Crème.

4 With a large spoon, dollop a drop of Marshmallow Crème on the top of each completely cooled cookie. Then place in the refrigerator for 30 minutes or until firmly set.

5 About 15 minutes before the Marshmallow Crème has set, prepare the Chocolate Shell Coating. Let the chocolate cool for about 15 minutes or until the bowl is relatively cool to the touch, so it won't melt the marshmallow top when dipping.

6 To assemble: Turn a cookie upside down and dip the top marshmallow portion into the melted chocolate. Use a candy-dipping fork or a plastic fork with the two middle prongs broken off to turn the cookie upside down and coat the sides until completely covered. Use the fork to remove the cookie from the chocolate and let any excess chocolate drip back into the bowl. Place back on the lined baking sheet to set. Once all the cookies have been dipped, place the baking sheet in the refrigerator for 30 minutes to harden the chocolate. Store covered in the refrigerator for up to 3 days.

Notes: *To make these dairy-free, use ghee or coconut oil rather than butter in the cookies. To make them egg-free, use the Egg-Free Marshmallow Crème. I prefer the egg-free crème for this recipe because it firms up and sticks to the cookies better, making dipping easier.*

Hazelnut Butter
SANDWICH COOKIES

PREP TIME: 35 minutes
COOK TIME : 20 to 25 minutes
SETTING TIME: 15 minutes
READY IN: 1 hour 10 minutes
YIELD: 2 dozen cookies

This was the first recipe I created for this book. I don't even remember what inspired me to make it. I think I was craving Nutella at the time. It happens. I feel so much older and wiser now, but these cookies still taste just as great as they did on day one. If you are a hazelnut fan, you will love this recipe.

FOR THE COOKIES

2 cups (185 g) sifted fine-ground blanched almond flour

1 tablespoon plus 2 teaspoons coconut flour

1½ teaspoons baking soda

1 teaspoon cream of tartar

¼ teaspoon fine-grain sea salt

12 ounces (340 g) unsalted dry-roasted hazelnuts, without skins, or raw hazelnuts

1 cup (150 g) coconut sugar

6 tablespoons (3 ounces/85 g) cold salted butter

2 large eggs, room temperature

1 teaspoon vanilla extract

Arrowroot flour or tapioca flour, for dusting

1 recipe Ganache (pages 369 to 370), any type

Ground hazelnuts, for garnish

1. Adjust an oven rack to the middle position and preheat the oven to 350°F (177°C). Line two baking sheets with parchment paper or nonstick baking mats; set aside. (*Note:* If working with only one baking sheet, allow it to cool completely between batches.)

2. In a large mixing bowl, combine the flours, baking soda, cream of tartar, and salt. Stir together using a fork until well combined; set aside.

3. If working with prepackaged dry-roasted hazelnuts, skip ahead to Step 4. If working with raw hazelnuts, roast them in the oven on a parchment-lined rimmed baking sheet for 10 minutes. Then wrap the freshly roasted hazelnuts in a dishcloth and roll them around on the countertop. Grinding the roasted nuts against each other helps the skins come off easily.

4. Put the hazelnuts in a high-powered food processor or blender and process for 3 to 5 minutes or until they turn into a smooth butter; set aside.

5. Put the coconut sugar and butter in medium-sized mixing bowl. Using a hand mixer set on low speed, cream them together for about 5 minutes or until crumbly (the mixture will resemble cooked ground meat). Then use a rubber spatula to transfer the hazelnut butter to the sugar and butter mixture and continue to beat on low until incorporated, about 1 minute. Add the eggs one at a time, mixing well after each addition, then add the vanilla and mix until combined.

6. Transfer the wet mixture to the dry flour mixture and beat on low until thoroughly combined.

7. Lay a piece of parchment paper on the counter and lightly dust it with arrowroot flour. Place the cookie dough on the dusted parchment and lightly dust the top of the dough with more arrowroot flour. Then place another sheet of parchment on top of the dough and roll it out to ¼ inch (6 mm) thick. Remove the top sheet of parchment. Using a small round cookie cutter, about 1½ to 1¾ inches (4 to 4.5 cm) in diameter, or a Wilton size D, closely stamp out rounds and arrange them on a lined baking sheet about 1½ inches (4 cm) apart, or 12 per sheet. Gather the scraps, cover with parchment again, and reroll. Repeat this process until no dough remains.

8. Bake each sheet separately for 10 to 12 minutes or until the edges of the cookies are lightly browned. Remove the parchment paper or baking mat from the baking sheet and let the cookies cool.

9 While the cookies are cooling, make the ganache.

10 To assemble: Turn half of the cookies upside down and spoon a dollop of ganache in the center of each cookie bottom. Dip the remaining cookies halfway into the chocolate and place back on the parchment paper. Gently reheat the chocolate if it starts to harden. Sprinkle the ground hazelnuts onto the halves dipped in chocolate, then sandwich the tops over the bottoms and press down. Let the cookies rest for about 15 minutes or until the chocolate has set. Store covered in the refrigerator for up to 3 days.

FLOURLESS DOUBLE
CHOCOLATE CHIP COOKIES

PREP TIME: 20 minutes
COOK TIME (PER BATCH): 10 minutes
READY IN: 30 minutes
YIELD: About 2 dozen cookies

These chocolate cookies are like the flourless chocolate cake of the cookie world. They are nut- and flour-free, with a dairy-free option as well. Most importantly, they are chocolate. Not just regular chocolate, but chocolate-covered chocolate.

1 cup (75 g) cacao powder or unsweetened cocoa powder

½ cup (75 g) coconut sugar

½ teaspoon baking soda

½ teaspoon fine-grain sea salt

1½ cups (10½ ounces/300 g) dark chocolate chips (63% to 85%), divided

2 tablespoons salted butter or melted coconut oil

2 large eggs, room temperature

1 teaspoon vanilla extract

Coarse or flake sea salt, for garnish (optional)

1. Adjust an oven rack to the middle position and preheat the oven to 350°F (177°C). Line three baking sheets with parchment paper or nonstick baking mats; set aside. [*Note:* Because the yield is large and these cookies spread when baked, you will need to bake the cookies in three rotations; if working with only one or two baking sheets, allow the pan(s) to cool completely between batches and keep the dough chilled between batches.]

2. In a large mixing bowl, combine the cacao powder, coconut sugar, baking soda, and salt. Stir together using a fork until well combined; set aside.

3. Melt 1 cup (200 g) of the chocolate chips and the butter in a double boiler over low heat or in a heatproof bowl set over a pan of gently simmering water. Stir frequently, using a rubber spatula, until completely melted and combined. Remove from the heat and set aside for about 5 to 7 minutes, until the bowl is relatively cool to the touch.

4. Using the rubber spatula or a whisk, mix the eggs and vanilla into the melted chocolate mixture. Then transfer the chocolate mixture to the cacao powder mixture and combine using a hand mixer set on low speed. Stir in the remaining ½ cup (100 g) of chocolate chips.

5. Use a small cookie scoop to transfer the dough onto the prepared baking sheets, spacing the cookies about 2 inches (5 cm) apart, up to 9 cookies per sheet.

6. Bake each sheet separately for 10 minutes or until a toothpick comes out clean when inserted into the middle of a cookie. Remove the parchment paper or baking mat from the baking sheet. Garnish the cookies with a sprinkle of sea salt, if desired, and let cool. Store covered at room temperature for up to 3 days.

Subs: For another dairy-free version, substitute palm shortening for the butter or coconut oil.

Soft Batch CHOCOLATE CHIP COOKIES

PREP TIME: 25 minutes
RESTING TIME: 1 hour
COOK TIME (PER BATCH): 10 to 12 minutes
READY IN: 1 hour 35 minutes
YIELD: 30 cookies

I don't discriminate among chocolate chip cookies. I like them all, but I especially like a good soft batch cookie. It took me over ten test batches to get these just right. They were too flat, too uneven, too crumbly, or too soft. Then the answer finally came to me one night as I was going to sleep. I knew exactly what needed to be done. When I made them the next day, they came out perfect. Trust me when I say that you shouldn't skip any steps. You can't rush perfection, especially when it comes to cookies. Who wants to wait for cookies, right? But trust me on this. The famous Jacques Torres Chocolate Chip Cookies require a twenty-four-hour resting period. I'm only going to make you rest the dough for an hour. Mainly because I love you, but mostly because we are working with a gluten-free flour, so we aren't waiting for proteins and starch enzymes to break down. I should have a PhD in Cookieology. I hope you enjoy these as much as I do!

12 tablespoons (6 ounces/170 g) salted butter

2 cups (185 g) sifted fine-ground blanched almond flour

¼ cup (40 g) coconut flour

1½ teaspoons baking soda

1 teaspoon cream of tartar

¼ teaspoon fine-grain sea salt

1 cup (135 g) sifted maple sugar

2 large eggs, room temperature

1 teaspoon vanilla extract

1½ cups (10½ ounces/300 g) chocolate chips

Notes: Sifting the almond flour and maple sugar is crucial. If you skip the sifting, the cookies will come out really rough-looking. Remember, we eat with our eyes first. (The coconut flour is already so fine that no sifting is required.)

This is another recipe that you can make now and bake later! Wrap the dough in plastic wrap, shape it into a log, and throw it in the freezer. When the urge strikes, remove the dough from the freezer and let stand for 5 to 10 minutes, then cut into ¾-inch (2-cm) slices and bake.

1 Brown the butter following the method described on page 360; let cool. Meanwhile, prepare the other ingredients.

2 In a large mixing bowl, combine the flours, baking soda, cream of tartar, and salt. Stir together using a fork until well combined; set aside. Put the maple sugar in a medium-sized mixing bowl.

3 Once the butter has cooled, use a rubber spatula to transfer it into the maple sugar bowl; scrape in the browned bits as well. Beat together the butter and sugar with a hand mixer set on low speed until combined, about 1 minute. Add the eggs one at a time, mixing well after each addition, then add the vanilla. Increase the mixer speed to high and continue to beat until smooth bubbles appear on the surface, about 1 minute.

4 Use the rubber spatula to transfer the egg mixture to the flour mixture. Beat on low until thoroughly combined. Mix in the chocolate chips by hand. Scrape down the sides of the bowl and cover with plastic wrap, pressing it directly on the surface of the dough. Place in the freezer to chill for 1 hour.

5 After about 45 minutes, adjust an oven rack to the middle position and preheat the oven to 350°F (177°C). Line three baking sheets with parchment paper or nonstick baking mats; set aside. (If working with only one or two baking sheets, allow to cool completely between batches.)

6 Once the dough is chilled, grab some dough and roll it between your palms to form a 1½-inch (4-cm) ball (golf ball size). Place the balls on the prepared baking sheets, spaced about 2 inches (5 cm) apart, or 12 per sheet. (The third batch will consist of about 6 cookies.) Bake each sheet separately for 10 to 12 minutes or until the cookies are lightly browned on the edges. Remove the parchment paper or baking mat from the baking sheet and let the cookies cool. Store covered at room temperature for up to 3 days.

DAIRY FREE*

caramel walnut
BROWNIE COOKIES

These cookies are nuts! Pun totally intended. If you took a brownie and turned it into a cookie, this would be it. Then, if you got even crazier with your brownie cookie and drizzled caramel over it and sprinkled walnuts across the top, well, this would definitely be it. Make this recipe. It's one of my favorites in the book. These cookies would be insane if you used them for ice cream sandwiches. D'oh, why didn't I think of that? Wait . . . I guess technically I did. Like just now. You're witnessing magic happen.

PREP TIME: 20 minutes
COOK TIME: 20 minutes
READY IN: 40 minutes
YIELD: 2 dozen cookies

1 recipe Salted Caramel Sauce (page 374)

1½ cups (10½ ounces/300 g) semisweet chocolate chips

¼ cup (55 g) palm shortening

1½ cups (140 g) sifted fine-ground blanched almond flour

2 tablespoons coconut flour

1 teaspoon cream of tartar

½ teaspoon baking soda

¼ teaspoon fine-grain sea salt

½ cup (75 g) coconut sugar

2 large eggs, room temperature

1 teaspoon vanilla extract

½ cup (60 g) raw walnuts, for garnish

Notes: To make these cookies dairy-free, make the Salted Caramel Sauce with ghee rather than butter.

To get that nice crackled brownie top look, as pictured, you have to use semisweet chocolate chips. Dark chocolate chips just don't work as well.

Pair these cookies with the Simple Vanilla Ice Cream on page 326 or the Best Chocolate Ice Cream on page 322 for killer ice cream sandwiches!

1 Prepare the Salted Caramel Sauce. Allow to cool, then refrigerate to thicken further.

2 Adjust an oven rack to the middle position and preheat the oven to 350°F (177°C). Line two baking sheets with parchment paper or nonstick baking mats; set aside. (*Note:* If working with only one baking sheet, allow it to cool completely between batches.)

3 Melt the chocolate chips and palm shortening in a double boiler over low heat or in a heatproof bowl set over a pan of gently simmering water. Stir frequently, using a rubber spatula, until completely melted and combined. Remove from the heat and let sit until the bowl is relatively cool to the touch. While waiting for the chocolate mixture to cool, prepare the other ingredients.

4 In a large mixing bowl, combine the flours, cream of tartar, baking soda, and salt. Stir together using a fork until well combined; set aside.

5 In a medium-sized mixing bowl, beat together the sugar and eggs with a hand mixer set on low speed until combined. Add the vanilla, increase the mixer speed to high, and continue to beat until bubbles appear on the surface, about 1 minute.

6 Use a rubber spatula to transfer the egg mixture to the cooled melted chocolate mixture. Stir until combined, then transfer the chocolate mixture to the almond flour mixture and beat using the hand mixer set on low speed until combined.

7 Use a small cookie scoop to transfer the dough evenly onto the prepared baking sheets, spacing the cookies about 1 inch (2.5 cm) apart, or 12 cookies per sheet. The dough will be more like a batter, but will hold its shape.

8 Bake each sheet separately for 10 minutes or until a toothpick comes out clean. Remove the parchment paper or baking mat from the baking sheet and let the cookies cool.

9 While cookies are cooling, chop the walnuts. Transfer the caramel sauce to a piping bag or to a resealable plastic bag with a corner cut off. Drizzle the caramel over the cooled cookies and garnish with a sprinkle of chopped walnuts. Store covered in the refrigerator for up to 3 days.

S'mores Chocolate Chip
COOKIE SANDWICHES

PREP TIME: 45 minutes
RESTING TIME: 1 hour
COOK TIME: 15 to 25 minutes
READY IN: 2 hours
YIELD: 10 cookie sandwiches

Again with the s'mores? I know, but I can't get enough. Since this recipe makes cookie sandwiches, it's technically different from my other s'mores creations. Yes, it is. This is another recipe that I saw floating around the Internet that I had to get my hands on. Literally. And my mouth. So I got to work and created my own grain-free version. I'm not gonna lie; these are over-the-top delicious.

1 recipe Soft Batch Chocolate Chip Cookies (page 300) or Simple Chocolate Chip Cookies (page 284)

1 recipe Ganache (pages 369 to 370), any type

1 recipe Marshmallow Crème, regular (page 366) or egg-free (page 368)

SPECIAL EQUIPMENT

Kitchen torch

MAKE AHEAD
CHOCOLATE CHIP COOKIES—
1 DAY AHEAD

1. Make the chocolate chip cookies. While the cookies are cooling, prepare the ganache; set aside.

2. Prepare the Marshmallow Crème immediately before assembling the cookie sandwiches. Transfer the crème to a piping bag fitted with the desired tip, or use a spoon to transfer the crème onto the sandwiches during assembly.

3. To assemble: Turn the cookies upside down and spoon a dollop of ganache onto the centers of half of the cookie bottoms. Then either pipe or spoon Marshmallow Crème into the centers of the remaining cookies. Sandwich a ganache-topped cookie together with a marshmallow-topped cookie, pressing down until the filling reaches the edges. Toast the edges of the Marshmallow Crème using a kitchen torch. These are best eaten immediately, but any remaining cookie sandwiches can be stored in the refrigerator for up to 3 days.

Notes: To make these dairy-free, use the Simple Chocolate Chip Cookies and the Dairy-Free Ganache.

My favorite way to prepare these cookie sandwiches, as pictured, is with Soft Batch Chocolate Chip Cookies, regular (egg white–based) Marshmallow Crème, and Dairy-Free Ganache.

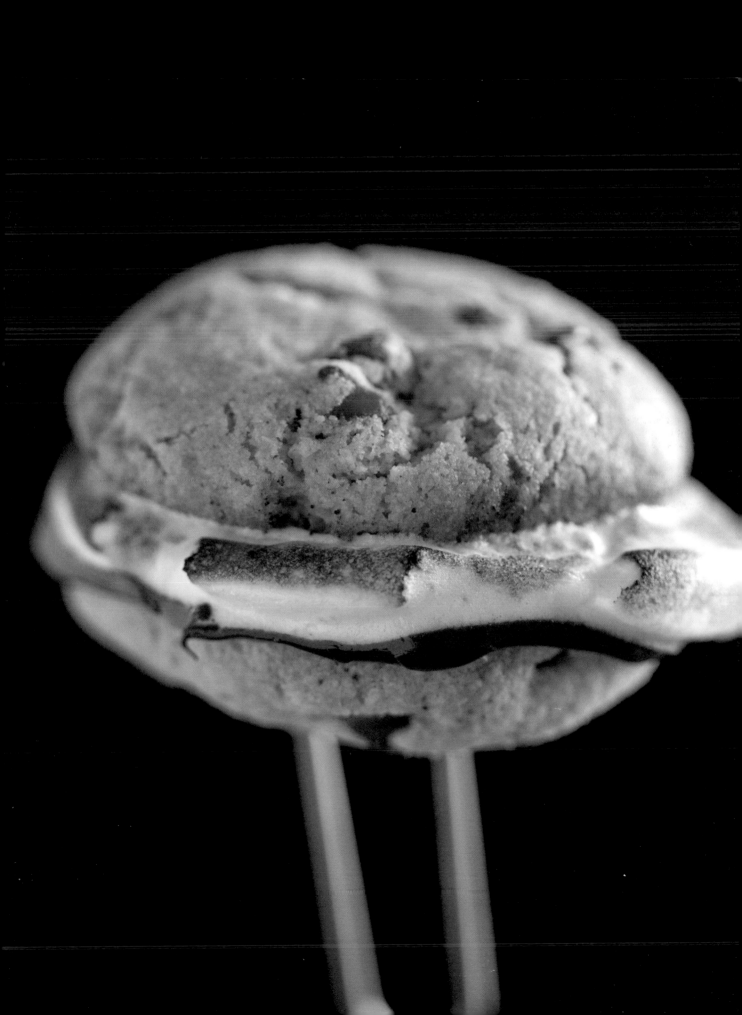

DAIRY FREE*

FRENCH MACARONS

PREP TIME: 20 minutes
RESTING TIME: 30 minutes to 1 hour
COOK TIME: 25 minutes
READY IN: 1 hour 15 minutes
YIELD: 2 dozen macarons

If you know anything about me, you know that French macarons are my reason for living. There are few things in life equal to the first bite of a French macaron. The way the shell cracks softly and releases its soft flavor center is one of life's greatest pleasures. Not only are French macarons gorgeous and fun to eat, but they are naturally gluten-free too. This is the only recipe in my book that includes refined sugar. The French macaron is very delicate and temperamental, and although it's best to avoid refined sugar whenever possible, using natural or alternative sweeteners can yield unsuccessful results. I've included this recipe because French macarons are a part of me, in the way that this book is a part of me, and if I didn't include a recipe for them, it just wouldn't feel right. I would be doing you a disservice as a reader and fellow food lover. Life is about enjoying the little things, and this recipe is meant to be made as a very special indulgence to share with your favorite people.

FOR THE SHELLS

¾ cup (70 g) sifted fine-ground blanched almond flour

1 cup (115 g) confectioners' sugar

2 large egg whites, room temperature

¼ teaspoon cream of tartar

¼ cup (50 g) caster sugar (see Notes)

FLAVORED SHELLS

Lemon—Add ½ teaspoon of lemon extract and natural yellow food coloring in Step 2.

Rose—Add ¼ teaspoon of rose water and natural red food coloring in Step 2.

Espresso—Add ½ teaspoon of instant espresso powder in Step 2. Sprinkle more espresso powder over the shell tops as a garnish before baking.

Chocolate—Add 3 tablespoons of unsweetened cocoa powder in place of ¼ cup of the almond flour in Step 1.

Pistachio—Use ½ cup (50 g) of sifted almond flour and add ¼ cup (20 g) of sifted pistachio meal in Step 1. Reserve the larger pieces of pistachios that remain after sifting to sprinkle as a garnish over the shell tops before baking.

Note: To make the pistachio meal, simply grind about ¼ cup (35 g) of raw, shelled pistachios in a small food processor until they are the texture of nut meal.

RECOMMENDED FILLINGS

One recipe of filling is enough to fill 2 dozen macarons. For dairy-free macarons, use the Dairy-Free Ganache or the Strawberry Sauce.

1 recipe Ganache (pages 369 to 370), any type

1 recipe Vanilla Buttercream (page 394), made with 1 cup (115 g) of confectioners' sugar

1 recipe Lemon Curd (page 388)

1 recipe Strawberry Sauce (page 378)

1 Line two baking sheets with parchment paper; set aside. In a medium-sized mixing bowl, combine the almond flour (or cocoa powder and/or pistachio meal, if making the chocolate or pistachio macarons) and confectioners' sugar. Stir together until combined, then pass through a fine-mesh sieve into another bowl. Toss any almond or sugar pebbles left behind. Set the mixture aside.

2 In a large metal mixing bowl or the bowl of a stand mixer, beat the egg whites until foamy. Then beat in the cream of tartar and one-third of the caster sugar. Continue to beat for about 1 minute, add half of the remaining sugar, and beat again. Then add the rest of the sugar and continue to beat until stiff glossy peaks form, about 7 to 8 minutes. At this time, mix in any desired flavoring or coloring.

3 Using a rubber spatula, fold the almond flour and sugar mixture into the egg whites and stir 60 to 75 times or until the batter is smooth and no lumps remain. It should look and move like lava.

4 Fit a piping bag with a Wilton 1A tip. Place the piping bag inside a tall glass and fold the edges of the bag over the glass. Transfer the batter into the piping bag using a rubber spatula. Evenly pipe 1½-inch (4-cm) circles onto the parchment-lined baking sheets, spaced 1 inch (2.5 cm) apart. When finished piping, tap the pan on the counter a few times to release any air bubbles. Let them sit for 30 minutes to 1 hour to dry and let the tops harden. This will allow the macarons to rise in the oven instead of spreading out, which will create the coveted "feet" on the bottoms. Before baking, the tops should appear matte and not stick to your fingertips when touched. If the environment is humid, this could take longer.

5 While waiting for the tops to set, make the desired filling. Then adjust an oven rack to the middle position and preheat the oven to 300°F (150°C). When ready, bake each sheet separately for 12 to 14 minutes, until the macarons are dry and have formed feet. Slide the parchment paper off the baking sheet and let the macarons cool.

6 To assemble: Carefully lift the shells off the parchment paper. Turn half of the shells upside down so that the flat bottoms are facing up. Pipe a small mound of filling into the centers of the cookie bottoms, then cover with the remaining shells. Storing the macarons in the refrigerator for 12 hours before eating is recommended, but optional.

Notes: French macarons can be temperamental. They are like beautiful women in that way, so treat them as such. Here are some tips:

- *Use room-temperature egg whites and cream of tartar to ensure that you obtain stiff peaks.*

- *Sifting the flour and confectioners' sugar through a sieve is crucial. You want the finest possible texture to create smooth, perfect shells.*

- *Do not undermix or overmix the batter. If you undermix, you will have peaks on the tops of your cookies after piping, and they will crack when baked. The batter should be running through the piping tip before you even get it over to the parchment paper. It should also spread slightly on the parchment paper after piping.*

- *Let the shells dry out before baking. Be patient and you will prevail. If you don't let the shells dry, they will crack and won't rise properly.*

- *Bake for the full amount of time, even if they look done; if you bake them for less time, they will stick to the parchment paper.*

- *My favorite brand of natural food coloring is Color Garden. Your other option is to leave them all-natural; they will taste exactly the same. If using standard food coloring, you need only 2 or 3 drops of color per batch.*

- *Caster sugar is a very fine baking sugar. It's not so fine that it's powdered like confectioners' sugar (aka powdered sugar), but its granules are very fine compared to those of regular sugar. Caster sugar is sometimes referred to as baker's sugar or ultra-fine pure cane sugar. You can find it in the baking aisle.*

Skillet
COOKIE SUNDAES

PREP TIME: 25 minutes
COOK TIME: 20 to 25 minutes
READY IN: 2½ hours
YIELD: Two 6-inch (15-cm) sundaes or one 10-inch (25-cm) sundae

This recipe is talking to you. Directly to you. It wants you to make it. Have you ever been to BJ's Restaurant and Brewhouse and had a Pizookie? This recipe is my take on that dessert. Up until a few years ago, I thought Pizookie was just a clever and fun-to-say word for a delicious treat. It actually stands for the words pizza *and* cookie, *which they smashed together because 1) smashing things is fun, and 2) they bake the cookie in a deep-dish pan, the same way they would a pizza, therefore it's a pizza cookie or "Pizookie"—ta-da! Look how I act like I thought of it myself.*

Butter or coconut oil, for the skillet(s)

1 recipe French Vanilla Ice Cream (page 330)

1 recipe Soft Batch Chocolate Chip Cookie dough (page 300) or Simple Chocolate Chip Cookie dough (page 284)

1. Prepare the French Vanilla Ice Cream and transfer it to the freezer to firm up.

2. Adjust an oven rack to the middle position and preheat the oven to 350°F (177°C). Grease two 6-inch (15-cm) or one 10-inch (25-cm) cast-iron skillet(s); set aside.

3. Make the chocolate chip cookie dough (if making the soft batch variety, skip the step of chilling the dough). Transfer the dough to the skillet(s) and bake for 20 to 25 minutes, until golden and a toothpick comes out clean when inserted into the center.

4. To assemble the sundaes, place a scoop of ice cream on the center of each cookie. To store leftovers, make sure that no ice cream is left on the cookies, then remove the cookies from the skillets, transfer to an airtight container or wrap in foil, and store at room temperature for up to 3 days.

Notes: To make these sundaes dairy-free, use the Simple Chocolate Chip Cookies and grease the skillet(s) with coconut oil rather than butter.

Not a plain-vanilla ice cream fan? Me neither. Jazz it up with any of the ice cream recipes in this book. It's your sundae; go wild!

Flourless Almond
BUTTER COOKIES

PREP TIME: 10 minutes
COOK TIME (PER BATCH): 10 to 12 minutes
READY IN: 20 minutes
YIELD: 1 dozen cookies

I once saw a recipe for flourless peanut butter cookies. They looked easy and sounded delicious, so I was really curious to see if almond butter would work. Guess what? It did! I also tested sunflower seed butter, and it works great too. You can eat these cookies plain or throw in some chocolate chips or nuts and get crazy! I think even dried cranberries would be good; they would taste like peanut butter and jelly sandwich cookies. Oh yeah, I just took it there.

1 cup (225 g) smooth almond butter

¼ cup (60 ml) raw honey

1 large egg, room temperature

2 tablespoons maple sugar

1 teaspoon vanilla extract

½ teaspoon baking soda

½ teaspoon fine-grain sea salt

⅛ teaspoon ground cinnamon

1. Adjust an oven rack to the middle position and preheat the oven to 350°F (177°C). Line two baking sheets with parchment paper or nonstick baking mats; set aside. (*Note:* If working with only one baking sheet, allow it to cool completely between batches.)

2. Place all the ingredients in the bowl of a stand mixer fitted with the paddle or whisk attachment and beat on medium speed until smooth and combined. Alternatively, place the ingredients in a medium-sized mixing bowl and beat using a hand mixer set on medium speed until smooth and combined.

3. Use a spoon to place large dollops of dough, each about 1 to 2 tablespoons, on the baking sheets, spacing them about 2 inches (5 cm) apart, or 6 per sheet. If precise circles are desired, use your fingertips to shape them. Bake each sheet separately for 10 to 12 minutes or until the bottoms of the cookies are browned. The cookies will be puffy when removed from the oven; they will solidify as they cool. Leave on the baking sheet until they are cool enough to move to a cooling rack with a spatula. Store covered at room temperature for up to 3 days.

Notes: I get the best results when I use Barney Butter smooth almond butter. It's hands-down my absolute favorite almond butter. Mainly because it looks and tastes just like peanut butter. It works the best in any almond butter recipe, but feel free to use any kind you prefer. If you decided to use peanut butter in its place, I promise I won't tell anyone; your secret is safe with me.

To make these cookies nut-free, use sunflower seed butter in place of the almond butter.

Hot Chocolate
COOKIES

PREP TIME: 45 minutes
COOK TIME: 20 minutes
SETTING TIME: 15 minutes
READY IN: 1 hour 20 minutes
YIELD: 20 cookies

1 recipe Chocolate Fudge Cookies (page 280)

1 recipe Marshmallow Crème, regular (page 366) or egg-free (page 368)

2 tablespoons chocolate shavings, for garnish

This recipe was inspired by a similar one I saw online around Christmastime. I just had to make my own version. Who doesn't want hot chocolate and cookies over the winter holidays? Combining the two pretty much made the most sense anything ever has in the whole history of life.

1 Make the Chocolate Fudge Cookies.

2 While the cookies are cooling, prepare the Marshmallow Crème.

3 To assemble: Use a large spoon to place a generous dollop of Marshmallow Crème on top of each cookie. Allow the crème to firm up (to expedite this process, place the marshmallow-topped cookies in the refrigerator for at least 15 minutes). Garnish with chocolate shavings. Store covered at room temperature for up to 3 days.

Notes: To make this recipe dairy-free, use ghee or coconut oil rather than butter in the cookies. To make it egg-free, use the Egg-Free Marshmallow Crème.

Chocolate Turtle THUMBPRINT COOKIES

PREP TIME: 30 minutes
COOK TIME: 20 minutes
READY IN: 50 minutes
YIELD: 2 dozen cookies

I brought these cookies to work as I was developing recipes for this book, and one of my co-workers, Dom, flipped out over them. Like, flipped out. After that, every single recipe I brought in was, "Good, but not Chocolate Turtle Thumbprint Cookie good." He still talks about them. I hope that you make them and enjoy them just as much. In fact, maybe you could make them and bring them to my office, and then I won't have to hear about them anymore. Just a thought.

1 recipe Salted Caramel Sauce (page 374)

1 recipe Chocolate Fudge Cookie dough (page 280)

1½ cups (6 ounces/170 g) raw pecans, coarsely chopped or pulsed in a food processor

2½ tablespoons chocolate chips, for drizzling (optional)

1 Make the Salted Caramel Sauce and let cool in the refrigerator while preparing the cookies.

2 Adjust an oven rack to the middle position and preheat the oven to 350°F (177°C). Line two baking sheets with parchment paper or nonstick baking mats; set aside. (*Note:* If working with only one baking sheet, allow it to cool completely between batches.)

3 Prepare the Chocolate Fudge Cookie dough. After chilling the dough in the freezer as directed in Step 4 on page 280, use a melon baller or teaspoon to scoop out ½-inch (1.25-cm) balls of dough. Roll each dough ball through the pecans until entirely coated, then place on a prepared baking sheet, spacing the cookies 1 inch (2.5 cm) apart, about 12 per sheet. Refrigerate the remaining dough between batches.

4 Bake each sheet separately for 10 minutes or until a toothpick comes out clean. Remove from the oven and let cool slightly on the baking sheet. Lightly press your thumb or a ½-teaspoon measuring spoon into the center of each cookie to make an indentation. Let the cookies cool completely.

5 Remove the caramel sauce from the refrigerator and transfer to a piping bag fitted with the desired tip (such as a Wilton 1A) or to a resealable plastic bag with a corner cut off. Pipe a dollop of caramel in the center of each cookie. Melt the chocolate chips (if using) in a microwave-safe bowl, then transfer the melted chocolate to a resealable plastic bag and snip off a corner. Squeeze to drizzle chocolate across the top of each cookie. Store covered at room temperature for up to 3 days.

Notes: *To make these cookies dairy-free, use ghee or coconut oil rather than butter in the cookie dough and ghee in the caramel sauce.*

Soft and Chewy
GINGERBREAD COOKIES

I'm not biased when it comes to gingerbread cookies. I like ones that snap and ones that are soft and chewy. I like them all. These cookies are soft, chewy, and perfect for the holiday season, but to be honest, I'd eat them in July too. I just want to eat them; I don't really care when.

PREP TIME: 25 minutes

RESTING TIME: 1 hour

COOK TIME: 35 minutes

READY IN: 2 hours

YIELD: 30 cookies

10 tablespoons (5 ounces/142 g) salted butter

2 cups (185 g) sifted fine-ground blanched almond flour

¼ cup (40 g) coconut flour

2 teaspoons ginger powder

1½ teaspoons baking soda

1 teaspoon cream of tartar

1 teaspoon ground cinnamon

½ teaspoon ground cloves

¼ teaspoon fine-grain sea salt

1 cup (150 g) coconut sugar

¼ cup (60 ml) blackstrap molasses

2 large eggs, room temperature

2 tablespoons melted coconut butter, for drizzling (optional)

1. Brown the butter following the method described on page 360; let cool. Meanwhile, prepare the other ingredients.

2. In a large mixing bowl, combine the flours, ginger, baking soda, cream of tartar, cinnamon, cloves, and salt. Stir together using a fork until well combined; set aside.

3. In a separate medium-sized mixing bowl, combine the coconut sugar and molasses. Mix together using a hand mixer set on low speed.

4. Once the butter has cooled, use a rubber spatula to transfer it to the coconut sugar bowl; use the spatula to scrape in the browned bits as well. Beat the butter and sugars together with the hand mixer on low until combined, about 1 minute. Add the eggs one at a time, mixing well after each addition.

5. Use the rubber spatula to transfer the egg mixture to the dry mixture. Beat on low until thoroughly combined. Scrape down the sides of the bowl and cover with plastic wrap, pressing it directly on the surface of the dough. Chill in the freezer for 1 hour or until firm.

6. After about 45 minutes, adjust an oven rack to the middle position and preheat the oven to 350°F (177°C). Line two baking sheets with parchment paper or nonstick baking mats; set aside. (*Note:* Because the yield is large and these cookies spread when baked, you will need to bake the cookies in four rotations; be sure to allow the baking sheets to cool completely between batches and keep the dough chilled.)

7. Once the dough is chilled, grab some dough and roll it between your palms to form 1-inch (2.5-cm) balls. Place the dough balls on the prepared baking sheets, spaced about 2 inches (5 cm) apart, or up to 9 cookies per sheet. Bake each sheet separately for 11 to 12 minutes or until the edges of the cookies are browned. Remove the parchment paper or baking mat from the baking sheet and let the cookies cool.

8. To garnish, transfer the melted coconut butter to a resealable plastic bag, snip off a corner, and drizzle the coconut butter over the cookies. Store covered at room temperature for up to 3 days.

CHAPTER 12

What's THE SCOOP?

DAIRY FREE*   NUT FREE

THE Best CHOCOLATE
ICE CREAM

I'm not kidding when I say that this is the best chocolate ice cream. You can't even tell that it's dairy-free; it tastes that good. I could probably eat the whole batch in one sitting if you dared me to. I would probably eat the whole batch anyway, even if you didn't dare me to. Don't judge. This ice cream is amazing with any sort of topping, from chocolate sauce to berry sauce to marshmallow crème for a rocky road version. You can really go nuts with it (literally!) or just eat it plain. Winning!

PREP TIME: 15 minutes
SETTING TIME: 1 to 2 hours
READY IN: 1 hour 15 minutes
YIELD: 1 pint (473 ml)

1 cup (7 ounces /170 g) chopped chocolate or chocolate chips

2 (13½-ounce/400-ml) cans full-fat coconut milk

4 large egg yolks

½ cup (65 g) maple sugar

2 teaspoons vanilla extract

¼ teaspoon fine-grain sea salt

⅛ teaspoon ground cinnamon

SPECIAL EQUIPMENT

Ice cream maker

MAKE AHEAD

ICE CREAM BASE—2 DAYS AHEAD:
STORE IN THE REFRIGERATOR UNTIL
READY TO CHURN

Subs: ½ cup (120 ml) of pure maple syrup in place of the maple sugar. Whisk the yolks alone until they have lightened in color. Continue with the recipe, adding the maple syrup in Step 5 when stirring in the vanilla, salt, and cinnamon.

Variation: **Dairy-Based Best Chocolate Ice Cream.** Substitute 1½ cups (350 ml) of whole milk and 1 cup (240 ml) of heavy cream for the coconut milk.

1 Place the chocolate in a large mixing bowl; set aside.

2 Heat the coconut milk in a large heavy-bottomed saucepan set over medium heat, stirring intermittently with a wooden spoon, until it reaches a simmer.

3 Meanwhile, in a large mixing bowl, whisk together the egg yolks and maple sugar until the yolks thicken and become a pale yellow.

4 When the coconut milk comes to a simmer, remove the pan from the heat. Temper the egg yolks by pouring one-third of the hot coconut milk into the egg and sugar mixture, whisking continually so that the egg yolks don't begin to cook, until combined. Then pour another one-third of the coconut milk into the egg mixture and continue to whisk. Once combined, transfer the egg mixture in the bowl to the saucepan with the remaining one-third of the coconut milk. Place the pan over medium-low heat, stirring constantly so that the egg doesn't cook on the bottom of the pan, until the mixture is thick enough to coat the wooden spoon, 7 to 10 minutes.

5 Pour the thickened mixture through a fine-mesh sieve over the chocolate to melt it. (The sieve will filter out any egg that may have cooked during the process.) Add the vanilla, salt, and cinnamon and stir using the wooden spoon until the chocolate is completely melted and the mixture is fully combined.

6 Press plastic wrap onto the surface of the mixture and place in the refrigerator for 1 to 2 hours or until cool. Alternatively, place in the freezer for 30 minutes or until cool.

7 Pour the mixture into the bowl of an ice cream maker and churn it, following the manufacturer's instructions. If firmer ice cream is desired, transfer to a container, cover, and place in the freezer for 30 minutes or until the desired firmness is reached. Store the ice cream in a covered container for up to 2 weeks.

DAIRY FREE* NUT FREE*

Double Chocolate
ICE CREAM SANDWICHES

PREP TIME: 35 minutes
RESTING TIME: 1½ to 2½ hours
COOK TIME: 10 minutes
READY IN: 2 hours 15 minutes
YIELD: 6 sandwiches

1 recipe The Best Chocolate Ice Cream (page 322)

1 recipe Chocolate Fudge Cookies (page 280) or Flourless Double Chocolate Chip Cookies (page 298)

SPECIAL EQUIPMENT
Ice cream maker

MAKE AHEAD

ICE CREAM BASE—2 DAYS AHEAD:
STORE IN THE REFRIGERATOR
UNTIL READY TO CHURN

COOKIES—1 DAY AHEAD

What's better than chocolate? Besides "nothing," your only answer should be "DOUBLE CHOCOLATE!" These ice cream sandwiches are chocolate overload in the best possible way.

1 Prepare the chocolate ice cream base, following Steps 1 through 6 on page 322.

2 While the ice cream mixture is chilling, make the cookies.

3 While the cookies are cooling, churn the ice cream by pouring the chilled ice cream mixture into the bowl of an ice cream maker and churn it, following the manufacturer's instructions. To firm up the ice cream and make it easier to scoop for sandwiches, transfer to a container, cover, and place in the freezer for 30 minutes or until the desired firmness is reached.

4 To assemble: Turn 6 cookies upside down on a sheet of parchment paper. Place a scoop of ice cream on each one. Then place another cookie on top of the ice cream and press down gently. Enjoy immediately. Another option is to assemble the ice cream sandwiches, wrap them individually and securely in parchment paper, and then place each wrapped sandwich in a large resealable plastic freezer bag to enjoy later. Let thaw on the counter for about 10 minutes before serving.

Notes: To make these sandwiches dairy-free, use ghee or coconut oil to make the Chocolate Fudge Cookies or use the Flourless Double Chocolate Chip Cookies. To make them nut-free, use the Flourless Double Chocolate Chip Cookies. The cookies featured in the photo are the Chocolate Fudge Cookies.

You will have leftover cookies since you are making a full batch and need only 12 of them to yield 6 ice cream sandwiches. You could make a half batch, but I suggest making the full recipe, because if you have ice cream left over, you can make more sandwiches. You can even repurpose the leftover cookies for another recipe or just enjoy them on their own. As I see it, if you're going to the trouble of baking cookies and churning ice cream, you might as well make the whole batch. If you want to make a half batch of the Chocolate Fudge Cookies, be advised that it will yield only 10 cookies, which would make just 5 ice cream sandwiches.

Simple Vanilla
ICE CREAM

PREP TIME: 15 minutes
SETTING TIME: 1 to 2 hours
READY IN: 1 hour 15 minutes
YIELD: 1 pint (473 ml)

This recipe is so simple and quick! For having no eggs, it still comes out quite creamy and doesn't taste "icy" at all. It's a great Paleo-friendly ice cream, especially for those who don't tolerate eggs well and can't use them in ice cream recipes. This was the first Paleo ice cream I ever made, and it holds a special place in my ice cream heart.

2 (13½-ounce/400-ml) cans full-fat coconut milk

½ cup (120 ml) pure maple syrup, any type

2 teaspoons vanilla extract

¼ teaspoon fine-grain sea salt

SPECIAL EQUIPMENT
Ice cream maker

1. Combine all the ingredients in the pitcher of a blender. Cover with the lid and blend until combined, then transfer the entire pitcher to the refrigerator to cool for 1 to 2 hours or overnight. Alternatively, place the pitcher in the freezer for 30 minutes or until cool. If the coconut cream separates, just put the pitcher back on the blender base and process until creamy and blended.

2. Pour the mixture into the bowl of an ice cream maker and churn it, following the manufacturer's instructions. If firmer ice cream is desired, transfer to a container, cover, and place in the freezer for 30 minutes or until the desired firmness is reached. Store the ice cream in a covered container for up to 2 weeks.

MAKE AHEAD

ICE CREAM BASE—2 DAYS AHEAD: STORE IN THE REFRIGERATOR UNTIL READY TO CHURN

Variation: **Dairy-Based Simple Vanilla Ice Cream.** *Substitute 1½ cups (350 ml) of whole milk and 1 cup (240 ml) of heavy cream for the coconut milk.*

COOKIE DOUGH
ICE CREAM SANDWICHES

PREP TIME: 30 minutes
SETTING TIME: 1 hour 50 minutes to 2 hours 50 minutes
READY IN: 2 hours 20 minutes
YIELD: 9 sandwiches

1 recipe French Vanilla Ice Cream (page 330) or Simple Vanilla Ice Cream (page 326)

1 recipe Cookie Dough Fudge (page 152)

SPECIAL EQUIPMENT
Ice cream maker

MAKE AHEAD

ICE CREAM BASE—2 DAYS AHEAD:
STORE IN THE REFRIGERATOR
UNTIL READY TO CHURN

COOKIE DOUGH LAYERS—1 WEEK
AHEAD: STORE COVERED IN THE
FREEZER UNTIL READY TO ASSEMBLE

Notes: To make these egg-free, use the Simple Vanilla Ice Cream.

This recipe is by far the most popular recipe on my blog, so of course I had to include it in my book. These ice cream sandwiches are like taking cookie dough and sandwiching ice cream between it. And then eating it. Yeah, it's like that. They are incredible. One of my all-time favorites!

1. Prepare the French Vanilla Ice Cream base by completing Steps 1 through 5 on page 330, or the Simple Vanilla Ice Cream base by completing Step 1 on page 326. While the ice cream base is chilling, work on the cookie dough layer.

2. Line an 8-inch (20-cm) square glass pan with parchment paper, leaving some overhang; set aside. Prepare the Cookie Dough Fudge, following Steps 2 through 4 on page 152.

3. Remove the chilled dough from the freezer and fold in the chocolate chips. Divide the dough in half. Take one half and press it evenly into the parchment-lined pan. Use the parchment paper to help remove it from the pan and set aside. Lay another piece of parchment paper in the pan, again leaving some overhang, and repeat the process with the remaining half of the dough. Then take the cookie dough layer that was set aside and put it on top of the layer that was just pressed. This ensures that the layers won't stick to each other. Place in the freezer for 20 minutes to set.

4. While the cookie dough layers are chilling, churn the ice cream: Pour the chilled mixture into the bowl of an ice cream maker and churn it, following the manufacturer's instructions. By the time the cookie dough layers are ready, the ice cream should be churned.

5. Remove the top layer of cookie dough using the parchment paper as grips; set aside. Use a rubber spatula or spoon to transfer and spread a layer of ice cream evenly over the bottom cookie dough layer. Then take the cookie dough layer that was set aside and flip it over, directly on top of the ice cream layer, with the parchment paper now on top. Remove the parchment paper and press down on the cookie dough with your fingertips until it is set in place. Cover and place in the freezer for 30 minutes to harden the ice cream.

6. When ready to serve, heat up a large chef's knife by placing it under hot running water. Dry the knife and use it to cut 9 ice cream sandwiches. Store any leftovers covered in the pan for up to 2 weeks. Let thaw on the counter for 5 to 10 minutes before serving.

DAIRY FREE NUT FREE

French Vanilla
ICE CREAM

PREP TIME: 15 minutes
SETTING TIME: 1 to 2 hours
READY IN: 1 hour 15 minutes
YIELD: 1 pint (473 ml)

Did you know that vanilla is the most popular ice cream flavor of all time? Vanilla ice cream is crucial to the balance of life. You absolutely have to have it for certain things, like topping brownies and warm-from-the-oven fruit cobblers and making ice cream sundaes and ice cream sandwiches. Sure, you could use other flavors, and I'm sure they'd be quite delicious, but there is just something classic about regular ol' vanilla ice cream.

2 (13½-ounce/400-ml) cans full-fat coconut milk

4 large egg yolks

½ cup (65 g) maple sugar

2 tablespoons raw honey

2 teaspoons vanilla extract

¼ teaspoon fine-grain sea salt

SPECIAL EQUIPMENT

Ice cream maker

1 Heat the coconut milk in a large heavy-bottomed saucepan set over medium heat, stirring intermittently with a wooden spoon, until it reaches a simmer.

2 Meanwhile, in a large mixing bowl, whisk together the egg yolks and maple sugar until the yolks thicken and become a pale yellow.

3 When the coconut milk comes to a simmer, remove from the heat. Temper the egg yolks by pouring one-third of the hot coconut milk into the egg and sugar mixture, whisking continually so that the egg yolks don't begin to cook, until combined. Then pour another one-third of the coconut milk into the egg mixture and continue to whisk. Once combined, transfer the egg mixture in the bowl to the saucepan with the remaining one-third of the coconut milk. Place the pan over medium-low heat, stirring constantly so that the egg doesn't cook on the bottom of the pan, and simmer until the mixture is thick enough to coat the wooden spoon, 7 to 10 minutes.

4 Pour the thickened mixture through a fine-mesh sieve over a clean mixing bowl. (The sieve will filter out any egg that may have cooked during the process.) Stir in the honey, vanilla, and salt until combined.

5 Press plastic wrap onto the surface of the mixture and place in the refrigerator for 1 to 2 hours or until cool. Alternatively, place in the freezer for 30 minutes or until cool.

6 Pour the mixture into the bowl of an ice cream maker and churn it, following the manufacturer's instructions. If firmer ice cream is desired, transfer to a container, cover, and place in the freezer for 30 minutes or until the desired firmness is reached. Store the ice cream in a covered container for up to 2 weeks.

Notes: For a dairy version, use 1½ cups (350 ml) of whole milk and 1 cup (240 ml) of heavy cream instead of the canned coconut milk.

Subs: ½ cup (120 ml) of pure maple syrup in place of the maple sugar. Whisk the yolks alone until they have lightened in color. Continue with the recipe, adding the maple syrup in Step 4 when stirring in the honey, vanilla, and salt.

Snickerdoodle
ICE CREAM SANDWICHES

PREP TIME: 35 minutes
RESTING TIME: 1½ to 2½ hours
COOK TIME: 11 to 12 minutes
READY IN: 2 hours 15 minutes
YIELD: 6 sandwiches

1 recipe Browned Butter Snickerdoodles (page 282)

1 recipe French Vanilla Ice Cream (page 330) or Simple Vanilla Ice Cream (page 326)

SPECIAL EQUIPMENT
Ice cream maker

MAKE AHEAD
BROWNED BUTTER
SNICKERDOODLES—1 DAY AHEAD

ICE CREAM BASE—2 DAYS AHEAD:
STORE IN THE REFRIGERATOR
UNTIL READY TO CHURN

First of all, snickerdoodles. Second of all, ice cream. Would you like me to go on? I thought so. This recipe is like cinnamon-covered vanilla heaven. The snickerdoodles are so soft, and when you take a bite, the ice cream just melts into a cookie cloud on your tongue. I could go on and on about it, but you should probably just make them and taste for yourself.

1 Prepare the Browned Butter Snickerdoodles through Step 4 on page 282. While waiting for the dough to set, prepare the French Vanilla Ice Cream base by completing Steps 1 through 4 on page 330 or the Simple Vanilla Ice Cream base by completing Step 1 on page 326. Place the ice cream base in the freezer for a quick 30-minute cool-down.

2 After the cookie dough has been in the freezer for about 45 minutes, preheat the oven to 350°F (177°C). Line two baking sheets with parchment paper or nonstick baking mats; set aside. (*Note:* If working with only one baking sheet, let it cool completely between batches.)

3 Roll the cookie dough in the sugar and cinnamon, then bake as instructed, following Steps 6 through 8 on page 282. While the cookies are cooling, make the ice cream: Pour the mixture into the bowl of an ice cream maker and churn it, following the manufacturer's instructions. To firm up the ice cream and make it easier to scoop for sandwiches, transfer to a container, cover, and place in the freezer for 30 minutes or until the desired firmness is reached.

4 To assemble: Turn 6 snickerdoodles upside down on a sheet of parchment paper. Place a scoop of ice cream on each one. Then place another snickerdoodle on top of the ice cream and press down gently. Enjoy immediately. Another option is to assemble the ice cream sandwiches, wrap them individually and securely in parchment paper, and then place each wrapped sandwich in a large resealable plastic freezer bag to enjoy later. Let thaw on the counter for about 10 minutes before serving.

Notes: To make these egg-free, use the Simple Vanilla Ice Cream.

You will have leftover cookies since you are making a full batch and need only 12 of them to yield 6 ice cream sandwiches. You could make a half batch, but I suggest making the full recipe, because if you have ice cream left over, you can make more sandwiches or even make another batch of ice cream if you have more people to serve. You can even repurpose the leftover cookies for another recipe or just enjoy them on their own. As I see it, you're going to all the trouble anyway, so you might as well make the whole batch.

Blackberry Swirl
GOAT CHEESE ICE CREAM

PREP TIME: 25 minutes
SETTING TIME: 1 to 2 hours
READY IN: 1 hour 25 minutes
YIELD: 1 pint (473 ml)

This recipe was inspired by some gelato that I had during my first trip to Austin, Texas, at a little gelato shop called Dolce Neve. They make gelato with milk that comes from grass-fed cows. The owners are from Italy too, so you know it's legit. While I was there, I ordered a blackberry and goat cheese gelato; it tasted like pure heaven. When I was thinking up ice cream flavors to include in my book, I knew I had to have this one.

FOR THE BLACKBERRY SAUCE

6 ounces (170 g) fresh blackberries (about ¾ cup)

2 tablespoons raw honey

1 tablespoon fresh-squeezed lemon juice

1 teaspoon vanilla extract

FOR THE ICE CREAM BASE

1½ cups (350 ml) whole milk

1 cup (240 ml) heavy cream

4 large egg yolks

½ cup (65 g) maple sugar

3 ounces (85 g) goat cheese, crumbled

2 tablespoons raw honey

1 teaspoon vanilla extract

¼ teaspoon fine-grain sea salt

SPECIAL EQUIPMENT

Ice cream maker

Notes: You can repurpose leftover blackberry sauce by drizzling it as a topping over the Almond Butter and Jelly Ice Cream Sandwiches on page 336.

MAKE AHEAD

BLACKBERRY SAUCE—1 DAY AHEAD

ICE CREAM BASE—2 DAYS AHEAD: STORE IN THE REFRIGERATOR UNTIL READY TO CHURN

1. Make the blackberry sauce: In the pitcher of a blender, combine the blackberries, honey, lemon juice, and vanilla. Blend until the mixture becomes liquid, then strain through a fine-mesh sieve set over a clean bowl to remove the seeds. Cover and place in the refrigerator.

2. In a large heavy-bottomed saucepan, bring the milk and cream to a simmer over medium heat, stirring intermittently with a wooden spoon.

3. Meanwhile, in a large mixing bowl, whisk together the egg yolks and maple sugar until the yolks thicken and become a pale yellow.

4. When the milk begins to simmer, remove the pan from the heat. Temper the egg yolks by pouring one-third of the hot milk into the egg and sugar mixture, whisking continually so that the egg yolks don't begin to cook, until combined. Then pour another one-third of the hot milk into the egg mixture while whisking. Once combined, transfer the egg mixture in the bowl to the saucepan with the remaining milk. Place the pan over medium-low heat, stirring constantly so that the egg doesn't cook on the bottom of the pan, and simmer until the mixture is thick enough to coat the wooden spoon, 7 to 10 minutes.

5. Place the goat cheese in a clean medium-sized mixing bowl. Pour the thickened milk and egg mixture through a fine-mesh sieve over the goat cheese in the mixing bowl. (The sieve will filter out any egg that may have cooked during the process.) Stir until combined. It's fine if some goat cheese crumbles remain. Stir in the honey, vanilla, and salt until combined.

6. Press plastic wrap onto the surface of the mixture and place in the refrigerator for 1 to 2 hours or until cool. Alternatively, place in the freezer for 30 minutes or until cool.

7. Pour the mixture into the bowl of an ice cream maker and churn it, following the manufacturer's instructions. Transfer half of the ice cream to a container, pour some of the blackberry sauce on top, and use a chopstick, butter knife, or toothpick to swirl it through the ice cream. Repeat with the remaining ice cream and more blackberry sauce. (There will likely be leftover blackberry sauce; drizzle it over the ice cream as a topping, if desired.) Cover and place in the freezer for 30 minutes or until the desired firmness is reached. Store the ice cream in a covered container for up to 2 weeks.

NUT FREE*

ALMOND BUTTER AND JELLY
ICE CREAM SANDWICHES

PREP TIME: 35 minutes
RESTING TIME: 1½ to 2½ hours
COOK TIME: 10 to 12 minutes
READY IN: 2 hours 15 minutes
YIELD: 6 sandwiches

1 recipe Blackberry Swirl Goat Cheese Ice Cream (page 334)

1 recipe Flourless Almond Butter Cookies (page 312)

SPECIAL EQUIPMENT

Ice cream maker

MAKE AHEAD

FLOURLESS ALMOND BUTTER COOKIES—1 DAY AHEAD

ICE CREAM BASE—2 DAYS AHEAD: STORE IN THE REFRIGERATOR UNTIL READY TO CHURN

Almond butter and jelly ice cream sandwiches! Get right out of town. The combination of almond butter and jelly doesn't sound quite as classic as peanut butter and jelly, but you get the gist. Your days of longing for the sandwiches from your childhood are over.

1 Prepare the base for the Blackberry Swirl Goat Cheese Ice Cream, following Steps 1 through 6 on page 334. While the base is chilling, make the Flourless Almond Butter Cookies. Allow the cookies to cool completely before assembling the sandwiches.

2 While the cookies are cooling, churn the ice cream, following Step 7 on page 334. To firm up the ice cream and make it easier to scoop for sandwiches, transfer to a container, cover, and place in the freezer for 30 minutes or until the desired firmness is reached.

3 To assemble: Turn 6 cookies upside down on the parchment paper. Place a scoop of ice cream on each one. If desired, spoon a dollop of leftover blackberry sauce over the ice cream. Then place another cookie on top of the ice cream and press down gently. Enjoy immediately. Another option is to assemble the ice cream sandwiches, wrap them individually and securely in parchment paper, and then place each wrapped sandwich in a large resealable plastic freezer bag to enjoy later. Let thaw on the counter for about 10 minutes before serving.

Notes: To make these sandwiches nut-free, make the Flourless Almond Butter Cookies with sunflower seed butter.

You will have leftover cookies since you are making a full batch and need only 12 of them to yield 6 ice cream sandwiches. You could make a half batch, but I suggest that you make the full recipe, because if you have ice cream left over, you can make more sandwiches or even make another batch of ice cream if you have more people to serve. You can even repurpose the leftover cookies for another recipe or just enjoy them on their own. As I see it, if you're going to the trouble of baking cookies, you might as well make the whole batch.

Sea Salt AND Honey
ICE CREAM

PREP TIME: 15 minutes
SETTING TIME: 1 to 2 hours
READY IN: 1 hour 15 minutes
YIELD: 1 pint (473 ml)

There is something romantic about this ice cream. I can't quite put my finger on it, but it's just so whimsical and carefree. I love the flavor of honey ice cream and the way the salt creates the perfect balance of salty and sweet.

2 (13½-ounce/400-ml) cans full-fat coconut milk

4 large egg yolks

¼ cup (35 g) maple sugar

½ cup (120 ml) raw honey

½ teaspoon fine-grain sea salt

Sea salt (fine to coarsely ground or flake), for garnish

SPECIAL EQUIPMENT

Ice cream maker

MAKE AHEAD

ICE CREAM BASE—2 DAYS AHEAD:
STORE IN THE REFRIGERATOR
UNTIL READY TO CHURN

1 In a large heavy-bottomed saucepan, bring the coconut milk to a simmer over medium heat, stirring intermittently with a wooden spoon.

2 Meanwhile, in a large mixing bowl, whisk together the egg yolks and maple sugar until the yolks thicken and become a pale yellow.

3 When the coconut milk comes to a simmer, remove the pan from the heat. Temper the egg yolks by pouring one-third of the hot coconut milk into the egg and sugar mixture, whisking continually so that the egg yolks don't begin to cook, until combined. Then pour another one-third of the hot coconut milk into the egg mixture and continue to whisk. Once combined, transfer the egg mixture in the bowl to the saucepan with the remaining coconut milk. Place the pan over medium-low heat, stirring constantly so that the egg doesn't cook on the bottom of the pan, and simmer until the mixture is thick enough to coat the wooden spoon, 7 to 10 minutes.

4 Pour the thickened mixture through a fine-mesh sieve set over a clean mixing bowl. (The sieve will filter out any egg that may have cooked during the process.) Stir in the honey and salt until combined.

5 Press plastic wrap onto the surface of the mixture and place in the refrigerator for 1 to 2 hours or until cool. Alternatively, place in the freezer for 30 minutes or until cool.

6 Pour the mixture into the bowl of an ice cream maker and churn it, following the manufacturer's instructions. If firmer ice cream is desired, transfer to a container, cover, and place in the freezer for 30 minutes or until the desired firmness is reached. Garnish with sea salt. Store the ice cream in a covered container for up to 2 weeks.

Notes: *Add a drizzle of honey over the ice cream as a topping.*

For a dairy version, substitute 1½ cups (350 ml) of whole milk and 1 cup (240 ml) of heavy cream for the coconut milk.

Chocolate-Covered Frozen ALMOND BUTTER Banana Bites

PREP TIME: 20 minutes
SETTING TIME: 2 to 4 hours
READY IN: 2 hours 20 minutes
YIELD: 20 bites

Could the name of this recipe be any longer? I couldn't help it! This recipe was inspired by a recipe I saw on a food blog for chocolate-covered bananas with sea salt sprinkled on them. I couldn't believe how genius it was, and so easy. You know me, though; I always have to take it up a notch. So I sliced the banana bites in half and added almond butter in the center. I know. To create a nut-free version, I also made a few with the Salted Caramel Sauce on page 374. So crazy delicious.

¼ cup (55 g) smooth almond butter

4 bananas, sliced crosswise into ½-inch (1.25-cm) pieces

1 recipe Chocolate Shell Coating (page 376)

2 teaspoons coarse or flake sea salt, for garnish

MAKE AHEAD

FROZEN BANANAS WITH ALMOND BUTTER—2 WEEKS AHEAD

SALTED CARAMEL SAUCE (VARIATION)—2 DAYS AHEAD

1 Line a baking sheet with parchment paper. Place the almond butter in a piping bag or in a resealable plastic bag with a corner cut off. Pipe a small dollop of almond butter in the center of half of the banana slices. Sandwich with the remaining banana slices and poke them through with a cocktail fork. Freeze for 2 to 4 hours or until frozen.

2 About 15 minutes before the bananas are ready, prepare the Chocolate Shell Coating. Holding onto the cocktail fork, dip a banana into the chocolate and coat evenly, allowing any excess chocolate to drip back into the bowl. Place the chocolate-covered banana on the parchment-lined baking sheet. Repeat the process until all the frozen bananas have been dipped in chocolate, then sprinkle sea salt on top of each one. Enjoy immediately or place back in the freezer to enjoy later. Store in a covered container for up to 2 weeks.

Notes: Depending on your freezer, the bananas could freeze in as little as 2 hours, or it might take up to 4 hours.

For a nut-free version, replace the almond butter with sunflower seed butter or ¼ cup (60 ml) of Salted Caramel Sauce (page 374).

Strawberry CHEESECAKE POPS

PREP TIME: 15 minutes
SETTING TIME: 4½ hours
READY IN: 4 hours 45 minutes
YIELD: 10 pops

½ cup (120 ml) whole milk

½ cup (120 ml) heavy cream

4 large egg yolks

½ cup (65 g) maple sugar

2 tablespoons raw honey

¼ teaspoon fine-grain sea salt

½ cup (60 g) gluten-free graham cracker crumbs (see Notes)

1 tablespoon salted butter, melted

¼ cup (60 ml) sour cream

2 ounces (55 g) cream cheese

10 strawberries (about 6½ ounces/185 g), quartered

SPECIAL EQUIPMENT

10 Popsicle molds and 10 Popsicle sticks

Notes: To make these pops dairy-free, replace the whole milk and heavy cream with 1 (13½-ounce/400-ml) can of full-fat coconut milk and omit the sour cream and cream cheese. Use dairy-free graham cracker crumbs.

I prefer Kinnikinnick Graham Style Crumbs, which are dairy-free and nut-free. You can find them at Whole Foods, Vitacost, and Amazon. Or you could make the Graham Cracker Crust on page 170, bake it, and then crumble it. Note, however, that my crust recipe is not dairy-free or nut-free.

I saw the idea for these pops on another food blog and had to make my own version. I think the original version had corn syrup in it. Yikes. So I cleaned it up a bit and made it better for your gluten-free enjoyment, with a dairy-free option as well. Look how much I love you.

1 In a large heavy-bottomed saucepan, bring the milk and cream to a simmer over medium heat, stirring intermittently with a wooden spoon.

2 Meanwhile, in a large mixing bowl, whisk together the egg yolks and maple sugar until the yolks thicken and become a pale yellow.

3 When the milk and cream come to a simmer, remove the pan from the heat. Temper the egg yolks by pouring one-third of the hot coconut milk into the egg and sugar mixture, whisking continually so that the egg yolks don't begin to cook, until combined. Then pour another one-third of the hot milk and cream into the egg mixture and continue to whisk. Once combined, transfer the egg mixture in the bowl to the saucepan with the remaining milk and cream. Place the pan over medium-low heat, stirring constantly so that the egg doesn't cook on the bottom of the pan, and simmer until the mixture is thick enough to coat the wooden spoon, 7 to 10 minutes.

4 Pour the thickened mixture through a fine-mesh sieve set over the pitcher of a blender. (The sieve will filter out any egg that may have cooked during the process.) Stir in the honey and salt with a spoon. Cover with the lid and refrigerate for 1 to 2 hours or until cool. Alternatively, place in the freezer for 30 minutes or until cool.

5 While the mixture is cooling, prepare the crust: Place the graham cracker crumbs and melted butter in a small bowl. Use a fork to stir and mash together until combined. Alternatively, a food processor will work: Process the crumbs and pour the melted butter in slowly until the mixture looks like wet sand. Set aside.

6 Once the egg and milk mixture has cooled, add the sour cream, cream cheese, and strawberries to the blender pitcher. Blend together until well combined and creamy.

7 Pour the mixture into the molds, leaving ½ to ¾ inch (1.25 to 2 cm) at the top for the graham cracker crust. Tap lightly on the counter to remove any air bubbles. Gently press the crust into the molds, being careful not to press too hard. Place a Popsicle stick in each slot. Cover and place in the freezer for 4 hours or overnight, until frozen. Remove from the freezer 10 minutes before serving to make it easier to remove the pops from their molds.

Coffee
ICE CREAM

PREP TIME: 15 minutes
SETTING TIME: 1 to 2 hours
READY IN: 1 hour 15 minutes
YIELD: 1 pint (473 ml)

My cat loves coffee ice cream. True story. He's loved it since he was a kitten. I feel somewhat responsible for this because I went through a sweatpants, chick flick, and Häagen-Dazs coffee ice cream phase. Now, if I ever eat coffee ice cream, he instantly appears out of thin air and badgers me until I let him lick the spoon. When I made and photographed this recipe, he would not leave me alone. I didn't think I was going to get the shot because he kept trying to jump on the table and eat the ice cream. For some reason he just loves coffee ice cream. He can't get enough of it. This recipe will totally replace your Häagen-Dazs. The sweatpants and chick flicks are out of my control, though.

2 (13½-ounce/400-ml) cans full-fat coconut milk

3 tablespoons instant espresso coffee

4 large egg yolks

½ cup (65 g) maple sugar

2 tablespoons raw honey

2 teaspoons vanilla extract

¼ teaspoon fine-grain sea salt

SPECIAL EQUIPMENT

Ice cream maker

Notes: I used Medaglia D'Oro instant espresso coffee granules. This product is widely available; you can find it at your local grocery store or on Amazon.

For a dairy version, substitute 1½ cups (350 ml) of whole milk and 1 cup (240 ml) of heavy cream for the coconut milk.

1. Place the coconut milk and instant espresso in a large heavy-bottomed saucepan set over medium heat, stirring intermittently with a wooden spoon until it reaches a simmer.

2. Meanwhile, in a large mixing bowl, whisk together the egg yolks and maple sugar until the yolks thicken and become a pale yellow.

3. When the coconut milk comes to a simmer, remove from the heat. Temper the egg yolks by pouring one-third of the hot coconut milk into the egg and sugar mixture, whisking continually so that the egg doesn't begin to cook, until combined. Then pour another one-third of the hot coconut milk into the egg mixture and continue to whisk. Once combined, transfer the egg mixture in the bowl to the saucepan with the remaining coconut milk. Place the pan over medium-low heat, stirring constantly so that the egg doesn't cook on the bottom of the pan, and simmer until the mixture is thick enough to coat the wooden spoon, 7 to 10 minutes.

4. Pour the thickened mixture through a fine-mesh sieve over a clean mixing bowl. (The sieve will filter out any egg that may have cooked during the process.) Stir in the honey, vanilla, and salt until combined.

5. Press plastic wrap onto the surface of the mixture and place in the refrigerator for 1 to 2 hours or until cool. Alternatively, place in the freezer for 30 minutes or until cool.

6. Pour the mixture into the bowl of an ice cream maker and churn it, following the manufacturer's instructions. If firmer ice cream is desired, transfer to a container, cover, and place in the freezer for 30 minutes or until the desired firmness is reached. Store the ice cream in a covered container for up to 2 weeks.

Subs: ½ cup (120 ml) of pure maple syrup in place of the maple sugar. Whisk the yolks alone until they have lightened in color. Continue with the recipe, adding the maple syrup in Step 4 when stirring in the honey, vanilla, and salt.

Variation: **Espresso Chip Ice Cream.** Add some chocolate chunks to your coffee ice cream halfway through churning to create an espresso chip flavor! The reason to add the chocolate pieces midchurn is that if the ice cream is still liquid, they will probably sink to the bottom and not be evenly distributed in the ice cream.

Salted Caramel
ICE CREAM

PREP TIME: 25 minutes
SETTING TIME: 1 to 2 hours
READY IN: 1 hour 25 minutes
YIELD: 1 pint (473 ml)

1½ cups (350 ml) whole milk

1 cup (240 ml) heavy cream

½ cup (75 g) coconut sugar

¼ cup (35 g) maple sugar

4 tablespoons (2 ounces/56 g) salted butter

4 large egg yolks

2 teaspoons vanilla extract

¼ teaspoon fine-grain sea salt

SPECIAL EQUIPMENT
Ice cream maker

Notes: To make this ice cream dairy-free, use 2 (13½-ounce/400-ml) cans of full-fat coconut milk in place of the whole milk and heavy cream, and substitute ghee for the butter.

Looking for a grass-fed version? Just use grass-fed versions of the milk and cream! I'm a huge fan of Organic Valley Grassmilk, available nationwide, and Organic Pastures raw dairy products, available only in California (with the exception of their cheese).

This is my favorite ice cream that I made for this book. It rivals a famous brand that runs about $13 a pint. Better yet, I don't even have to leave the house; I can stay in my sweats while I wait for it to churn. Stretchy pants and ice cream just go together, kind of like sea salt and caramel.

1. Place the milk and cream in a large heavy-bottomed saucepan set over medium heat, stirring intermittently with a wooden spoon until it reaches a simmer.

2. Meanwhile, combine the sugars and butter in a medium-sized saucepan set over medium-low heat. Whisk intermittently until the sugars are combined and the butter starts to melt. Continue to stir occasionally as the butter melts and the sugars begin to absorb it. When the butter is completely melted and the sugar is heated, the mixture will become smooth instead of granular. Start to whisk vigorously until it's completely smooth and has the look and texture of caramel. Turn the heat down to low and check on the milk. The caramel needs to stay slightly warm or the sugar will start to become granular again.

3. When the milk has come to a simmer, remove the pan from the heat and pour one-third of the hot milk into the warm caramel. Whisk together, then add another one-third of the milk to the caramel and whisk again. Once combined, transfer the milk and caramel mixture to the saucepan with the remaining one-third of the milk and place the pan over medium-low heat for a few minutes, until it starts to simmer.

4. While you are heating the milk and caramel mixture, whisk the egg yolks in a medium-sized mixing bowl until they have lightened in color and become a pale yellow.

5. When the milk mixture comes to a simmer, remove the pan from the heat. Temper the egg yolks by pouring one-third of the milk mixture into the whisked yolks, whisking continually so that the yolks don't begin to cook, until combined. Then pour another one-third of the milk mixture into the egg mixture and continue to whisk. Once combined, transfer the egg mixture in the bowl to the saucepan with the remaining one-third of the milk mixture. Place the pan back over medium-low heat, stirring constantly so that the egg doesn't cook on the bottom of the pan, and simmer until the mixture is thick enough to coat the wooden spoon, 7 to 10 minutes.

6. Pour the thickened mixture through a fine-mesh sieve into a clean mixing bowl. (The sieve will filter out any egg that may have cooked during the process.) Stir in the vanilla and salt until combined. Press plastic wrap on the surface of the mixture and place in the refrigerator for 1 to 2 hours or until cool. Alternatively, place in the freezer for 30 minutes or until cool.

7. Pour the mixture into the bowl of an ice cream maker and churn it, following the manufacturer's instructions. If firmer ice cream is desired, transfer to a container, cover, and place in the freezer for 30 minutes or until the desired firmness is reached. Store the ice cream in a covered container for up to 2 weeks.

DAIRY FREE   EGG FREE   NUT FREE

peach
SORBET

PREP TIME: 5 minutes
SETTING TIME: 30 minutes
READY IN: 35 minutes
YIELD: 1 pint (473 ml)

Pureeing frozen fruit is probably the easiest way to make a frozen dessert. You just throw it in a food processor and let it do its thing, no ice cream maker required. Frozen banana ice cream was one of the first desserts I made when I started eating Paleo, and I have been using the same method with other frozen fruits ever since. This sorbet would also be great in a mixed berry blend or with just strawberries.

3 peaches, peeled if desired, diced, and frozen, or 2 cups (16 ounces/ 454 g) bagged frozen sliced peaches

¼ cup (60 ml) full-fat canned coconut milk

2 tablespoons raw honey

1 tablespoon fresh-squeezed lemon juice

1 Combine all the ingredients in the bowl of a food processor. Process until smooth, about 5 minutes. Then transfer the mixture to another container and place in the freezer to harden for 30 minutes or until the desired firmness is reached. Store the sorbet in a covered container for up to 2 weeks.

Notes: *If you prefer your sorbet more tart, add additional lemon juice 1 teaspoon at a time to taste. Throwing in some frozen raspberries would also lend a nice subtle tartness to this sorbet.*

DAIRY FREE EGG FREE NUT FREE

Blackberry
CABERNET SORBET

PREP TIME: 5 minutes
SETTING TIME: 1 to 2 hours
READY IN: 1 hour 5 minutes
YIELD: 1 pint (473 ml)

I first came across this sorbet when I was living in San Jose, California, in 2002. There was a little restaurant down the street from my apartment on San Fernando Street called Stratta Grill and Bar. The restaurant has long since closed, but I will never forget a dessert they served there; it was one of the best I've ever had in my entire life. It was a chocolate molten lava cake topped with a scoop of blackberry Cabernet sorbet. I still remember the way the tartness of the sorbet paired with the chocolate and how the cold and warmth mingled together on my tongue to create an experience like no other.

2 (6-ounce/170-g) cartons fresh blackberries

1 cup (240 ml) Cabernet Sauvignon

1 cup (240 ml) water

½ cup (65 g) maple sugar

2 tablespoons raw honey

2 teaspoons fresh-squeezed lemon juice

¼ cup (1½ ounces/40 g) fresh raspberries (optional)

SPECIAL EQUIPMENT

Ice cream maker

1 Combine all the ingredients in the pitcher of a blender. Cover with the lid and puree until well blended. Pour the mixture through a fine-mesh sieve into a medium-sized mixing bowl. (The sieve will catch any seeds.) Press plastic wrap onto the surface of the mixture and place in the refrigerator for 1 to 2 hours or until cool. Alternatively, place in the freezer for 30 minutes or until cool.

2 Pour the mixture into the bowl of an ice cream maker and churn it, following the manufacturer's instructions. If firmer sorbet is desired, transfer to a container, cover, and place in the freezer for 30 minutes or until the desired firmness is reached. Store the sorbet in a covered container for up to 2 weeks.

Notes: I like to include raspberries in this sorbet because it brightens the color and adds a subtle tartness that I love, evening out the sweetness of the blackberries. They are completely optional. I also recommend using fresh instead of frozen berries because the frozen ones will make the texture more like a smoothie, which may not work well in your ice cream maker. Another option for frozen berries would be to let them thaw and drain any excess juices or water.

To enjoy this sorbet on a cone, you can buy a gluten-free brand like Goldbaum's or Let's Do . . . Gluten-Free Sugar Cones. You can also make your own!

MINT *Chip* ICE CREAM BARS

PREP TIME: 15 minutes
SETTING TIME: 4½ hours
READY IN: 4 hours 45 minutes
YIELD: 10 bars

There are certain flavors that chocolate was just mint to be with. See what I did there? Mint, meant. You're clever, you get it. Mint is unquestionably one of those flavors that was destined to be with chocolate. These decadent ice cream bars are the perfect marriage of the two flavors.

FOR THE ICE CREAM

2 (13½-ounce/400-ml) cans full-fat coconut milk

4 large egg yolks

½ cup (65 g) maple sugar

2 tablespoons raw honey

¼ teaspoon fine-grain sea salt

½ teaspoon vanilla extract

⅛ teaspoon peppermint extract

2 (3-ounce/170-g) mint dark chocolate bars, finely chopped, divided

4 drops natural green food coloring (optional)

FOR THE COATING

½ recipe Chocolate Shell Coating (page 376)

SPECIAL EQUIPMENT

10 Popsicle molds and 10 Popsicle sticks

Notes: My favorite mint dark chocolate bars are Alter-Eco brand. You can find them at Whole Foods, Sprouts, and Amazon.

The food coloring is completely optional. I prefer the Color Garden brand of natural food coloring; you can find it at Sprouts and on Amazon.

For a dairy version, substitute 1½ cups (350 ml) of whole milk and 1 cup (240 ml) of heavy cream for the coconut milk.

1. Place the coconut milk in a large heavy-bottomed saucepan set over medium heat, stirring intermittently with a wooden spoon until it reaches a simmer.

2. Meanwhile, in a large mixing bowl, whisk together the egg yolks and maple sugar until the yolks thicken and become a pale yellow.

3. When the milk comes to a simmer, remove from the heat. Temper the egg yolks by pouring one-third of the hot coconut milk into the egg and sugar mixture, whisking continually so that the egg yolks don't begin to cook, until combined. Then pour another one-third of the hot milk into the egg mixture and continue to whisk. Once combined, transfer the egg mixture in the bowl to the saucepan with the remaining milk. Place the pan over medium-low heat, stirring constantly so that the egg doesn't cook on the bottom of the pan, and simmer until the mixture is thick enough to coat the wooden spoon, 7 to 10 minutes. Be sure to stir constantly to make sure that the egg doesn't cook on the bottom of the pan.

4. Pour the mixture through a fine-mesh sieve into a clean mixing bowl. (The sieve will filter out any egg that may have cooked during the process.) Stir in the honey, salt, vanilla, and peppermint extract until combined.

5. Press plastic wrap onto the surface of the mixture and place in the refrigerator for 1 to 2 hours or until cool. Alternatively, place in the freezer for 30 minutes or until cool.

6. Once the egg mixture is cold, stir in half of the chopped mint chocolate and the food coloring, if using. Transfer the mixture to a container with a spout for pouring, like the pitcher of a blender or a large glass measuring cup. Pour the mixture into the molds. Tap lightly on the counter to remove any air bubbles, then place a Popsicle stick in each slot. Cover and freeze for 4 hours or overnight, until frozen.

7. Fifteen minutes before removing the ice cream bars from the freezer, prepare a half batch of the Chocolate Shell Coating. When the coating has cooled slightly, remove the bars from the freezer and let sit for 10 minutes to make it easier to remove them from their molds. While waiting, line a baking sheet with parchment paper and transfer the remaining half of the chopped mint chocolate to a bowl.

8. Remove an ice cream bar from its mold and, holding it over the pan of chocolate coating, use a spoon to drizzle the coating onto the bar. Then sprinkle some of the chocolate pieces across the wet chocolate coating. Place the finished bar on the parchment. Repeat with the remaining bars. Enjoy immediately or place in the freezer to set and enjoy later. Store in a covered container for up to 2 weeks.

Pumpkin
ICE CREAM

PREP TIME: 15 minutes
SETTING TIME: 1 to 2 hours
READY IN: 1 hour 15 minutes
YIELD: 1 pint (473 ml)

Mmm, pumpkin. This recipe is like eating pumpkin pie, but in ice cream form. I love it when my favorite foods are in ice cream form. When I was a kid, I always wished that I would have to have my tonsils removed because rumor had it, you got to eat ice cream for every meal. Any fan of pumpkin is sure to love this recipe. It is great in the fall, but let's be real, we don't need it to be fall to eat pumpkin. Am I right or am I right?

2 (13½-ounce/400-ml) cans full-fat coconut milk

1 teaspoon pumpkin pie spice

½ teaspoon ground cinnamon

⅛ teaspoon Chinese five spice

4 large egg yolks

½ cup (65 g) maple sugar

1 tablespoon light molasses (not blackstrap)

2 teaspoons vanilla extract

¼ teaspoon fine-grain sea salt

1 cup (240 ml) pumpkin puree, chilled

SPECIAL EQUIPMENT

Ice cream maker

1 Place the coconut milk, pumpkin pie spice, cinnamon, and Chinese five spice in a large heavy-bottomed saucepan set over medium heat, stirring intermittently with a wooden spoon until it reaches a simmer.

2 Meanwhile, in a large mixing bowl, whisk together the egg yolks and maple sugar until the yolks thicken and become a pale yellow.

3 When the coconut milk comes to a simmer, remove from the heat. Temper the egg yolks by pouring one-third of the hot coconut milk into the egg and sugar mixture, whisking continually so that the egg yolks don't begin to cook, until combined. Then pour another one-third of the hot milk into the egg mixture and continue to whisk. Once combined, transfer the egg mixture to the saucepan with the remaining one-third of the coconut milk. Place the pan over medium-low heat, stirring constantly so that the egg doesn't cook on the bottom of the pan, and simmer until the mixture is thick enough to coat the wooden spoon, 7 to 10 minutes.

4 Pour the thickened mixture through a fine-mesh sieve into a clean mixing bowl. (The sieve will filter out any egg that may have cooked during the process.) Stir in the molasses, vanilla, and salt until combined.

5 Press plastic wrap onto the surface of the mixture and place in the refrigerator for 1 to 2 hours or until cool. Alternatively, place in the freezer for 30 minutes or until cool.

6 Transfer the mixture to a blender, add the pumpkin puree, and blend until combined. Pour the blended mixture into the bowl of an ice cream maker and churn it, following the manufacturer's instructions. If firmer ice cream is desired, transfer to a container, cover, and place in the freezer for 30 minutes or until the desired firmness is reached. Store the ice cream in a covered container for up to 2 weeks.

Notes: For a dairy version, substitute 1½ cups (350 ml) of whole milk and 1 cup (240 ml) of heavy cream for the coconut milk.

Subs: ½ cup (120 ml) of pure maple syrup in place of the maple sugar. Whisk the yolks alone until they have lightened in color. Continue with the recipe, adding the maple syrup in Step 4 with the molasses, vanilla, and salt.

Pumpkin GINGERbREAD
ICE CREAM SANDWICHES

PREP TIME: 35 minutes
RESTING TIME: 1½ to 2½ hours
COOK TIME: 11 to 12 minutes
READY IN: 2 hours 15 minutes
YIELD: 6 sandwiches

1 recipe Soft and Chewy Gingerbread Cookies (page 318)

1 recipe Pumpkin Ice Cream (page 354)

SPECIAL EQUIPMENT
Ice cream maker

MAKE AHEAD

SOFT AND CHEWY GINGERBREAD COOKIES—1 DAY AHEAD

PUMPKIN ICE CREAM BASE—2 DAYS AHEAD; STORE IN THE REFRIGERATOR UNTIL READY TO CHURN

This recipe is like shoving the holidays into your mouth and eating them in one bite. Yeah, it's like that.

1. Prepare the Soft and Chewy Gingerbread Cookies through Step 4 on page 318. While waiting for the dough to set, make the Pumpkin Ice Cream base by completing Steps 1 through 4 on page 354. Place the ice cream base in the freezer for a quick 30-minute cool-down.

2. After the cookie dough has been in the freezer for about 45 minutes, preheat the oven to 350°F (177°C). Line two baking sheets with parchment paper or nonstick baking mats; set aside. (*Note:* If working with only one baking sheet, allow it to cool completely between batches.)

3. Bake the cookies as instructed in Step 7 on page 318; do not garnish with coconut butter. While the cookies are cooling, churn the ice cream: Pour the base mixture into the bowl of an ice cream maker and churn it, following the manufacturer's instructions. To firm up the ice cream and make it easier to scoop for sandwiches, transfer to a container, cover, and place in the freezer for 30 minutes or until the desired firmness is reached.

4. To assemble: Turn 6 cookies upside down. Place a scoop of ice cream on each one. Then place another cookie on top of the ice cream and press down gently. Enjoy immediately. Another option is to assemble the ice cream sandwiches, wrap them individually and securely in parchment paper, and then place each wrapped sandwich in a large resealable plastic freezer bag to enjoy later. Let thaw on the counter for about 10 minutes before serving.

Notes: You will have leftover cookies since you are making a full batch and need only 12 of them to yield 6 ice cream sandwiches. You could make a half batch, but I suggest that you make the full recipe, because if you have ice cream left over, you can make more sandwiches or even make another batch of ice cream if you have more people to serve. You can even repurpose the leftover cookies for another recipe or just enjoy them on their own. As I see it, you're going to all the trouble anyway, so you might as well make the whole batch.

Whisky BUSINESS

Browned
BUTTER

COOK TIME: 10 minutes
RESTING TIME: 15 to 20 minutes
READY IN: 25 minutes

Sound the trumpets, all hail browned butter! Browned butter is EVERYTHING. It's so simple to make: You literally just melt butter and let it cook a while, but the flavor you get is like nothing else in the universe. It's absolute perfection. There are few things in life that I love as much as I love browned butter, and the number of recipes in this book that use it will tell you the same story.

Grass-fed butter, any amount
(see Notes)

1 Put the butter in a medium-sized heavy-bottomed saucepan over medium-low heat. Stir intermittently using a rubber spatula. As the butter melts, it will start to bubble and foam. As it continues to cook, it will turn from lemon yellow to amber in color and will go from a loud bubble to a quiet simmer. When the butter is ready, brown specks will have formed at the bottom of the pan, and some of the specks will start to rise in the foam. The butter will also have a pleasant nutty aroma.

2 Remove the pan from the heat and let cool for 15 to 20 minutes, until the pan is cool to the touch, before using in a recipe (unless otherwise directed). When transferring the browned butter from the saucepan, be sure to use a rubber spatula to scrape all the browned bits off the bottom of the pan—that's where a lot of the flavor is. The browned butter will harden when cooled. If it won't be used soon after being made, store it in a covered container in the refrigerator like regular butter, and gently reheat to liquefy before using, making sure that it doesn't get too hot.

Notes: *This recipe can be used to make any amount of browned butter. The specific amount required for each recipe in this book is noted in the recipe in which the browned butter is used.*

Almond Butter
CENTER

PREP TIME: 5 minutes
READY IN: 5 minutes
YIELD: 1 cup (228 g)

This dairy-free almond butter center is so good, it makes peanut butter centers jealous. This recipe is a great substitute in anything that calls for peanut butter filling. Use it for cookies and confections; you won't be missing peanut butter anytime soon.

1 cup (225 g) smooth almond butter

2 tablespoons maple sugar

1 tablespoon coconut flour

1 teaspoon vanilla extract

1 In a medium-sized mixing bowl, combine all the ingredients using a whisk or hand mixer set on low speed. Store any leftovers in the refrigerator for up to 2 weeks.

Notes: If you use a natural almond butter, there may be more oil in it. If the Almond Butter Center is too runny because of that extra oil, try refrigerating it for 15 to 20 minutes to thicken further before using.

Variation: **Reese's-Style Almond Butter Center.** Add 1 to 2 tablespoons of ghee and ⅛ teaspoon of salt to lend more of a "Reese's" flavor. It sounds strange, but ghee and almond butter taste really good together. Some ghee is stronger in flavor than others, so start with 1 tablespoon, taste, and add up to 1 tablespoon more to get the flavor profile you like.

DAIRY FREE EGG FREE NUT FREE

Maple SUGAR

COOK TIME: 20 minutes
READY IN: 30 minutes
YIELD: About 1½ cups (280 g)

I was so nervous to make maple sugar for the first time. It was a totally irrational fear, but to me it seemed like such a weird process that I had convinced myself that it wouldn't work and I wouldn't be able to do it. I also wasn't thrilled about wasting that much maple syrup if it didn't work out. All my fear and hesitation was for nothing—not only was the process super simple, it was actually fun! I liked watching it go through the various stages and was so happy with the result. I will never pay for store-bought maple sugar again. Making your own is way more cost-effective, and it comes out so much better. Don't be intimidated; give this recipe a whirl!

2 cups (16 ounces/475 ml) pure maple syrup, light color

SPECIAL EQUIPMENT
Candy thermometer

1 Pour the maple syrup into a large heavy-bottomed saucepan and set the heat to medium-high. The syrup will begin to bubble vigorously and rise in the pan as it heats up; stir if needed to keep it from rising too high or place a wooden spoon across the top of the pan. Boil until the syrup reaches 257°F to 262°F (125°C to 128°C), or a few degrees past the hard ball stage on a candy thermometer, about 20 minutes.

2 Once the syrup reaches temperature, remove from the heat and start stirring vigorously with a wooden spoon. (Wood will not scratch the saucepan.) Continue to stir until the syrup lightens and thickens in texture, 5 to 7 minutes, and eventually becomes granulated, similar in look and feel to brown sugar. The transformation from liquid to granulated sugar happens very quickly.

3 Sift the sugar to remove the larger clumps, then process the larger clumps in a food processor until they become granulated. Store the maple sugar in an airtight container. Use 1:1 in place of white sugar.

Notes: You want the maple syrup to reach a temperature between 257°F and 262°F (125°C and 128°C), or 45° to 50°F (25° to 28°C) over boiling temperature. In most places water boils at 212°F (100°C), but this can change due to humidity or elevation. To test, boil a pot of water, taking note of the temperature at which it boils, then add 45° to 50°F (25° to 28°C) to that.

You can use a stand mixer to make maple sugar, but I find that the process goes super quick by hand, and you can work on toning your arms!

Want to make a super large batch? Use a 32-ounce (950-ml) bottle of maple syrup and a stockpot. This quantity of syrup will yield about 3 cups (420 g) of sugar.

The best way to clean your pot after making maple sugar is to fill the pot with water and set it over medium heat. The heated water will turn the sugar back to liquid, and cleanup will be a breeze.

MARSHMALLOW CRÈME

PREP TIME: 5 minutes
COOK TIME: 10 to 12 minutes
READY IN: 15 minutes
YIELD: 2 cups (170 g)

After much marshmallow research and deliberation, I discovered that there are really only two ways to make homemade marshmallow crème: either with egg whites or without. I wanted an egg-free recipe for those with egg sensitivities as well as a traditional recipe, so I got to work and tested four different versions. This recipe and the egg-free version that follows were the winners by far. They taste just like store-bought marshmallow crème!

½ cup (120 ml) cold water

⅓ cup (80 ml) light-colored raw honey

¼ cup (60 ml) pure maple syrup, any type

¼ teaspoon fine-grain sea salt

2 large egg whites

¼ teaspoon cream of tartar

2 teaspoons vanilla extract

SPECIAL EQUIPMENT
Candy thermometer

1. In a large heavy-bottomed saucepan, combine the water, honey, maple syrup, and salt. Whisk together and heat over medium-high heat while preparing the egg whites.

2. In a large mixing bowl or the bowl of a stand mixer, combine the egg whites and cream of tartar. Using a hand mixer or the stand mixer fitted with the whisk attachment, beat together on high speed until soft peaks form; set aside.

3. By now the honey mixture should be bubbling vigorously and rising in the pan. Whisk again and boil until the mixture reaches 240°F (116°C) on a candy thermometer, 10 to 12 minutes. Once it reaches temperature, remove from the heat.

4. With the mixer on low, very slowly pour the hot honey mixture down the side of the bowl into the egg whites. After all the honey mixture has been poured in, increase the speed to high and continue to beat until the mixture becomes white, thick, and glossy. When ribbons start to form and hold their shape, add the vanilla and mix until combined. Use immediately. If the crème is allowed to sit for too long, it will begin to weep and the egg whites will eventually separate into a pool of liquid at the bottom of the bowl.

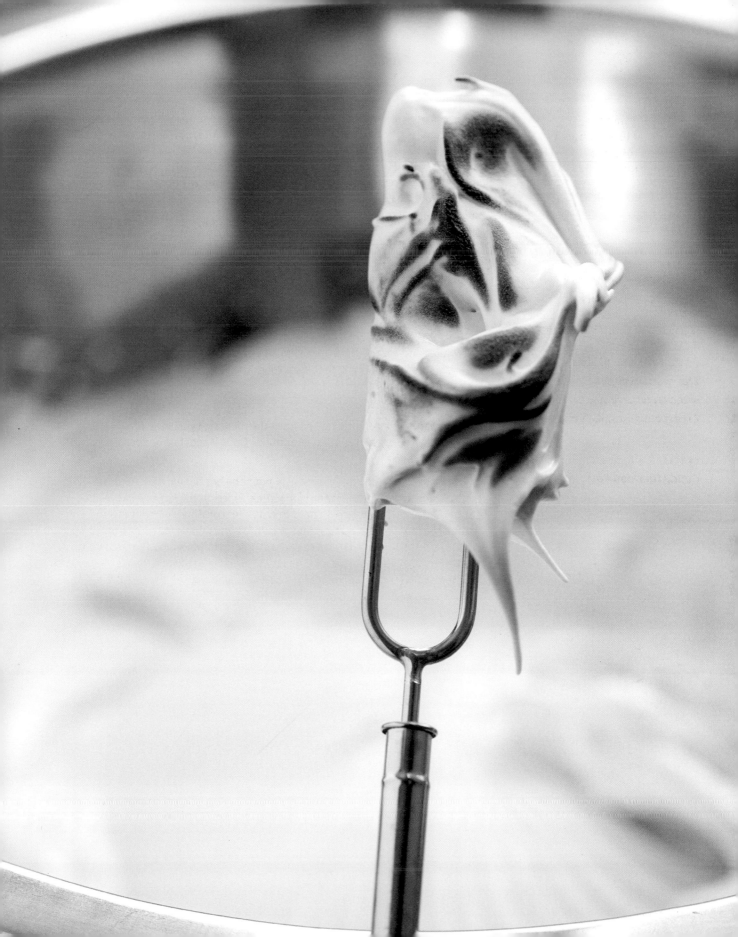

Egg-Free
MARSHMALLOW CRÈME

PREP TIME: 5 minutes
COOK TIME: 10 to 12 minutes
READY IN: 15 minutes
YIELD: 1½ cups (128 g)

1 cup (240 ml) cold water, divided

⅓ cup (80 ml) light-colored raw honey

¼ cup (35 g) maple sugar

¼ teaspoon fine-grain sea salt

2 tablespoons, or 2 (¼-ounce/7-g) envelopes, unflavored gelatin, 225 bloom strength

2 teaspoons vanilla extract

SPECIAL EQUIPMENT
Candy thermometer

Subs: Maple syrup in place of the maple sugar.

1. In a large heavy-bottomed saucepan, combine ½ cup (120 ml) of the water with the honey, maple sugar, and salt. Whisk together and heat over medium-high heat while preparing the gelatin.

2. Pour the remaining ½ cup (120 ml) of water into a large mixing bowl or the bowl of a stand mixer. Sprinkle the gelatin over the water, then pour in the vanilla. Stir gently using a spoon until the mixture resembles applesauce; set aside and tend to the honey mixture.

3. The honey mixture will start to bubble vigorously and rise in the pan; whisk intermittently. Boil until the mixture reaches 240°F (116°C) on a candy thermometer, 10 to 12 minutes. Once it reaches temperature, remove from the heat.

4. Using a hand mixer or the stand mixer (fitted with the whisk attachment) set on low speed, very slowly pour the hot honey mixture down the side of the bowl into the gelatin mixture. Once all the mixture has been poured in, increase the speed to high and continue to beat until the mixture turns white and thickens and ribbons start to form. Use immediately; the crème will continue to thicken as it sits and will become too firm to use easily. If it starts to firm up, beat it again on high until it becomes smooth again. If the mixture sits out too long and firms up too much, it may not be salvageable.

Ganache
THREE WAYS

The answer to life's most complicated questions is simple: ganache. You can use ganache for anything, and I do. Simply defined, ganache is a glaze, icing, sauce, or filling for pastries made with chocolate and, traditionally, cream. I've included three versions for you: one made with butter, one made with coconut milk for a dairy-free option, and one for the primal folks that contains heavy cream. Any one of these recipes can be used anywhere that ganache is called for. Ganache is so easy to make and will turn any common recipe into royalty.

GANACHE

1. Melt the chocolate chips and butter in a double boiler over low heat or in a heatproof bowl set over a pan of gently simmering water. Stir frequently, using a rubber spatula, until completely melted and combined.

2. Leftover ganache can be kept covered in the refrigerator for a couple of weeks or can be frozen for up to 3 months. Reheat it over simmering water or by placing it in a heatproof storage container and soaking it in a hot water bath until it reaches a pourable consistency.

PREP TIME: 5 minutes
READY IN: 15 minutes
YIELD: 1½ cups (350 ml)

1 (12-ounce/340-g) bag chocolate chips

8 tablespoons (4 ounces/115 g) salted butter

PRIMAL GANACHE

1. Melt the heavy cream and chocolate chips in a double boiler over low heat or in a heatproof bowl set over a pan of gently simmering water. Stir frequently, using a rubber spatula, until completely melted and combined. Stir in the salt.

2. Leftover ganache can be kept covered in the refrigerator for a couple of weeks or can be frozen for up to 3 months. Reheat it over simmering water or by placing it in a heatproof storage container and soaking it in a hot water bath until it reaches a pourable consistency.

PREP TIME: 5 minutes
READY IN: 15 minutes
YIELD: 1 cup (350 ml)

½ cup (120 ml) heavy cream

3 ounces (85 g) dark chocolate chips (63% to 85% cacao)

3 ounces (85 g) semisweet chocolate chips

⅛ teaspoon fine-grain sea salt

Notes: You don't have to use both dark and semisweet chocolate chips. If you have only one kind on hand, that's fine. I like the flavor complexity of both chocolates together. Look at me, all fancy pants.

DAIRY-FREE GANACHE

PREP TIME: 5 minutes
READY IN: 15 minutes
YIELD: 1½ cups (350 ml)

1 (12-ounce/340-g) bag chocolate chips

½ cup (120 ml) canned full-fat coconut milk

1. Melt the chocolate chips and coconut milk in a double boiler over low heat or in a heatproof bowl set over a pan of gently simmering water. Stir frequently, using a rubber spatula, until completely melted and combined.

2. Leftover ganache can be kept covered in the refrigerator for a couple of weeks or can be frozen for up to 3 months. Reheat it over simmering water or by placing it in a heatproof storage container and soaking it in a hot water bath until it reaches a pourable consistency.

Whipped CREAM

PREP TIME: 10 minutes
READY IN: 15 minutes
YIELD: 1½ cups (120 g)

Whipped cream is the easiest thing to make, and maybe the most delicious. I would be lying if I said that I'd never made whipped cream to eat by itself. Don't judge. It's delicious.

1 cup (240 ml) heavy cream, well chilled

1 tablespoon pure maple syrup, any type

1 teaspoon vanilla extract

1 Place a large mixing bowl and the whisk attachment(s) for your hand mixer in the freezer to chill for at least 10 minutes.

2 Put the cream, maple syrup, and vanilla in the chilled bowl. Beat on low speed until combined, then increase the speed to high. Continue to beat on high until stiff peaks form.

Subs: Honey in place of the maple syrup.

Whipped COCONUT CREAM

DAIRY FREE   EGG FREE   NUT FREE

Whipped coconut cream is a great dairy-free alternative to traditional whipped cream, and it's just as easy to make: All you need to do is throw a few cans of coconut milk in the refrigerator overnight. As the milk chills, the cream, due to its fat content, solidifies, separates from the water, and rises to the top. Be sure to check out the Polite Provisions section on page 50 for my preferred brands; they work great every time.

PREP TIME: 10 minutes
READY IN: 15 minutes
YIELD: About 2 cups (160 g)

1 The night before you make the whipped coconut cream, place the cans of coconut milk in the refrigerator.

2 At least 10 minutes before preparing the whipped coconut cream, place a large mixing bowl and the whisk attachment(s) for your hand mixer in the freezer to chill.

3 Open the very well chilled cans, scrape the thick cream layer off the top, and place the cream in the chilled mixing bowl. Discard the water at the bottom of the can or reserve it for other uses. Beat the cream on high speed until it becomes airy with soft peaks. Then add the maple syrup, vanilla, and salt and beat to combine.

2 (13½-ounce/400-ml) cans full-fat coconut milk

1 tablespoon pure maple syrup, any type

1 teaspoon vanilla extract

⅛ teaspoon fine-grain sea salt

Notes: To increase your odds of success, I highly recommend that you put a few extra cans of coconut milk in the refrigerator. Sometimes you get what we in the industry call a "dud" can, in which the cream layer does not separate from the watery layer. To have the best chance of getting a whippable cream, place multiple cans in the refrigerator at the same time. It's likely that two of them will be workable. I've been known to put six cans in the refrigerator at once!

I like to add a pinch of salt to balance out the flavor. I suggest trying it with and without salt to see which way you prefer it.

Salted
CARAMEL SAUCE

PREP TIME: 5 minutes
COOK TIME: 10 minutes
READY IN: 15 minutes
YIELD: ¾ cup (180 ml)

½ cup (65 g) maple sugar

¼ cup (40 g) coconut sugar

½ cup (120 ml) canned full-fat coconut milk, room temperature

4 tablespoons (2 ounces/56 g) salted butter or ¼ cup (55 g) ghee

½ teaspoon vanilla extract

⅛ teaspoon fine-grain sea salt

The first time I made caramel sauce, it was an accident. I was trying to make frosting, and when I tasted it I was like, "Um, I think I just made caramel sauce." So I messed around with the recipe a bit to perfect it. For thicker caramel, just throw it in the refrigerator or freezer. Use it on anything, love it on everything.

1 In a medium-sized heavy-bottomed saucepan, combine the sugars, coconut milk, and butter. Over low heat, whisk gently in one direction so that the butter doesn't separate, until the butter has melted, the sugar has dissolved, and the mixture is combined. Turn the heat up to medium and bring to a soft boil, then add the vanilla and salt and whisk until combined.

2 Increase the heat to medium-high and bring the mixture to a full boil. Let boil for 2 minutes. Remove from the heat and whisk gently until it becomes a smooth liquid again. Place back over the heat and boil for an additional 2 minutes to thicken further. Remove from the heat and whisk until the mixture becomes a smooth liquid again. Repeat this process a total of four times. The caramel should be the consistency of thick soup.

3 Let cool slightly and transfer to a jar. The caramel will continue to thicken as it cools. Refrigerate to cool and thicken completely, or freeze for extra-thick caramel. As the caramel comes back up to room temperature, it will begin to thin slightly and return to a pourable state. Store in the refrigerator or freezer in a covered container for up to 2 weeks.

Notes: To make this sauce dairy-free, use ghee rather than butter.

If your butter or ghee breaks, it's because the temperature changed too rapidly. Try to keep the boiling temperature at around 212°F (100°C), but not over 240°F (116°C), or the soft ball stage on a candy thermometer. It's important that your ingredients come to temperature together. Stirring in only one direction will also help keep the butter from separating. You can save a separated caramel by whisking vigorously and then transferring it to a bowl. Place the bowl in the freezer and whisk every 10 minutes or so until the caramel comes together and firms up. As it gets colder, the butter will harden and become easier to mix in.

Are you in a hurry for thick caramel? Transfer the finished caramel to a small metal mixing bowl, throw it in the freezer, and stir occasionally until completely cool and thick, about 20 minutes.

*Variation: **Browned Butter Salted Caramel Sauce.** Before beginning the recipe, brown the butter following the method on page 360. Use a rubber spatula to transfer the browned butter to a medium-sized mixing bowl, scraping up the browned bits as well. Place the bowl in the freezer to harden for 15 to 20 minutes, then proceed with the recipe as written.*

Chocolate
SHELL COATING

PREP TIME: 5 minutes
READY IN: 15 minutes
YIELD: About 2 cups (475 ml)

Who doesn't love chocolate shell coating? Find me the person; it's a fool's errand, I tell you. This recipe is great for everything from ice cream to candy making. I love using it for chocolate-dipped anything. The coconut oil makes the chocolate so smooth and silky, and it hardens perfectly. This is a very popular recipe in my house, just as I'm sure it will be in yours.

2 cups (14 ounces/400 g) chocolate chips

¼ cup (60 ml) melted coconut oil

1 Melt the chocolate chips in a double boiler over low heat or in a heatproof bowl set over a pan of gently simmering water. Stir frequently, using a rubber spatula, until the chocolate is completely melted and smooth. Remove from the heat and stir in the coconut oil. Let sit until the bowl is relatively cool to the touch.

2 Store in a covered container at room temperature for up to 2 weeks. If the mixture hardens, reheat over simmering water or in the microwave for 30 seconds until it becomes liquid again.

STRAWBERRY SAUCE

PREP TIME: 5 minutes
COOK TIME: 25 to 30 minutes
READY IN: 30 minutes
YIELD: ¾ cup (180 ml)

This strawberry sauce is so versatile. It can be used as a spread on biscuits, as a filling for bars, tarts, and pies, or as a topping over ice cream. Now I want to eat all of that. I use this sauce in a lot of recipes throughout this book as a replacement for store-bought jams and jellies that contain refined sugar. I hope you enjoy it as much as I do.

2 cups (16 ounces/455 g) strawberries, hulled and sliced

¼ cup (60 ml) raw honey

2 tablespoons fresh-squeezed lemon juice

1 In a large heavy-bottomed saucepan, combine the strawberries, honey, and lemon juice. Mash the strawberries until they are well combined with the rest of the ingredients. Bring the mixture to a boil over medium-high heat. Continue to boil, stirring intermittently, until the sauce has reduced and thickened, 25 to 30 minutes. Remove from the heat.

2 If not using the sauce right away, transfer to a jar and store in the refrigerator for up to 3 weeks.

Notes: Looking for a fun recipe that uses this sauce? Check out the Strawberry Meringue Tartlets on page 194!

STRAWBERRY
CREAM CHEESE FROSTING

PREP TIME: 15 minutes
READY IN: 30 minutes
YIELD: 2 cups (365 g)

This frosting is great when you need something pink but don't want to use food coloring. It's also awesome because it tastes great with both chocolate cake and white or yellow cake. Not like you need any convincing; I'm just saying.

½ cup (120 ml) Strawberry Sauce (page 378)

1 (8-ounce/225-g) package cream cheese, softened

8 tablespoons (4 ounces/115 g) unsalted butter, softened

2 tablespoons maple sugar

MAKE AHEAD
STRAWBERRY SAUCE—
2 WEEKS AHEAD

1. Prepare the Strawberry Sauce and let cool to room temperature.

2. In a medium-sized mixing bowl, using a hand mixer set on low speed, beat together the cream cheese, butter, and maple sugar until smooth and combined. Add the Strawberry Sauce in ¼-cup (60-ml) increments, beating well after each addition. Then turn the speed to high and continue to beat until smooth and creamy.

3. Transfer to a piping bag fitted with the desired tip, or use an offset spatula to spread the frosting. Store any leftover frosting in a covered container in the refrigerator for up to 1 week. If the frosting is too firm to pipe or spread after removing it from the refrigerator, allow it to sit at room temperature for about 20 minutes or until soft. Beat again on low using a hand mixer, if needed.

Notes: Cakes and pastries made with cream cheese frostings must be kept refrigerated; they can be left out at room temperature for only about an hour.

Subs: ½ cup (120 ml) of store-bought, no-sugar-added strawberry fruit spread in place of the Strawberry Sauce.

Light-colored raw honey for the maple sugar.

STRAWBERRY Lemonade
MERINGUE FROSTING

PREP TIME: 25 minutes
RESTING TIME: 30 minutes
READY IN: 55 minutes
YIELD: 2 cups (170 g)

This is one of my favorite dairy-free frostings. It's great for summer and delicious on vanilla cake. It tastes just like the pink Starburst. I'm totally serious; it's insane. It's like a strawberry explosion in your mouth. This frosting would also be delicious on top of a strawberry or lemon tart.

1 recipe Strawberry Sauce (page 378)

½ cup (120 ml) raw honey

½ cup (120 ml) pure maple syrup, dark

⅓ cup (80 ml) water

4 large egg whites, room temperature

¼ teaspoon cream of tartar

⅛ teaspoon fine-grain sea salt

2 tablespoons vanilla extract

½ teaspoon lemon extract

SPECIAL EQUIPMENT
Candy thermometer

MAKE AHEAD
STRAWBERRY SAUCE—
2 WEEKS AHEAD

1 Prepare the Strawberry Sauce. Transfer to a storage container and place in the refrigerator for 30 minutes or until cold.

2 In a large heavy-bottomed saucepan, combine the honey, maple syrup, and water. Whisk together and heat over medium-high heat while preparing the egg whites.

3 In a large mixing bowl, using a hand mixer set on low speed, beat together the egg whites, cream of tartar, and salt until combined. Gradually increase the speed to high and continue to beat until soft peaks form, about 3 to 5 minutes; set aside.

4 By now the honey mixture should be bubbling vigorously and rising in the pan. Whisk again and let boil until the mixture reaches 238° to 240°F (114 to 116°C) on a candy thermometer, about 10 minutes. Once it reaches temperature, remove from the heat.

5 Set the mixer to low speed and very slowly pour the hot honey mixture down the side of the mixing bowl into the egg whites. After all the honey mixture has been poured in, increase the speed to high and continue to beat until the mixture has thickened and doubled in size and the bowl is cool to the touch. Then add the cold Strawberry Sauce, vanilla, and lemon extract and beat until combined.

6 Transfer to a piping bag fitted with the desired tip, or use an offset spatula to spread the frosting. Store any leftover frosting in a covered container in the refrigerator for up to 3 days. Since this is a meringue-type frosting, the egg whites may start to separate. If that happens, whip using a hand mixer on high until recombined.

Subs: *1 cup (240 ml) of store-bought, no-sugar-added strawberry fruit spread in place of the Strawberry Sauce.*

Peaches
AND CREAM

PREP TIME: 5 minutes
COOK TIME: 30 to 40 minutes
READY IN: 35 minutes
YIELD: 1½ cups (350 ml)

2 large yellow peaches, pitted and sliced

½ cup (120 ml) canned full-fat coconut milk or sour cream

¼ cup (60 ml) raw honey

¼ cup (60 ml) fresh-squeezed lemon juice

⅛ teaspoon fine-grain sea salt

½ teaspoon vanilla extract

I'm a huge peaches and cream fan. I could literally eat it every day and never get sick of it. This recipe would be great as a topping for Paleo pancakes or waffles or just eaten with biscuits. And who are we kidding, it would be great mixed into ice cream too.

1 In a large heavy-bottomed saucepan, combine the sliced peaches, coconut milk, honey, lemon juice, and salt. Gently mash and mix the peaches until they are combined with the rest of the ingredients.

2 Bring the mixture to a boil over medium-high heat. Continue to boil, stirring intermittently, until the mixture has reduced and thickened and barely any liquid remains in the pan, about 30 to 40 minutes. Remove from the heat and stir in the vanilla. If not using right away, transfer to a jar for storage and refrigerate for up to 1 week.

Notes: To make this dairy-free, use coconut milk rather than sour cream.

Subs: Two (15-ounce/425-g) cans of yellow peaches in water or natural fruit juice instead of fresh peaches.

Sour
CHERRY COMPOTE

PREP TIME: 5 minutes
COOK TIME: 20 to 30 minutes
READY IN: 25 minutes
YIELD: 1½ cups (355 ml)

Confession time: I'm not a huge fan of regular cherries, but for some reason I really love tart cherries. I think I just like tart fruit in general. I'm such a weirdo. This Sour Cherry Compote in insanely delicious; I could eat it by the spoonful. I mainly use it for my Sour Cherry Crumble Bars (page 112). They are good. Tart cherry good.

2 (14½-ounce/411-g) cans tart red cherries in water (see Notes)

¼ cup (60 ml) raw honey

¼ cup (60 ml) fresh-squeezed lemon juice

1 In a large heavy-bottomed saucepan set over medium-high heat, combine 1 full can of cherries and its water and 1 drained can of cherries, along with the honey and lemon juice. Mash together until the cherries are combined with the rest of the ingredients. Let the mixture boil and reduce, stirring intermittently, for about 20 to 30 minutes, until barely any liquid remains in the pan.

2 Once the mixture has reduced and thickened, remove from the heat. If not using the compote right away, transfer to a covered jar and store in the refrigerator for up to 2 weeks.

Notes: My go-to brand of canned tart cherries in water is Oregon Specialty Fruit, available at most grocery stores, Amazon, and Walmart. Instead of canned cherries, you could use 14 ounces (400 g) of frozen tart cherries or fresh tart cherries (about 2 cups [310 g], pitted and stemmed). If using frozen or fresh cherries, add about 1 cup (240 ml) of water to the mixture as well since you aren't getting the liquid from the cans.

Lemon CURD

PREP TIME: 5 minutes
SETTING TIME: 20 minutes
READY IN: 25 minutes
YIELD: 2 cups (450 g)

Lemon curd is a magical thing. You can eat it plain, use it as a tart filling, drizzle it over muffins, layer it between cakes—essentially, you can put it on anything. I recommend using Meyer lemons in this curd because they are sweeter than common supermarket lemons.

½ cup (65 g) maple sugar

¼ cup (20 g) grated Meyer lemon zest

¾ cup (180 ml) fresh-squeezed Meyer lemon juice (about 4 lemons)

2 tablespoons raw honey

4 large eggs

⅛ teaspoon fine-grain sea salt

12 tablespoons (6 ounces/170 g) unsalted cold butter, cubed

SPECIAL EQUIPMENT
Candy thermometer

1 Combine the maple sugar and lemon zest in a medium-sized mixing bowl. Mix together with a spoon until combined; set aside.

2 In a large heatproof mixing bowl, combine the lemon juice, honey, eggs, and sugar-zest mixture. Place the bowl over a saucepan half filled with water set over medium heat. As the water starts to simmer, stir constantly using a whisk until the mixture thickens to a puddinglike texture and reaches 160°F (71°C) on a candy thermometer, about 10 minutes. Remove from the heat and press the curd through a fine-mesh sieve into a blender pitcher. Add the salt, then blend on low, adding the butter a few cubes at a time. After all the butter has been added, continue to blend until the mixture becomes light and creamy.

3 Use the curd as a glaze on cake or transfer to a prepared tart crust and place in the refrigerator for about 20 minutes to cool and set. If not using the curd right away, transfer it to a bowl and cover with plastic wrap, pressing directly on the surface. The curd will stay fresh for about 1 week.

ITALIAN
MERINGUE

This meringue is so easy to throw together and yields amazing results every time. There are actually three types of meringue: French, Swiss, and Italian. Each one uses a different method. When it comes to meringue, I prefer the Italian method. I get the most stable results and no weeping. Weeping is when the meringue starts to form a pool of liquid underneath itself when layered on top of a dessert. The taste of this meringue is also fabulous, of course, and it toasts perfectly under a kitchen torch. It's great on tarts and pies, and even as a frosting on cakes.

½ cup (120 ml) raw honey

½ cup (20 ml) pure maple syrup, dark

⅓ cup (80 ml) water

4 large egg whites, room temperature

¼ teaspoon cream of tartar

⅛ teaspoon fine-grain sea salt

SPECIAL EQUIPMENT
Candy thermometer

1 In a large heavy-bottomed saucepan, combine the honey, maple syrup, and water. Whisk together and heat over medium-high heat while preparing the egg whites.

2 In a large mixing bowl using a hand mixer set on low speed, beat together the egg whites, cream of tartar, and salt until combined. Gradually increase the speed to high and continue to beat until soft peaks form, 3 to 5 minutes; set aside.

3 By now the honey mixture should be bubbling vigorously and rising in the pan; whisk again and let it boil until the mixture reaches 238° to 240°F (114 to 116°C) on a candy thermometer, about 10 minutes. Once it reaches temperature, remove from the heat.

4 Set the hand mixer to low and very slowly pour the hot honey mixture down the side of the mixing bowl into the egg whites. After all the honey mixture has been poured in, increase the speed to high and continue to beat until the mixture has thickened and doubled in size and the bowl is cool to the touch. Use immediately.

NUT FREE

Swiss Meringue BUTTERCREAM

PREP TIME: 10 minutes
RESTING TIME: 15 minutes
READY IN: 25 minutes
YIELD: About 2 cups (240 g)

Swiss Meringue Buttercream is a great for piping. It always comes out beautifully. Anytime I want to pipe roses on a cake or cupcakes, I use a buttercream; it is so easy to work with and tastes fantastic. This buttercream tastes great with white and almond cakes.

5 large egg whites, room temperature

1 cup (130 g) maple sugar

2 tablespoons light-colored raw honey

16 tablespoons (8 ounces/225 g) unsalted butter, softened

2 teaspoons vanilla extract

SPECIAL EQUIPMENT
Candy thermometer

1. Combine the egg whites, maple sugar, and honey in a large heatproof mixing bowl. Mix together using a whisk until completely combined. Set the bowl over a simmering pot of water on the stove and cook, stirring constantly so that the egg doesn't cook on the bottom of the pan, until the mixture reaches 160°F (71°C). Remove from the heat and continue to whisk until slightly cooled. Place in the freezer for 15 minutes or until cool to the touch, anywhere between 55° and 65°F (12° and 18°C). While waiting for the egg and sugar mixture to cool, prepare the butter.

2. In a large mixing bowl, beat the butter with a hand mixer set on medium-high speed for about 2 minutes, until the butter lightens in color. With the mixer on, beat the cooled egg white mixture into the butter in three additions, beating well after each addition. Then add the vanilla and continue to beat until smooth and creamy.

3. Transfer to a piping bag fitted with the desired tip, or use an offset spatula to spread the frosting. This buttercream is best used right away, but any remaining can be stored in an airtight container in a cool, dry place for up to 2 days. Do not store in the refrigerator; the cold will cause the butter to harden.

Notes: *I'm not a fan of making any frosting ahead of time and storing it, because it can be difficult to get the right consistency again. This is particularly true of buttercreams. It's always best to use frostings soon after making them.*

Vanilla
BUTTERCREAM

PREP TIME: 5 minutes
READY IN: 5 minutes
YIELD: About 2 cups (240 g)

Sometimes you just need to whip up some frosting at a moment's notice. This is the frosting for you! Not only does it taste and work like traditional buttercream, but it's incredibly easy to make. You can thank me later.

16 tablespoons (8 ounces/225 g) unsalted butter, softened

1 cup (135 g) sifted maple sugar

⅛ teaspoon fine-grain sea salt

1 tablespoon milk (see Notes)

1 teaspoon vanilla extract

1 In the bowl of a stand mixer fitted with the whisk attachment, combine the butter, maple sugar, and salt. Beat on medium speed until combined. Add the milk and vanilla and continue to beat on high until the butter has lightened and the mixture has become fluffy and creamy, 3 to 5 minutes, scraping down the sides of the bowl and the whisk as needed.

2 Transfer to a piping bag fitted with the desired tip, or use an offset spatula to spread the frosting. Store any remaining frosting in an airtight container in a cool, dry place for up to 2 days. Do not store in the refrigerator; the cold will cause the butter to harden.

Notes: *This recipe can be made with any type of milk: full-fat canned coconut milk, almond milk, cow's milk, heavy cream, or half-and-half. It really just needs a liquid addition to make the texture ultra creamy.*

If you don't have a stand mixer, this frosting can be made with a hand mixer; follow the same process using a large mixing bowl.

Chocolate
BUTTERCREAM

PREP TIME: 5 minutes
READY IN: 15 minutes
YIELD: About 2 cups (240 g)

This is my favorite frosting to use on cake. It tastes just like frosting made with refined sugar, so I never feel like I'm missing out on anything. Ever. Lick the bowl; you won't regret it.

1 cup (7 ounces/200 g) chocolate chips

16 tablespoons (8 ounces/225 g) unsalted butter, softened

½ cup (75 g) coconut sugar, sifted

1 teaspoon vanilla extract

1. Melt the chocolate chips in a double boiler over low heat or in a heatproof bowl set over a pan of gently simmering water. Stir frequently, using a rubber spatula, until the chocolate is completely melted and smooth. Remove from the heat and let cool slightly.

2. In a large mixing bowl, beat together the butter and coconut sugar with a hand mixer set on medium-high speed until the butter is light and fluffy and the sugar is incorporated, about 2 minutes. Add the vanilla and continue to beat until mixed. Make sure that the melted chocolate has cooled enough so it doesn't melt the butter when added, then add the chocolate to the butter mixture in three additions, beating well after each addition. Continue to beat until smooth.

3. Transfer to a piping bag fitted with the desired tip, or use an offset spatula to spread the frosting. Store any remaining frosting in an airtight container in a cool, dry place for up to 2 days. Do not store in the refrigerator; the cold will cause the butter to harden.

Notes: Be sure to sift the sugar for this recipe. Coconut sugar is very granular; sifting it will break down the grain and help incorporate the sugar into the butter. If you skip this step, the frosting may be slightly gritty.

If for some reason the frosting is too soft, just place it in the refrigerator or freezer for a few minutes to firm up, then beat it again with a hand mixer.

Cream Cheese
FROSTING

PREP TIME: 5 minutes
READY IN: 5 minutes
YIELD: About 2 cups (455 g)

Cream cheese frosting is a delicious frosting for cakes and cupcakes. Not to mention that it's really easy to make and even easier to work with. If I'm not catering to a dairy-free crowd, it's usually my first choice for frosting. I also like it because it gives me a blank canvas to decorate with and get really creative.

1 (8-ounce/225-g) package cream cheese, softened

4 tablespoons (2 ounces/56 g) unsalted butter, softened

½ cup (70 g) sifted maple sugar

2 tablespoons light-colored raw honey

1 teaspoon vanilla extract

1 Place the cream cheese and butter in a medium-sized mixing bowl. Beat together using a hand mixer set on medium speed until fluffy and combined. Gradually add the maple sugar, beating well after each addition. Then add the honey and vanilla and continue to mix until smooth and creamy.

2 Transfer to a piping bag fitted with the desired tip, or use an offset spatula to spread the frosting. Store any leftover frosting in a covered container in the refrigerator for up to 1 week. If the frosting is too firm to pipe or spread after removing it from the refrigerator, allow it to sit at room temperature for about 20 minutes, until soft. Beat again on low using a hand mixer, if needed.

Notes: Cakes and pastries made with cream cheese frostings must be kept refrigerated; they can be left out at room temperature for only about an hour.

EGG FREE · NUT FREE

ELDERFLOWER
MASCARPONE FROSTING

PREP TIME: 10 minutes
READY IN: 10 minutes
YIELD: About 2 cups (455 g)

I adore elderflower liqueur. The flavor is absolutely perfect. I'm a huge fan of St. Germaine, and I love to use it any way I can. Mostly in champagne or with gin, but my drinking habits aside, I also love to use it in baking. It makes the best frosting. It's great with vanilla cake and insane with lemon cake. Get crazy with it.

16 ounces (455 g) mascarpone cheese

¼ cup (60 ml) light-colored raw honey

2 tablespoons St. Germaine elderflower liqueur

1 tablespoon heavy cream, plus more if needed

½ teaspoon lemon extract

1 Combine all the ingredients in a medium-sized mixing bowl and beat together using a hand mixer set on low speed until smooth and creamy. If the frosting is too thick, add more heavy cream a tablespoon at a time until the desired consistency is reached.

2 Transfer to a piping bag fitted with the desired tip, or use an offset spatula to spread the frosting. Store any leftover frosting in a covered container in the refrigerator for up to 1 week. If the frosting is too firm to pipe or spread after removing it from the refrigerator, allow it to sit at room temperature for about 20 minutes, until soft. Beat again on low using a hand mixer, if needed.

Notes: Cakes and pastries made with cheese-based frostings must be kept refrigerated; you can leave them out at room temperature for only about an hour.

MASCARPONE AND
GOAT CHEESE FROSTING

PREP TIME: 10 minutes
READY IN: 10 minutes
YIELD: About 2 cups (565 g)

16 ounces (455 g) mascarpone cheese

4 ounces (115 g) goat cheese

2 tablespoons light-colored raw honey

½ cup (65 g) maple sugar

This frosting is similar to cream cheese frosting but has its own unique flavor. It pairs so well with chocolate and white cake. It also pairs well with berry-filled cakes.

1. In a medium-sized mixing bowl, beat together the mascarpone, goat cheese, and honey using a hand mixer set on low speed, until combined. Gradually add the maple sugar and continue to beat until smooth and creamy.

2. Transfer to a piping bag fitted with the desired tip, or use an offset spatula to spread the frosting. Store any leftover frosting in a covered container in the refrigerator for up to 1 week. If the frosting is too firm to pipe or spread after removing it from the refrigerator, allow it to sit at room temperature for about 20 minutes, until soft. Beat again on low using a hand mixer, if needed.

Notes: Cakes and pastries made with cheese-based frostings must be kept refrigerated; they can be left out at room temperature for only about an hour.

Lemon
MERINGUE BUTTERCREAM

PREP TIME: 10 minutes
RESTING TIME: 10 to 15 minutes
READY IN: 20 minutes
YIELD: About 2 cups (240 g)

This is such a great recipe for anything lemon flavored that may need a little frosting love. I recommend making the Limoncello Cupcakes (page 219) and using this frosting on top, piped into roses with a Wilton 1M tip. That's all. I'll mind my own business now.

5 large egg whites, room temperature

1 cup (130 g) maple sugar

2 tablespoons light-colored raw honey

16 tablespoons (8 ounces/225 g) unsalted butter, softened

3 tablespoons fresh-squeezed lemon juice

2 teaspoons vanilla extract

2 teaspoons grated lemon zest

¼ teaspoon lemon extract

SPECIAL EQUIPMENT

Candy thermometer

1 Combine the egg whites, maple sugar, and honey in a large heatproof mixing bowl. Mix together using a whisk until completely combined. Set over a simmering pot of water on the stove and stir constantly until the mixture reaches 160°F (71°C), about 10 minutes. Remove from the heat and continue to whisk until slightly cooled. Place in the freezer for 10 to 15 minutes or until cool to the touch, anywhere between 55° and 65°F (12° and 18°C). While waiting for the egg and sugar mixture to cool, prepare the butter.

2 In a large mixing bowl, beat the butter with a hand mixer set on medium-high speed for about 2 minutes, until the butter lightens in color. With the mixer on, beat the cooled egg white mixture into the butter in three additions, beating well after each addition. Then add the lemon juice, vanilla, lemon zest, and lemon extract and continue to beat until smooth and creamy.

3 Transfer to a piping bag fitted with the desired tip, or use an offset spatula to spread the frosting. Store any remaining frosting in an airtight container in a cool, dry place for up to 2 days. Do not store in the refrigerator; the cold will cause the butter to harden.

Lemon
GLAZE

PREP TIME: 5 minutes
READY IN: 5 minutes
YIELD: ½ cup (120 ml)

This glaze is great over anything—cookies, cakes, muffins, quick breads, you name it. If I had only two words to describe this recipe, I would say simple and charming.

2 tablespoons melted coconut butter

2 tablespoons light-colored raw honey, melted

¼ cup plus 2 tablespoons (90 ml) canned full-fat coconut milk

2 tablespoons fresh-squeezed lemon juice

1 teaspoon grated lemon zest

1 In a small mixing bowl, stir together the melted coconut butter and honey until combined. Stir in the coconut milk. Add the lemon juice and zest and stir until all the ingredients are combined.

2 Pour the glaze over cakes, muffins, and quick breads. To harden the glaze after pouring, transfer the baked good to the refrigerator to set for 15 to 20 minutes. Store any leftover glaze in a covered container at room temperature for up to 2 weeks. If it thickens, microwave it for 15 to 30 seconds and stir until the glaze becomes a liquid consistency again.

Lemon
CREAM CHEESE FROSTING

PREP TIME: 10 minutes
READY IN: 10 minutes
YIELD: 1 cup (455 g)

Let's face it: I really like cream cheese frosting. I feel you should have plenty of flavors ready to go in your cream cheese frosting lineup. Your lemon desserts will thank you. And the people eating your lemon desserts. You might even make some new friends because people you don't know will want to be your friend just so they can eat your lemon desserts. It could happen. Lemon Cream Cheese Frosting is a powerful thing.

1 (8-ounce/225-g) package cream cheese, softened

½ cup (65 g) maple sugar

1 tablespoon plus 2 teaspoons fresh-squeezed lemon juice

1 tablespoon light-colored raw honey

1 teaspoon grated lemon zest

1. Combine all the ingredients in a medium-sized mixing bowl. Beat together using a hand mixer set on low speed until smooth and creamy.

2. Transfer to a piping bag fitted with the desired tip, or use an offset spatula to spread the frosting. Store any leftover frosting in a covered container in the refrigerator for up to 1 week. If the frosting is too firm to pipe or spread after removing it from the refrigerator, allow it to sit at room temperature for about 20 minutes or until soft. Beat again on low using a hand mixer, if needed.

Notes: Cakes and pastries made with cream cheese frosting must be kept refrigerated; they can be left out at room temperature for only about an hour.

NUT FREE

Eggnog Bliss
MERINGUE BUTTERCREAM

PREP TIME: 10 minutes
RESTING TIME: 10 to 15 minutes
READY IN: 20 minutes
YIELD: About 2 cups (240 g)

As you may have noticed, I have a slight thing for eggnog. When developing the recipes for this book, I wanted to make sure that I had all my eggnog bases covered, especially in the frosting department. This eggnog buttercream is amazing. It's great on cakes and even cookies. Keep it in your arsenal for the holidays. You will impress everyone, including the bah humbugs.

5 large egg whites, room temperature

½ cup (120 ml) eggnog

½ cup (65 g) maple sugar

16 tablespoons (8 ounces/225 g) unsalted butter, softened

2 tablespoons light-colored raw honey

½ teaspoon vanilla extract

¼ teaspoon ground nutmeg

SPECIAL EQUIPMENT
Candy thermometer

1 Combine the egg whites, eggnog, and maple sugar in a large heatproof mixing bowl. Mix together using a whisk until completely combined. Set over a simmering pot of water on the stove and stir constantly until the mixture reaches 160°F (71°C). Remove from the heat and continue to whisk until slightly cooled. Place in the freezer for 10 to 15 minutes or until cool to the touch, anywhere between 55° and 65°F (12° and 18°C). While waiting for the egg and sugar mixture to cool, prepare the butter.

2 In a large mixing bowl, beat the butter with a hand mixer set on medium-high speed for about 2 minutes, until it lightens in color. With the mixer on, beat the cooled egg white mixture into the butter in three additions, beating well after each addition. Then add the honey, vanilla, and nutmeg and continue to beat until smooth and creamy.

3 Transfer to a piping bag fitted with the desired tip, or use an offset spatula to spread the frosting. Store any remaining frosting in an airtight container in a cool, dry place for up to 2 days. Do not store in the refrigerator; the cold will cause the butter to harden.

Notes: Don't panic if you whisk constantly and still get some cooked egg at the bottom of the bowl. It won't affect your frosting, and you can always pass the mixture through a fine-mesh sieve to collect the egg "gunk." I usually just pour in my egg whites with egg gunk and all, and it gets beaten into the butter anyway. I'll leave it up to you!

Dairy-Free Eggnog, MERINGUE FROSTING

PREP TIME: 10 minutes
RESTING TIME: 10 to 15 minutes
READY IN: 20 minutes
YIELD: About 2 cups (160 g)

Everyone needs eggnog. Even dairy-free people need eggnog. I made a batch of my dairy-free Eggnog Cupcakes (page 272) topped with this frosting, and everyone loved them; no one even knew that they were dairy-free. #winning

5 large egg whites, room temperature

½ cup (120 ml) dairy-free eggnog (see Notes)

⅓ cup (50 g) maple sugar

1 cup (230 g) palm shortening

¼ cup (60 ml) light-colored raw honey

1 tablespoon coconut flour

1½ teaspoons vanilla extract

½ teaspoon ground nutmeg

¼ teaspoon ground cinnamon

SPECIAL EQUIPMENT
Candy thermometer

1   Combine the egg whites, eggnog, and maple sugar in a large heatproof mixing bowl. Mix together using a whisk until completely combined. Set over a simmering pot of water on the stove and stir constantly until the mixture reaches 160°F (71°C). Remove from the heat and continue to whisk until slightly cooled. Place in the freezer for 10 to 15 minutes or until cool to the touch, anywhere between 55° and 65°F (12° and 18°C). While waiting for the egg and sugar mixture to cool, prepare the other ingredients.

2   In a large mixing bowl, combine the palm shortening, honey, coconut flour, vanilla, nutmeg, and cinnamon. Beat with a hand mixer set on medium-high speed for about 2 minutes, until combined. With the mixer on, beat the cooled egg mixture into the shortening mixture in three additions, beating well after each addition. Continue to beat until smooth and creamy.

3   Transfer to a piping bag fitted with the desired tip, or use an offset spatula to spread the frosting. This frosting should be used right away; it does not store well.

Notes: My favorite dairy-free eggnog is Almond Milk Holiday Nog from Califia Farms. A nut-free and dairy-free eggnog to use would be So Delicious Dairy-Free Coconut Milk Eggnog.

Don't panic if you whisk constantly and still get some cooked egg at the bottom of the bowl. It won't affect your frosting, and you can always pass the mixture through a fine-mesh sieve to collect the egg "gunk." I usually just pour in my egg whites with egg gunk and all, and it gets beaten into the mix anyway.

Palm shortening, like butter, hardens when refrigerated, so if you desire a thicker frosting, place the frosting in the fridge for 10 to 20 minutes.

Eggnog
CREAM CHEESE FROSTING

PREP TIME: 10 minutes
READY IN: 10 minutes
YIELD: About 2 cups (455 g)

If you make this frosting and then eat it all before you actually frost anything, I won't judge. This frosting is so tasty. It's great on Eggnog Cupcakes (page 272) and on Holiday Spice Cake (page 274). It's also really easy to make. Everyone loves easy.

1 (8-ounce/225-g) package cream cheese, softened

8 tablespoons (4 ounces/115 g) unsalted butter, softened

½ cup (65 g) maple sugar

½ cup (120 ml) eggnog

1 teaspoon vanilla extract

¼ teaspoon ground nutmeg

1 Combine the cream cheese, butter, and maple sugar in a medium-sized mixing bowl. Beat together using a hand mixer set on low speed until combined, then gradually increase the speed and continue beating until the mixture is smooth. Then beat in the eggnog, vanilla, and nutmeg and continue to beat until smooth and creamy.

2 Transfer to a piping bag fitted with the desired tip, or use an offset spatula to spread the frosting. Store any leftover frosting in a covered container in the refrigerator for up to 1 week. If the frosting is too firm to pipe or spread after removing it from the refrigerator, allow it to sit at room temperature for about 20 minutes or until soft. Beat again on low using a hand mixer, if needed.

Notes: Cakes and pastries made with cream cheese frostings must be kept refrigerated; they can be left out at room temperature for only about an hour.

ACKNOWLEDGMENTS

"To succeed in life, you need two things: ignorance and confidence."
—Mark Twain

I had no idea what I was getting myself into when I started this project. There are so many people I need to thank who helped me along the way to make this book possible. They really aren't kidding when they say, "It takes a village." I would like to thank:

First and foremost, God, for leading me down this strange and wonderful path. Thank you for the abundance of peonies that I needed in the dead of winter for cake shots and for the out-of-season figs . . . I will be forever grateful.

Juli Bauer, without whom this book would never have been possible, thank you for believing in me and my little blog from day one. Thank you for constantly supporting me, giving encouragement, and offering advice. Thank you for making me believe I could do this and for talking me down from many a ledge. You are the type of person who lights up a room with your presence; you are my absolute favorite person in the world to be goofy with. I'm so happy we've made a lifelong friendship because of food.

Brad Hermanns, thank you for wiping away the failed recipes and frustration when they rolled down my cheeks, for getting takeout when I was too tired to cook, for tasting every single recipe even though you don't like sweets, for cleaning up after me for the last year, and for getting me ingredients when I needed them. You are so patient and so thoughtful. You take care of me so well. I never could have done this without you. Thank you for always supporting me in every single thing that I do and still loving me in the process.

"They say love is blind. I disagree. Infatuation is blind, love is all-seeing and accepting. Love is seeing the flaws and blemishes and accepting them. Love is accepting the bad habits and mannerisms, and working around them. Love is recognizing all the fears and insecurities, and knowing your role is to comfort. Love is working through all the challenges and painful times. Infatuation is fragile and will shatter when life is not perfect. Love is strong and it strengthens because it is real."

—Author Unknown

Stacy Struss, the Merriam-Webster dictionary defines the word *friend* as "a person who helps support someone or something." You have been a friend in the truest sense of the word and so much more. I can't thank you enough for your constant support, assistance, and friendship throughout this entire process. This book is as much a part of you as it is me; you can surely be found sprinkled through its pages. Thank you for being my foodie soul mate. You just get me in a way that few others do and I appreciate it more than you'll ever know.

Mom, thank you for always encouraging me to pursue my interests and never letting me believe my goals were out of reach. Without that I doubt this book would have been possible. **Dad and Heidi,** thank you for not laughing at me when I told you I wanted to pursue photography as a career and for buying me my first camera. Thank you for always challenging me to do my best. Thanks to **Linda "Mom" Thowsen** for all the vintage props, grammar lessons, and hugs along the way.

My friends and family, thank you for still inviting me to stuff even though you knew I would say no because "I have to work on the book." Thank you for being so understanding about unreturned phone calls and long periods of absence on my part, and thank you most of all for your tremendous outpouring of support and encouragement. I'm so lucky to have you all in my life. You mean the world to me. Thanks to **Jennifer Barajas-Waldrop** for sending over great recipe ideas and feedback. Thank you to **Marin Hughes** for giving me the push I needed to start a blog in the first place.

My entire GoPro Family, you guys are so boss. Thank you for tasting all the recipes I brought in, giving me feedback, and creating a "Vanessa Recipe Donation Jar" in the kitchen. You guys are incredible, and I'm so lucky to have you in my world. Special shout-outs to **Joe Van-Dalsem** and **Peter Barnes** for the patient instructions, answering of dumb questions, software, equipment lending, and tech support, and **Brian Smith** for the Jedi editing skills.

Everyone at Victory Belt, especially **Erich Krauss, Michele Farrington, Sean Farrington,** and **Susan Lloyd.** Erich, for taking a chance on an unknown kid and geeking out with me several times over food and book ideas. Michele, for being so incredibly helpful and answering all my freak-out emails with nothing but patience and grace. Sean, for translating my vision perfectly, and Susan, for just being awesome. Thank you to my editors, **Holly Jennings,** for not making me feel like that big of an idiot and offering great ideas to help make the book that much better, and **Pam Mourouzis,** for being so exceedingly helpful and somehow keeping all my thoughts, needs, and wants organized; you are magic. Thank you all for being so excited to be in my corner.

Bill and Hayley Staley, for being such a supportive force in the Paleo community. Thank you for always helping out, answering questions, sharing expertise, and never expecting anything in return. You are truly genuine people and so greatly appreciated.

The Sic at 6, I'd go to war with you. You've been there from the start. Thanks for the friendship forged through blood, sweat, and booze and for constantly supporting me in all my Paleo endeavors.

Patty Brutlag, for the camera, digital photography lessons by frantic late night phone calls, and for making me look beautiful in my book. You are truly an inspiration to all photographers out there.

The Woody Show, Woody, Ravey, Greg, and Menace, given the choice of anyone in the world, I'd have you as my dinner guests. I've been listening to you guys since the Bay Area days and probably now more than ever since you've been back in Los Angeles. Although I know we don't technically know each other (I did meet Menace at BFD one year, that counts, right?), it would feel strange not to thank you. I know you guys hate anything healthy, but I also know you love food. You were there in the kitchen with me while I made every recipe in this book. Thanks for making me laugh and helping me to get through the hardest thing I've ever done in my life, with a smile on my face. You made the hours pass like minutes and in all honesty I don't think I could have done it without you.

We're totally legal best friends for life now, dead to real. Love you guys. Live life and party!

To my fellow food bloggers, you amaze me with your passion and creativity every single day. I am constantly wowed and awed by you. I have only succeeded in writing a book because I've had support from all of you. Thank you.

To my readers, I wouldn't be here if it weren't for you! Thank you for reading my blog, trying my recipes, leaving me comments and feedback, and helping me grow not only as a baker, but also as a person. Special shout-out to TSL! Thank you for commenting on every blog post and making me feel like I actually know what I'm doing.

RESOURCES

Curious about the science and theories behind the Paleo diet? Check out these great books:

» Hartwig, Dallas, and Melissa Hartwig. *It Starts with Food: Discover the Whole30 and Change Your Life in Unexpected Ways.* Las Vegas, NV: Victory Belt Publishing, 2012.

» Sanfilippo, Diane. *Practical Paleo: A Customized Approach to Health and a Whole-Foods Lifestyle.* Las Vegas, NV: Victory Belt Publishing, 2012.

» Wolf, Robb. *The Paleo Solution: The Original Human Diet.* Las Vegas, NV: Victory Belt Publishing, 2010.

RECIPE INDEX

 70
FROSTED "OATMEAL" BREAKFAST SQUARES

 72
SOUTHERN BISCUITS

 74
BISCUITS AND CAJUN SAUSAGE GRAVY

 76
PESTO RELOADED

 78
EASY IMMERSION BLENDER MAYONNAISE

 80
FRENCH ONION AND BACON TART

82
CHILES RELLENOS CASSEROLE

 84
BACON CHEESEBURGER STUFFED POTATOES

 86
CHIPOTLE COLESLAW

 88
BBQ PULLED PORK NACHOS

 90
DUCK FAT FRIES

 92
LOADED MASHED CAULIFLOWER

94
PESTO CAPRESE

 96
BACON JALAPEÑO DEVILED EGGS

 98
BROWNED BUTTER SAGE AND GOAT CHEESE SPAGHETTI SQUASH

 100
PIZZA SOUP

 102
CHIPOTLE CHICKEN SALAD

 104
SHEPHERD'S POT PIE

 108
S'MORES BARS

 110
BETTER THAN BOX BROWNIES

 112
SOUR CHERRY CRUMBLE BARS

 114
SAMOA BARS

 116
BILLIONAIRE BARS

 118
S'MORES DONUTS

 120
SKILLET BROWNIE SUNDAE WITH BROWN SUGAR BACON CRUMBLES

 122
PEACHES AND CREAM BARS

 124
BARELY LEGAL BARS

 126
BROWNIE CRUMB DONUTS

 128
ROCKY ROAD BROWNIES

130
PUMPKIN BREAD

 132
DONUT SHOP DONUTS

 136
CHOCOLATE CHIP COOKIE BOTTOM

 140
WHITE CHOCOLATE

 142
CHOCOLATE

 144
CHOCOLATE-DIPPED POTATO CHIPS

 146
ALMOND BUTTER CUPS

148
SALTED CARAMEL CUPS

 150
WHITE CHOCOLATE CARAMEL CASHEW CLUSTERS

 152
COOKIE DOUGH FUDGE

 154
COOKIE DOUGH CUPS

 156
CHOCOLATE-COVERED TOFFEE

 158
BROWN SUGAR BACON

 160
"REESE'S" DESSERT SHOOTERS

 162
CARAMEL CRÈME BRÛLÉE

 166
OLD-FASHIONED FLAKY PIE CRUST

 168
FAUXREO CRUST

 170
GRAHAM CRACKER CRUST

 172
SIMPLE CRUST

 174
HOLIDAY SPICED CRUST

 176
PUMPKIN PIE

178
MISSISSIPPI MUD PIE

CLEAN EATING WITH A DIRTY MIND   419

180	182	184	186	188	190	192	194

 S'MORES PIE   EGGNOG CHIFFON PIE   MEYER LEMON MERINGUE TARTLETS   TUXEDO TART   BLUEBERRY LEMON TARTLETS   BROWNED BUTTER CARAMEL BANANA TART   SPICED MAPLE PEAR TART   STRAWBERRY MERINGUE TARTLETS

    CLASSIC YELLOW CAKE   WHITE CAKE   ALMOND CAKE    LIMONCELLO POUND CAKE   BLACKBERRY ELDERFLOWER CAKE   HOT FUDGE SUNDAE CUPCAKES   CHOCOLATE CUPCAKES

 CRÈME BRÛLÉE CUPCAKES   "REESE'S" CUPCAKES    CARAMEL MAPLE FIG CAKE   STRAWBERRY CHEESECAKE CAKE   DEATH BY CHOCOLATE CAKE   SALTED CARAMEL CUPCAKES   NO-BAKE STRAWBERRY CHEESECAKE JARS   S'MORES CUPCAKES

 CHOCOLATE DREAM CHEESECAKE   KEY LIME CHEESECAKE CUPS   ROCKY ROAD CUPCAKES   MOLTEN CHOCOLATE LAVA CAKE   SALTED CARAMEL CHEESECAKE BITES   "REESE'S" CHEESECAKE   BOURBON BUTTER PECAN CUPCAKES   CHOCOLATE-COVERED STRAWBERRY CUPCAKES

 RED, WHITE, AND BLUEBERRY CUPCAKES   SPOOKY HALLOWEEN CAKE   PEPPERMINT MOCHA CUPCAKES   EGGNOG CUPCAKES   HOLIDAY SPICE CAKE      CHOCOLATE FUDGE COOKIES    BROWNED BUTTER SNICKERDOODLES

 SIMPLE CHOCOLATE CHIP COOKIES    SHORTBREAD COOKIES    ALMOND BUTTER PATTIES   PALEO MOONPIES   STRAWBERRIES AND CREAM COOKIES   DEVIL'S FOOD COOKIES   HAZELNUT BUTTER SANDWICH COOKIES   FLOURLESS DOUBLE CHOCOLATE CHIP COOKIES

 SOFT BATCH CHOCOLATE CHIP COOKIES   CARAMEL WALNUT BROWNIE COOKIES   S'MORES CHOCOLATE CHIP COOKIE SANDWICHES   FRENCH MACARONS   SKILLET COOKIE SUNDAES   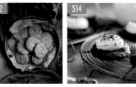 FLOURLESS ALMOND BUTTER COOKIES    HOT CHOCOLATE COOKIES   CHOCOLATE TURTLE THUMBPRINT COOKIES

318 SOFT AND CHEWY GINGERBREAD COOKIES

322 THE BEST CHOCOLATE ICE CREAM

324 DOUBLE CHOCOLATE ICE CREAM SANDWICHES

326 SIMPLE VANILLA ICE CREAM

328 COOKIE DOUGH ICE CREAM SANDWICHES

330 FRENCH VANILLA ICE CREAM

332 SNICKERDOODLE ICE CREAM SANDWICHES

334 BLACKBERRY SWIRL GOAT CHEESE ICE CREAM

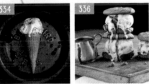

336 ALMOND BUTTER AND JELLY ICE CREAM SANDWICHES

338 SEA SALT AND HONEY ICE CREAM

340 CHOCOLATE-COVERED FROZEN ALMOND BUTTER BANANA BITES

342 STRAWBERRY CHEESECAKE POPS

344 COFFEE ICE CREAM

346 SALTED CARAMEL ICE CREAM

348 PEACH SORBET

350 BLACKBERRY CABERNET SORBET

352 MINT CHIP ICE CREAM BARS

354 PUMPKIN ICE CREAM

356 PUMPKIN GINGERBREAD ICE CREAM SANDWICHES

360 BROWNED BUTTER

362 ALMOND BUTTER CENTER

364 MAPLE SUGAR

366 MARSHMALLOW CRÈME

368 EGG-FREE MARSHMALLOW CRÈME

369 GANACHE—THREE WAYS

372 WHIPPED CREAM

373 WHIPPED COCONUT CREAM

374 SALTED CARAMEL SAUCE

376 CHOCOLATE SHELL COATING

378 STRAWBERRY SAUCE

380 STRAWBERRY CREAM CHEESE FROSTING

382 STRAWBERRY LEMONADE MERINGUE FROSTING

384 PEACHES AND CREAM

386 SOUR CHERRY COMPOTE

388 LEMON CURD

390 ITALIAN MERINGUE

392 SWISS MERINGUE BUTTERCREAM

394 VANILLA BUTTERCREAM

396 CHOCOLATE BUTTERCREAM

398 CREAM CHEESE FROSTING

400 ELDERFLOWER MASCARPONE FROSTING

402 MASCARPONE AND GOAT CHEESE FROSTING

404 LEMON MERINGUE BUTTERCREAM

406 LEMON GLAZE

408 LEMON CREAM CHEESE FROSTING

410 EGGNOG BLISS MERINGUE BUTTERCREAM

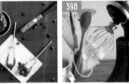

412 DAIRY-FREE EGGNOG MERINGUE FROSTING

414 EGGNOG CREAM CHEESE FROSTING

DAIRY-FREE

EGG-FREE

NUT-FREE

NUT FREE

GENERAL INDEX

CONVERSION GUIDE

If you'd like to print out a copy of this chart to hang in your kitchen, you can find a downloadable PDF on my blog at www.cleaneatingwithadirtymind.com/conversionguide.

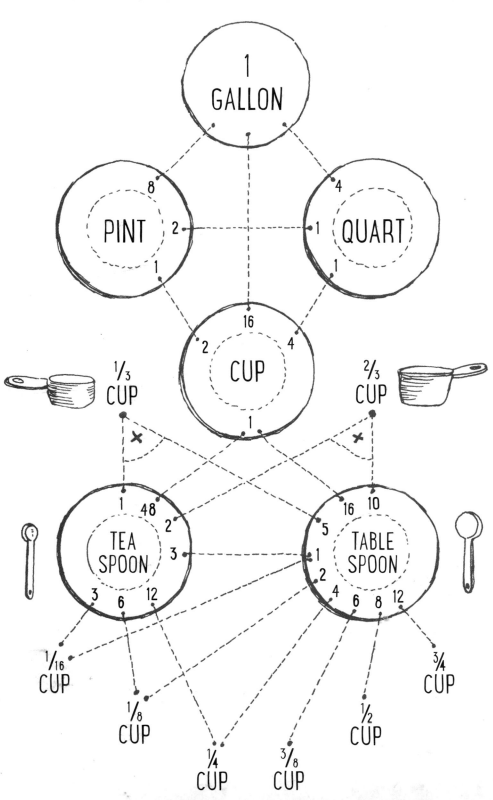